Aviation Maintenance Technician Certification Series

NO COST REVISION/UPDATE SUBSCRIPTION PROGRAM

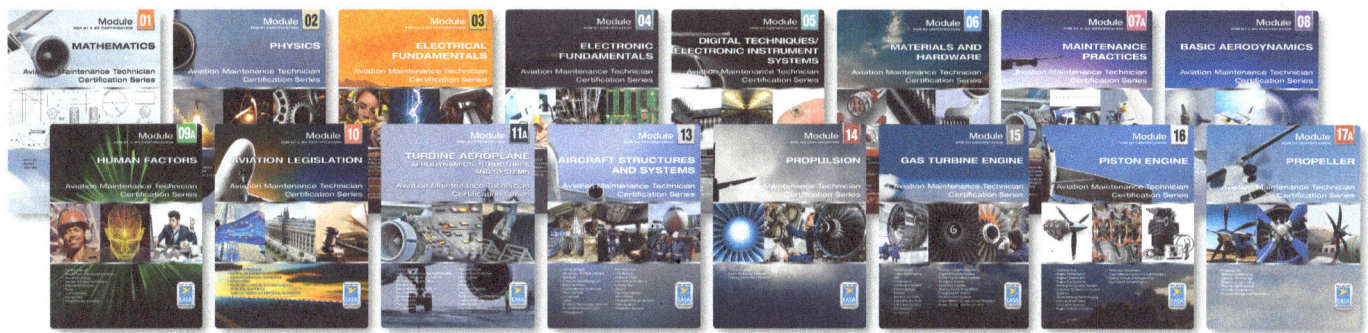

Complete EASA Part-66 Aviation Maintenance Technician Certification Series

NO COST REVISION/UPDATE PROGRAM

Aircraft Technical Book Company offers a revision/update program to all who purchase an EASA Module from the EASA Aviation Maintenance Technician Certification Series. The update is good for two (2) years from time of registration of any EASA Module or EASA bundled kit. If a revision occurs within two (2) years from date of registration, we will send you the revised eBook FREE of cost to your registered email.

HERE IS HOW TO SIGN UP FOR YOUR SUBSCRIPTION

Please send an email to *info@actechbooks.com* with the following information:

1. Name
2. Email
3. Order Number and/or School

Please know that we try to keep our records as current as possible. If your email address changes please let us know so we can update your account.

If you have any questions about this process please contact us at: *info@actechbooks.com*

MODULE 04

FOR B2 CERTIFICATION

ELECTRONIC FUNDAMENTALS

Aviation Maintenance Technician Certification Series

72413 U.S. Hwy 40
Tabernash, CO 80478-0270 USA

www.actechbooks.com

+1 970 726-5111

AVIATION MAINTENANCE TECHNICIAN CERTIFICATION SERIES

Author   James W. Wasson, Ph.D
Layout/Design   Michael Amrine

About the author:

Dr. James W. Wasson, an accomplished author, is founder and President of Growth Strategies International LLC providing Aerospace and Defense Management Consulting Services to the U.S. Air Force, U.S. Navy and Boeing. He is also a Technology Commercialization Business Consultant to the University of South Carolina Small Business Development Center.

Dr. Wasson was Chief Technology Officer (CTO) at BAE Systems Inc., where he planned and directed new avionics systems product development. He has 20 years of experience as Director of Avionics Engineering, Program Management and Business Development at Smiths Aerospace (now GE Aviation) and as Avionics Engineering Manager at McDonnell Douglas (now Boeing).

He was Chairman of the Graduate Business and Management College for the University of Phoenix West Michigan Campuses and Adjunct Professor. He has a PhD and MBA in International Business Management and a BS in Engineering Technology. He is a licensed FAA Airframe & Powerplant Mechanic and Private Pilot.

Copyright © 2016 — Aircraft Technical Book Company. All Rights Reserved.

No part of this publication may be reproduced, stored in a retrieval system, transmitted in any form or by any means, electronic, mechanical, photocopying, recording or otherwise, without the prior written permission of the publisher.

To order books or for Customer Service, please call +1 970 726-5111.

www.actechbooks.com

Printed in the United States of America

For comments or suggestions about this book, please call or write to:
1.970.726.5111 | comments@actechbooks.com

WELCOME

The publishers of this Aviation Maintenance Technician Certification Series welcome you to the world of aviation maintenance. As you move towards EASA certification, you are required to gain suitable knowledge and experience in your chosen area. Qualification on basic subjects for each aircraft maintenance license category or subcategory is accomplished in accordance with the following matrix. Where applicable, subjects are indicated by an "X" in the column below the license heading.

For other educational tools created to prepare candidates for licensure, contact Aircraft Technical Book Company.

We wish you good luck and success in your studies and in your aviation career!

REVISION LOG

VERSION	EFFECTIVE DATE	DESCRIPTION OF CHANGE
001	2016 01	Module Creation and Release
002	2017 02	Format Update

FORWARD

PART-66 and the Acceptable Means of Compliance (AMC) and Guidance Material (GM) of the European Aviation Safety Agency (EASA) Regulation (EC) No. 1321/2014, Appendix 1 to the Implementing Rules establishes the Basic Knowledge Requirements for those seeking an aircraft maintenance license. The information in this Module of the Aviation Maintenance Technical Certification Series published by the Aircraft Technical Book Company meets or exceeds the breadth and depth of knowledge subject matter referenced in Appendix 1 of the Implementing Rules. However, the order of the material presented is at the discretion of the editor in an effort to convey the required knowledge in the most sequential and comprehensible manner. Knowledge levels required for Category A1, B1, B2, and B3 aircraft maintenance licenses remain unchanged from those listed in Appendix 1 Basic Knowledge Requirements. Tables from Appendix 1 Basic Knowledge Requirements are reproduced at the beginning of each module in the series and again at the beginning of each Sub-Module.

How numbers are written in this book:
This book uses the International Civil Aviation Organization (ICAO) standard of writing numbers. This method displays large numbers by adding a space between each group of 3 digits. This is opposed to the American method which uses commas and the European method which uses periods. For example, the number one million is expressed as so:

ICAO Standard	1 000 000
European Standard	1.000.000
American Standard	1,000,000

SI Units:
The International System of Units (SI) developed and maintained by the General Conference of Weights and Measures (CGPM) shall be used as the standard system of units of measurement for all aspects of international civil aviation air and ground operations.

Prefixes:
The prefixes and symbols listed in the table below shall be used to form names and symbols of the decimal multiples and submultiples of International System of Units (SI) units.

MULTIPLICATION FACTOR		PREFIX	SYMBOL
1 000 000 000 000 000 000	= 10^{18}	exa	E
1 000 000 000 000 000	= 10^{15}	peta	P
1 000 000 000 000	= 10^{12}	tera	T
1 000 000 000	= 10^{9}	giga	G
1 000 000	= 10^{6}	mega	M
1 000	= 10^{3}	kilo	k
100	= 10^{2}	hecto	h
10	= 10^{1}	deca	da
0.1	= 10^{-1}	deci	d
0.01	= 10^{-2}	centi	c
0.001	= 10^{-3}	milli	m
0.000 001	= 10^{-6}	micro	μ
0.000 000 001	= 10^{-9}	nano	n
0.000 000 000 001	= 10^{-12}	pico	p
0.000 000 000 000 001	= 10^{-15}	femto	f
0.000 000 000 000 000 001	= 10^{-18}	atto	a

International System of Units (SI) Prefixes

EASA LICENSE CATEGORY CHART

	Module Number and Title	A1 Airplane Turbine	B1.1 Airplane Turbine	B1.2 Airplane Piston	B1.3 Helicopter Turbine	B1.4 Helicopter Piston	B2 Avionics
1	Mathematics	X	X	X	X	X	X
2	Physics	X	X	X	X	X	X
3	Electrical Fundamentals	X	X	X	X	X	X
4	Electronic Fundamentals		X	X	X	X	X
5	Digital Techniques / Electronic Instrument Systems	X	X	X	X	X	X
6	Materials and Hardware	X	X	X	X	X	X
7A	Maintenance Practices	X	X	X	X	X	X
8	Basic Aerodynamics	X	X	X	X	X	X
9A	Human Factors	X	X	X	X	X	X
10	Aviation Legislation	X	X	X	X	X	X
11A	Turbine Aeroplane Aerodynamics, Structures and Systems	X	X				
11B	Piston Aeroplane Aerodynamics, Structures and Systems			X			
12	Helicopter Aerodynamics, Structures and Systems				X	X	
13	Aircraft Aerodynamics, Structures and Systems						X
14	Propulsion						X
15	Gas Turbine Engine	X	X		X		
16	Piston Engine			X		X	
17A	Propeller	X	X	X			

GENERAL KNOWLEDGE REQUIREMENTS
MODULE 04 SYLLABUS AS OUTLINED IN PART-66, APPENDIX 1

Level 1
A familiarization with the principal elements of the subject.
Objectives:
a. The applicant should be familiar with the basic elements of the subject.
b. The applicant should be able to give a simple description of the whole subject, using common words and examples.
c. The applicant should be able to use typical terms.

Level 2
A general knowledge of the theoretical and practical aspects of the subject and an ability to apply that knowledge.
Objectives:
a. The applicant should be able to understand the theoretical fundamentals of the subject.
b. The applicant should be able to give a general description of the subject using, as appropriate, typical examples.
c. The applicant should be able to use mathematical formula in conjunction with physical laws describing the subject.
d. The applicant should be able to read and understand sketches, drawings and schematics describing the subject.
e. The applicant should be able to apply his knowledge in a practical manner using detailed procedures.

Level 3
A detailed knowledge of the theoretical and practical aspects of the subject and a capacity to combine and apply the separate elements of knowledge in a logical and comprehensive manner.
Objectives:
a. The applicant should know the theory of the subject and interrelationships with other subjects.
b. The applicant should be able to give a detailed description of the subject using theoretical fundamentals and specific examples.
c. The applicant should understand and be able to use mathematical formula related to the subject.
d. The applicant should be able to read, understand and prepare sketches, simple drawings and schematics describing the subject.
e. The applicant should be able to apply his knowledge in a practical manner using manufacturer's instructions.
f. The applicant should be able to interpret results from various sources and measurements and apply corrective action where appropriate.

PART-66 - APPENDIX I
BASIC KNOWLEDGE REQUIREMENTS

LEVELS

B2

Sub-Module 01 - Semiconductors

4.1.1 - Diodes

(a) Diode symbols;
Diode characteristics and properties;
Diodes in series and parallel;
Main characteristics and use of silicon controlled rectifiers (thyristors), light emitting diode, photo conductive diode, varistor, rectifier diodes;
Functional testing of diodes.

2

(b) Materials, electron configuration, electrical properties;
P and N type materials: effects of impurities on conduction, majority and minority characters;
PN junction in a semiconductor, development of a potential across a PN junction in unbiased, forward biased and reverse biased conditions;
Diode parameters: peak inverse voltage, maximum forward current, temperature, frequency, leakage current, power dissipation;
Operation and function of diodes in the following circuits: clippers, clampers, full and half wave rectifiers, bridge rectifiers, voltage doublers and triplers;
Detailed operation and characteristics of the following devices: silicon controlled rectifier (thyristor), light emitting diode, Schottky diode, photo conductive diode, varactor diode, varistor, rectifier diodes, Zener diode.

2

4.1.2 - Transistors

(a) Transistor symbols;
Component description and orientation;
Transistor characteristics and properties.

2

(b) Construction and operation of PNP and NPN transistors;
Base, collector and emitter configurations;
Testing of transistors;
Basic appreciation of other transistor types and their uses;
Application of transistors: classes of amplifier (A, B, C);
Simple circuits including: bias, decoupling, feedback and stabilization;
Multistage circuit principles: cascades, push-pull, oscillators, multivibrators, flip-flop circuits.

2

4.1.3 - Integrated Circuits

(a) Description and operation of logic circuits and linear circuits/operational amplifiers;

-

Description and operation of logic circuits and linear circuits;
Introduction to operation and function of an operational amplifier used as: integrator, differentiator, voltage follower, comparator;
Operation and amplifier stages connecting methods: resistive capacitive, inductive (transformer), inductive resistive (IR), direct;
Advantages and disadvantages of positive and negative feedback.

2

PART-66 - APPENDIX I
BASIC KNOWLEDGE REQUIREMENTS

LEVELS

B2

4.2 - Printed Circuit Boards
   Description and use of printed circuit boards.

2

4.3 - Servomechanisms
(a) Understanding of the following terms: Open and closed loop systems, feedback, follow up, analogue transducers;
Principles of operation and use of the following synchro system components/features: resolvers, differential, control and torque, transformers, inductance and capacitance transmitters.

—

(b) Understanding of the following terms: Open and closed loop, follow up, servomechanism, analogue, transducer, null, damping, feedback, deadband;
Construction operation and use of the following synchro system components: resolvers, differential, control and torque, E and I transformers, inductance transmitters, capacitance transmitters, synchronous transmitters;
Servomechanism defects, reversal of synchro leads, hunting.

2

CONTENTS

ELECTRONIC FUNDAMENTALS

Welcome	iii
Revision Log	iii
Forward	iv
EASA License Category Chart	v
General Knowledge Requirements	v
Contents	vii

SUB-MODULE 01
SEMICONDUCTORS

Knowledge Requirements	1.1
Semiconductors	1.2
Characteristics And Properties	1.2
Semiconductor Materials	1.3
Electron Behavior In Valence Shells	1.4
Effects of Impurities on P and N Type Materials	1.5
Majority And Minority Carriers	1.6
PN Junctions And The Basic Diode	1.7
Unbiased PN Junction	1.7
Forward-Bias PN Junction	1.8
Reverse-Biased PN Junction	1.9
Semiconductor Diodes	1.9
Diode parameters	1.9
Diode Symbols	1.10
Diode Identification	1.11
Types Of Diodes	1.11
Signal Diodes	1.12
Photodiodes	1.13
Light Emitting Diodes	1.13
Power Rectifier Diodes	1.15
Schottky Diodes	1.16
Varistor	1.16
Varactor Diodes	1.17
Diode Maintenance And Testing	1.19
Diodes In Series And Parallel	1.21
Clipper Circuit	1.21
Clamper Circuit	1.22
Half-Wave Rectifier Circuit	1.22
Full-Wave Rectifier Circuit	1.23
Bridge Rectifier Circuit	1.23
Voltage Doublers And Triplers	1.24
Transistors	1.25
Description, Characteristics, Properties and Symbols	1.25
Testing of Transistors	1.26
Construction And Operation Of Transistors	1.28
Bipolar Junction Transistors	1.28
Unipolar Junction Transistors	1.28
Field Effect Transistors	1.30
Metal Oxide Field Effect Transistors	1.31
Multi-Layer Semiconductor Devices	1.32
Shockley Diodes	1.32
Silicon Controlled Rectifiers	1.32
DIACS And TRIACS	1.34
Simple Circuits	1.34
Biasing	1.34
Configurations	1.36
Common-Emitter Configuration	1.36
Common-Collector Configuration	1.36
Common-Base Configuration	1.36
Basic Amplifier Circuits	1.37
Class A Amplifiers	1.37
Class AB Amplifiers	1.38
Class B Amplifier	1.38
Class C Amplifier	1.38
Cascade Amplifiers	1.39
Feedback And Stabilization	1.39
Direct Coupling	1.39
Resistive-Capacitive Coupling	1.40
Impedance Coupling	1.40
Transformer Coupling	1.40
Push Pull Amplifiers	1.41
Oscillators	1.41
Mutivibrators	1.43
Flip-flop Circuits	1.43
Integrated Circuits	1.43
Binary Numbering System	1.44
Place Values	1.46
Binary Number System Conversion	1.46
Binary-Coded Decimals	1.47
Logic Gates	1.48
NOT Gate	1.48
Buffer Gate	1.48
AND Gate	1.49
OR Gate	1.49
NAND Gate	1.50
NOR Gate	1.51
Exclusive OR Gate	1.51
Exclusive NOR Gate	1.51
Negative Logic Gates	1.51
Aircraft Logic Gate Applications	1.51
Logic Circuits	1.53
Adder Logic Circuits	1.53
Flip-Flop Logic Circuits	1.53
Comparator Logic Circuits	1.55

CONTENTS

Encoder Logic Circuits	1.56
Decoder Logic Circuits	1.57
Linear Circuits And Operational Amplifiers	1.57
Positive and Negative Feedback	1.61
Voltage Follower Circuit	1.61
Multivibrator Circuit	1.62
Integrator Circuit	1.62
Differentiator Circuit	1.63
Scale Of Integration	1.63
Questions	1.67
Answers	1.68

SUB-MODULE 02
PRINTED CIRCUIT BOARDS

Knowledge Requirements	2.1
Printed Circuit Boards	2.2
PCB Manufacturing Process	2.2
Single-Layer Boards	2.2
Double-Layered Boards	2.2
Multi-Layer Ed Boards	2.5
PCB Repair	2.6
Risks And Possible Damage	2.6
Anti-Static Protection	2.8
Controlled Environment	2.8
Static-Safe Workstation	2.8
Anti-Static Wrist Straps	2.8
Grounding Test Stations	2.9
Ionizers	2.9
Special Handling	2.10
Questions	2.11
Answers	2.12

SUB-MODULE 03
SERVOMECHANISMS

Knowledge Requirements	3.1
Servomechanisms	3.2
Feedback: Open-Loop And Closed-Loop Systems	3.2
Analog Transducers	3.4
Synchro Systems	3.5
DC Selsyn Systems	3.5
AC Synchro Systems	3.6
Torque Synchro Systems	3.8
Control Synchro Systems And Synchronous Transmitters	3.8
Differential Synchro Systems	3.9
Resolver Synchro Systems	3.10
E-I Inductive Transmitters	3.10
Capacitance Transmitters	3.11
Stability: Null Hunting, Deadband, And Damping	3.12
Servomechanism Defects	3.13
Questions	3.15
Answers	3.16
Acronym Index	A.1
Index	I.1

SUB-MODULE 01

PART-66 SYLLABUS LEVELS
CERTIFICATION CATEGORY → **B2**

Sub-Module 01
SEMICONDUCTORS
Knowledge Requirements

4.1 - Semiconductors

4.1.1. - Diodes
(a) Diode symbols; Diode characteristics and properties; Diodes in series and parallel;   2
Main characteristics and use of silicon controlled rectifiers (thyristors), light emitting diode, photo conductive diode, varistor, rectifier diodes;
Functional testing of diodes.

(b) Materials, electron configuration, electrical properties;   2
P and N type materials: effects of impurities on conduction, majority and minority characters;
PN junction in a semiconductor, development of a potential across a PN junction in unbiased, forward biased and reverse biased conditions;
Diode parameters: peak inverse voltage, maximum forward current, temperature, frequency, leakage current, power dissipation;
Operation and function of diodes in the following circuits: clippers, clampers, full and half wave rectifiers, bridge rectifiers, voltage doublers and triplers;
Detailed operation and characteristics of the following devices: silicon controlled rectifier (thyristor), light emitting diode, Schottky diode, photo conductive diode, varactor diode, varistor, rectifier diodes, Zener diode.

4.1.2 - Transistors
(a) Transistor symbols;
Component description and orientation;   2
Transistor characteristics and properties.

(b) Construction and operation of PNP and NPN transistors;
Base, collector and emitter configurations;   2
Testing of transistors;
Basic appreciation of other transistor types and their uses;
Application of transistors: classes of amplifier (A, B, C);
Simple circuits including: bias, decoupling, feedback and stabilization;
Multistage circuit principles: cascades, push-pull, oscillators, multivibrators, flip-flop circuits.

4.1.3 - Integrated Circuits

(a) Description and operation of logic circuits and linear circuits/operational amplifiers;

(b) Description and operation of logic circuits and linear circuits;
Introduction to operation and function of an operational amplifier used as: integrator, differentiator, voltage follower, comparator; Operation and amplifier stages connecting methods: resistive capacitive, inductive (transformer), inductive resistive (IR), direct;
Advantages and disadvantages of positive and negative feedback.

SEMICONDUCTORS

Semiconductors are the building blocks of modern electronics. These devices are electronic components, much like resistors, capacitors, transformers and relays, except that they exploit the electron behavior of semiconductor materials. Since the late 1950's, semiconductor devices have replaced thermionic devices (i.e., vacuum tubes) in most applications. They use electronic conduction in the "solid state", as opposed to the gaseous state such as occurs during thermionic emission in a high vacuum. As such, semiconductors are often referred to as solid-state devices. *(Figure 1-1)*

CHARACTERISTICS AND PROPERTIES

The key characteristics that have allowed solid-state devices to replace vacuum tubes in most applications are their small size and weight, low operating voltages, lower power dissipation, higher reliability and extremely long life. In addition, there is no warm up-period required since semiconductors are absent a cathode heater. However, semiconductors typically do not perform as well as vacuum tubes for high-power, high-frequency operation, such as television broadcasting, and they are much more vulnerable to Electro-Static Discharge (ESD) during handling and operation.

Figure 1-1. Solid-state semiconductor devices.

ESD is the transfer of electrostatic charges between bodies at different potentials caused by direct contact or induced by an electrostatic field. If a solid-state component that is charged is then suddenly grounded, the charge will dissipate to ground, but in the process, the component will be damaged due to excessive heat from breakdown of the dielectric material within the component. Care must be taken to discharge any static electricity from the person handling the component and the workstation before touching sensitive semiconductor devices.

Semiconductor materials, such as silicon and germanium, exhibit unique properties whereby the conductivity of these materials can be varied and over wide ranges by subtle changes in temperature, light intensity, and impurity content. Semiconductors are manufactured both as single discrete devices, such as diodes and transistors, and as fully Integrated Circuits, which can consist of millions or billions of discrete components manufactured and interconnected on a single semiconductor substrate or wafer. Their long life, reliability, and resilience in harsh environments make them ideal for use in avionics.

The key to the function of solid-state devices is in the electrical behavior of semiconductors. To understand semiconductors, the following sections will review what makes a material an insulator or a conductor, followed by an explanation for how materials of limited conductivity are constructed and some of their many uses.

SEMICONDUCTOR MATERIALS

The periodic table, shown in *Figure 1-2*, is a tabular arrangement of the chemical elements, organized on the basis of their atomic number (number of protons in the nucleus), electron configurations, and recurring chemical properties. Elements are presented in order of increasing atomic number, which is typically listed with the chemical symbol in each box.

Elemental semiconductors, known as metalloids on the periodic table, are made from a group of materials having electrical conductivities that lie between metal conductors and non-metal insulators. These group IV elements, such as Carbon (C), Silicon (Si), Germanium (Ge) etc., are known as elemental or single-element semiconductors. Silicon is by far the most widely used material in semiconductor devices. Its combination of low raw material cost, relatively simple processing, and

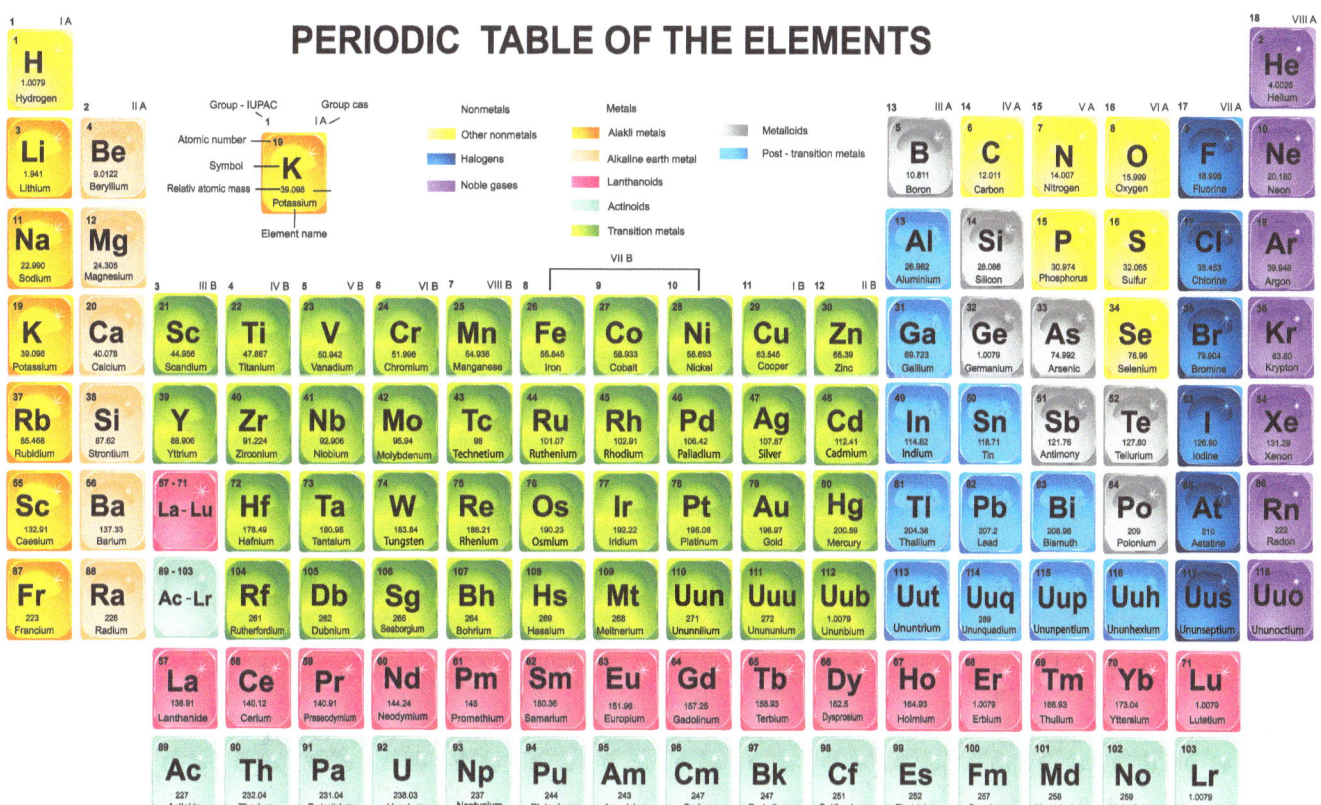

Figure 1-2. Periodic table of elements.

a useful temperature range make it ideal for use among many applications. Germanium was widely used early on; however, its thermal sensitivity makes it less useful than silicon. Germanium is often combined with silicon to make very high-speed Silicon-Germanium (SiGe) devices. In addition, Silicon is often combined with Carbon to form Silicon-Carbide (SiC) devices for high-power and high-temperature applications.

Compound semiconductors do not appear in nature, but are synthesized using two or more elements from groups II through VI of the periodic table. Compound semiconductors that can be synthesized using elements from 3rd and 5th group of the periodic table include Gallium-Arsenide (GaAs), Gallium-Phosphide (GaP), Gallium-Nitride (GaN), Gallium-Aluminum-Arsenide (GaAlAs), Indium-Phosphorus (InP), and Indium-Antimony (InSb). The color of light that emits from a Light Emitting Diode depends on which of these compounds are used.

Compound semiconductors that are synthesized using elements from 2nd and 6th group include Cadmium-Selenium (CdSe), Cadmium-Tellurium (CdTe), Cadmium-Mercury-Tellurium (CdHgTe), and Zinc-Sulfer (ZnS). Light detectors, such as photocells, are typically made from InSb or CdSe compounds. Any combination of elements, such as zinc, cadmium, boron, aluminum, gallium, indium, carbon, silicon, germanium, tin, phosphorous, arsenic, antimony, sulfur, selenium, and tellurium, can be formed in to compound semiconductors with various properties.

ELECTRON BEHAVIOR IN VALENCE SHELLS

An atom of any material has a characteristic number of electrons orbiting the nucleus of the atom. The arrangement of the electrons occurs in somewhat orderly orbits called rings or shells. The closest shell to the nucleus can only contain two electrons. If the atom has more than two electrons, they are found in the next orbital shell away from the nucleus. This second shell can only hold eight electrons. If the atom has more than ten electrons (2 + 8), they orbit in a third shell farther out from the nucleus. This third shell is filled with eight electrons and then a fourth shell starts to fill if the element still has more electrons. However, when the fourth shell contains eight electrons, the number of electrons in the third shell begins to increase again until a maximum of 18 is reached. *(Figure 1-3)*

Shell or Orbit Number	1	2	3	4	5
Maximum Number of Electrons	2	8	18	32	50

Figure 1-3. Maximum number of electrons in each orbital shell of an atom.

The outer most orbital shell of any atom's electrons is called the valence shell. The number of electrons in the valence shell determines the chemical properties of the material. When the valence shell has the maximum number of electrons, it is complete and the electrons tend to be bound strongly to the nucleus. Materials with this characteristic are chemically stable. It takes a large amount of force to move the electrons in this situation from one atom valence shell to that of another. Since the movement of electrons is called electric current, substances with complete valence shells are known as good insulators because they resist the flow of electrons (i.e., electricity). Most insulators are compounds of two or more elements that share electrons to fill their valence shells. *(Figure 1-4)*

In atoms with an incomplete valence shell, that is, those without the maximum number of electrons in their valence shell, the electrons are bound less strongly to the nucleus. The material is chemically disposed to combine with other materials or other identical atoms to fill in the unstable valence configuration and bring the number of electrons in the valence shell to maximum. Two or more substances may share the electrons in their valence shells and form a covalent bond. A covalent bond is the method by which atoms complete their valence shells by sharing valence electrons with other atoms.

Electrons in incomplete valence shells may also move freely from valence shell to valence shell of different atoms or compounds. In this case, these are known as free electrons. As stated, the movement of electrons

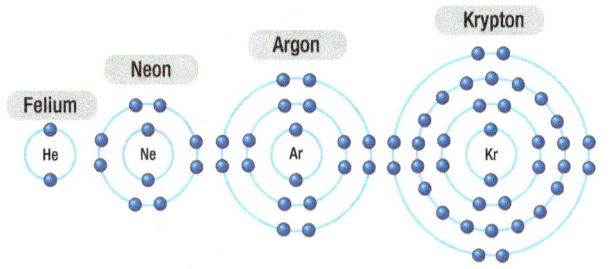

Figure 1-4. Elements with full valence shells are good insulators.

is known as electric current or current flow. When electrons move freely from atom to atom or compound to compound, the substance is known as a conductor. *(Figure 1-5)*

Not all materials are pure elements, that is, substances made up of one kind of atom. Compounds occur when two or more different types of atoms combine. They create a new substance with different characteristics than any of the component elements. When compounds form, valence shells and their maximum number of electrons remain the rule of physics. The new compound molecule may either share electrons to fill the valence shell or free electrons may exist to make it a good conductor.

Silicon is an atomic element that contains four electrons in its valence shell. It tends to combine readily with itself and form a lattice of silicon atoms in which adjacent atoms share electrons to fill out the valance shell of each to the maximum of eight electrons. The periodic arrangement of atoms in a crystal is a called a lattice. This unique symmetric alignment of silicon atoms results in a crystalline structure. *(Figure 1-6)*

Once bound together, the valence shells of each silicon atom are complete. In this state, movement of electrons does not occur easily. There are no free electrons to move to another atom and no space in the valence shells to accept a free electron. Therefore, silicon in this form is somewhat of an insulator.

EFFECTS OF IMPURITIES ON P AND N TYPE MATERIALS

Since silicon in its ultra-pure form is an insulator, it must be transformed into a semi-conductive material by adding some impurities to the silicon - this process is known as doping. Arsenic (As), phosphorus (P), or some other element with five valence electrons in each atom is mixed into the molten silicon. Selective cooling of the molten material causes solidification to occur across a particular crystal direction. Crystal growth is enhanced by placing a small "seed" crystal at the end which is cooled first. The seed crystal is lowered into the molten material and is raised slowly allowing the crystal to grow onto the seed. The crystal pulled and rotated slowly from the melt as it grows into the shape of an ingot. *(Figure 1-7)*

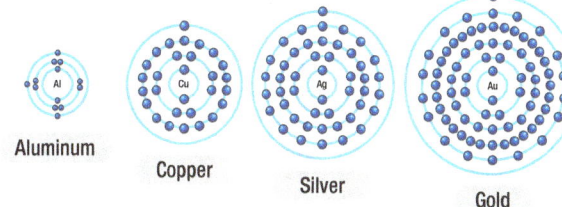

Figure 1-5. The valence shells of elements that are good conductors have 1 or 3 electrons.

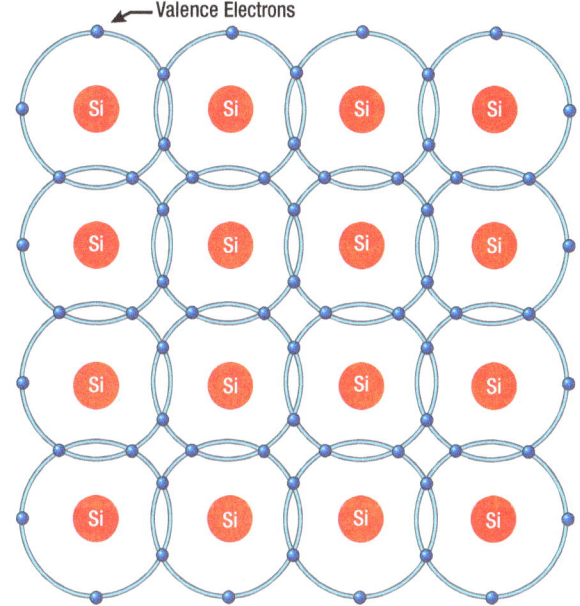

Figure 1-6. The silicon atoms with just the valence shell electrons share.

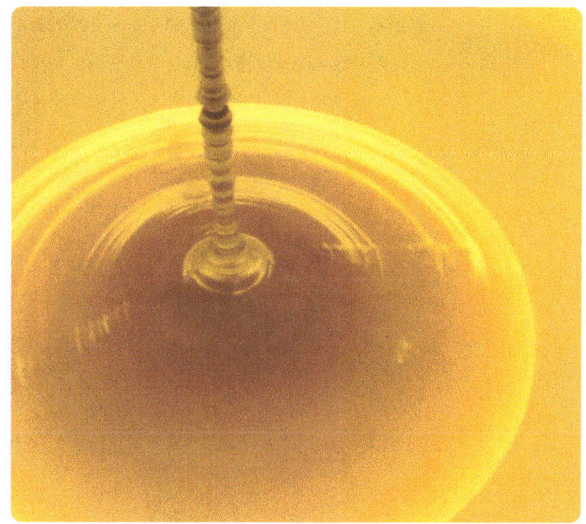

Figure 1-7. Silicon crystals are grown from molten silicon. Impurities added to the molten mixture determine if the crystal will be P-type or N-type material.

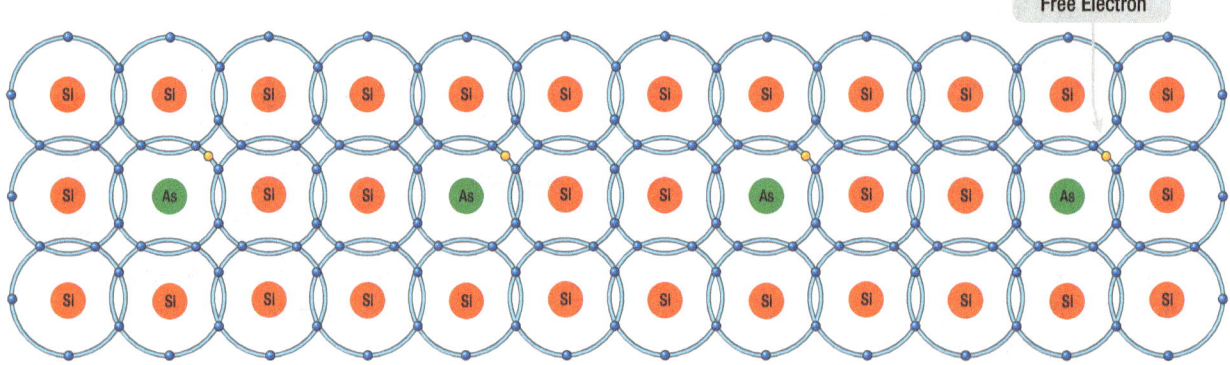

Figure 1-8. Silicon atoms doped with arsenic form a lattice work of covalent bonds. Free electrons exist in the material from the arsenic atom's 5th valence electron. These are the electrons that flow when the semiconductor material, known as N-type or donor material, is conducting.

The result is a silicon lattice with flaws. The elements bond, but numerous free electrons are present in the material from the 5th electron that is part of the valence shell of the doping element atoms. These free electrons can now flow under certain conditions. Thus, the silicon becomes semi-conductive.

When silicon is doped with an element or compound containing five electrons in its valence shell, the result is a negatively charged material due to the excess free electrons, and the fact that electrons are negatively charged. This is known as an N-type semiconductor material. It is also known as a donor material because, when it is used in electronics, it donates the extra electrons to current flow. *(Figure 1-8)*

Doping silicon can also be performed with an element that has only three valence electrons, such as boron, gallium, or indium. Valence electron sharing still occurs, and the silicon atoms with interspersed doping element atoms form a lattice molecular structure. However, in this case, there are many valence shells where there are only seven electrons and not eight. This greatly changes the properties of the material. The absence of the electrons, called holes, encourages electron flow due to the preference to have eight electrons in all valence shells. Therefore, this type of doped silicon is also semi-conductive. It is known as P-type material or as an acceptor since it accepts electrons in the holes under certain conditions. *(Figure 1-9)*

MAJORITY AND MINORITY CARRIERS

Both N-type and P-type semiconductors are able to conduct electricity. In the N-type material, current flows primarily like it does in any conductor. The valence electrons move from one valence shell to another as they progress through the material. Due to the surplus of electrons, the electrons are considered the majority current carriers in N-type semiconductors. Any movement of current in N-type material by the filling of holes is considered the minority current carrier.

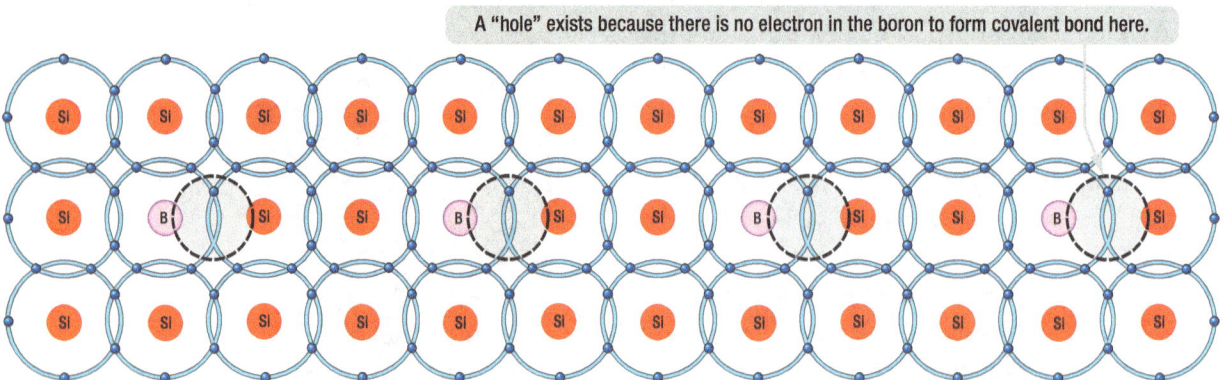

Figure 1-9. The lattice of boron doped silicon contains holes where the three boron valence shell electrons fail to fill in the combined valence shells to the maximum of eight electrons. This is known as P-type semiconductor material or acceptor material.

In P-type material, current primarily flows by valence electrons filling holes that exist in the doped lattice. This makes holes the majority carrier in P-type material. Any current flow in P-type material that occurs without holes (valence electrons exchanging with other valence electrons) is known as the minority carrier.

Figure 1-10 shows the progression of a hole moving through a number of atoms. Notice that the hole illustrated at the far left of the top depiction of the figure attracts the next valance electron into the vacancy, which then produces another vacancy called a hole in the next position to the right. Once again, this vacancy attracts the next valance electron. This exchange of holes and electrons continues to progress, and can be viewed in one of two ways: electron movement or hole movement.

For electron movement, illustrated by the top depiction of *Figure 1-10*, the electron is shown as moving from the right to the left through a series of holes. In the second depiction in the figure, the motion of the vacated hole can be seen as migration from the left to the right, called hole movement. The valence electron in the structure will progress along a path detailed by the arrows. Holes, however, move along a path opposite that of the electrons.

Combining N-type and P-type semiconductor material in certain ways can produce very useful results. The following section will discuss what occurs at the junction of the N-type and P-type material when a voltage is applied.

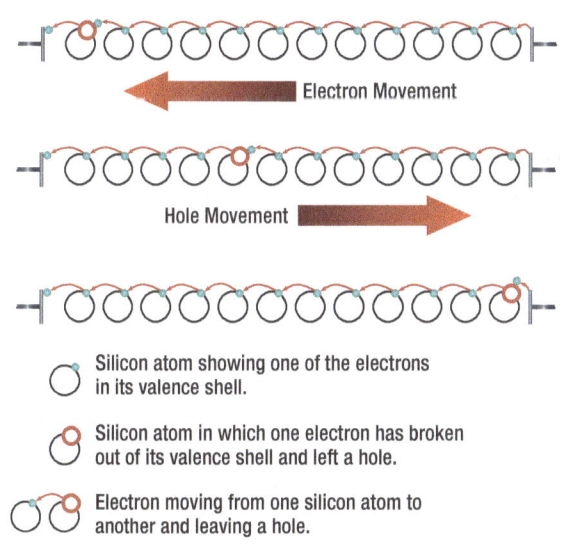

Figure 1-10. A hole moving through atoms.

PN JUNCTIONS AND THE BASIC DIODE

A single type of semiconductor material by itself is not very useful. But, applications have been developed when P-type and N-type materials are joined that have revolutionized electrical and electronic devices. The boundary where the P-type material touches the N-type material is called the PN junction. Interesting and useful phenomenon occur at this contact region. Furthermore, when joined, the entire two-element semiconductor device becomes a basic diode.

A diode is an electrical device that allows current to flow in one direction through the device but not the other. Because of this, the semiconductor diode is used in electronic circuits to convert Alternating Current (AC) into Direct Current (DC). Thus, the PN semiconductor device can act as a rectifier. An explanation of what happens at the PN junction and how it affects the entire PN semiconductor device follows. A glass encased semiconductor diode is shown in *Figure 1-11*.

UNBIASED PN JUNCTION

Figure 1-12 illustrates the electrical characteristics of an unbiased diode, which means that no external voltage is applied. The P side in the illustration is shown to have many holes, while the N-side shows many electrons. When the P and N material contact each other, the electrons on the N-side tend to diffuse out in all directions. Some of the electrons enter the P region. With so many holes in the P material, the electrons soon drop into a hole. When this occurs, the hole then disappears. A negatively charged ion is created since there is now one more electron than the number of protons in the nucleus of the boron (or gallium or indium) atom to which the hole belonged.

Figure 1-11. A silicon diode, the square crystal silicon can be seen between the two leads.

Meanwhile, in the N material near the junction, the valence electrons that departed for the P-type material leave behind a band of positive ions since there are now more positively charged protons in the nucleus of the arsenic (or phosphorous, etc.) atoms than there are electrons in their shells. Thus, each time an electron crosses the PN junction, it creates a pair of ions. In *Figure 1-12*, this is shown in the area outlined by the dash lines. The circled plus signs and the circled negative signs are the positive and negative ions, respectively. These ions are fixed in the crystal and do not move around like electrons or holes in the conduction band. They constitute the depletion zone where neither excess electrons nor excess holes exist. The ions create an electrostatic field across the junction between the oppositely charged ions.

Because holes and electrons must overcome this field to cross the junction, the electrostatic field is usually called a barrier or potential hill. As the diffusion of electrons and holes crosses the junction, the strength of the electrostatic field increases until it becomes strong enough to prevent more electrons or holes from crossing over. At this point, a state of equilibrium exists and there is no further movement across the junction. The PN junction and the entire PN device is said to be unbiased.

FORWARD-BIAS PN JUNCTION

The two semiconductors joined at the PN junction form a diode that can be used in an electrical circuit. When a voltage source (e.g., battery) is attached to the diode with the negative terminal connected to the N-type semiconductor material and the positive terminal connected to the P-type material, it is said to have forward bias and electricity can flow in the circuit. *(Figure 1-13)*

The voltage opposes the electrostatic field at the junction and reduces the potential hill. The positive potential of the battery forces holes in the P-type material toward the junction. The negative potential of the battery forces free electrons in the N-type material towards the opposite side of the junction. The depletion zone becomes very narrow and electrons in the N-type material flow across into the P-type material. There, they combine with holes. The electron and holes continuously come together resulting in current flow. These majority carriers in each semiconductor material increase in number as voltage is increased. This increases

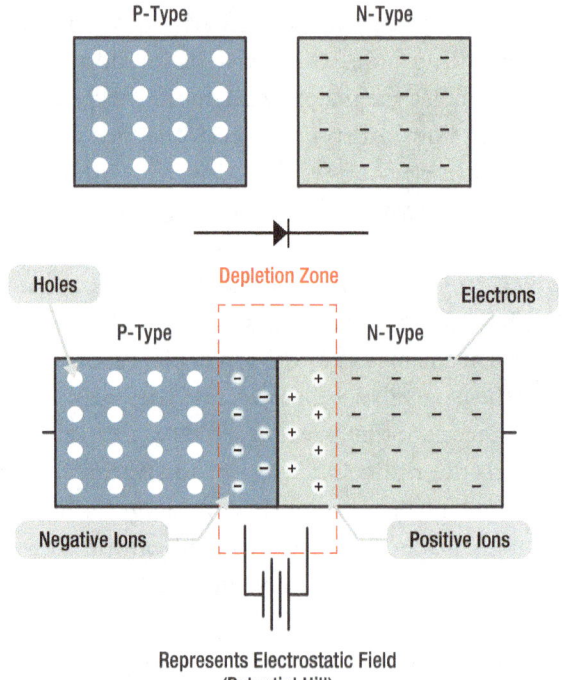

Figure 1-12. An unbiased PN junction – the depletion zone creates a barrier that electrons or holes must overcome for current to flow. The electrostatic field that forms that barrier is shown by a battery circuit involving the positive and negative ions in the depletion zone.

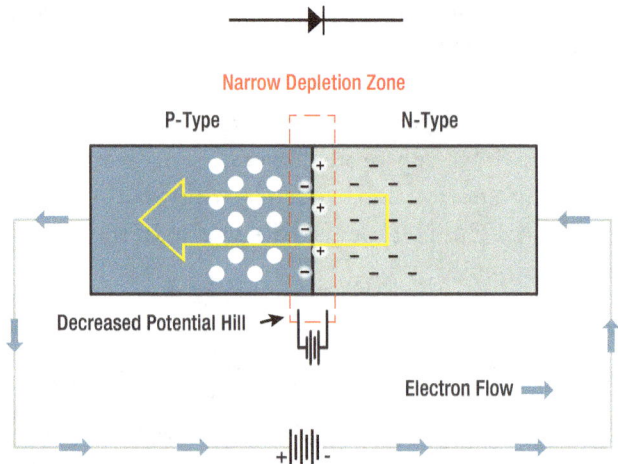

Figure 1-13. The flow of current and the PN junction of a forward biased semiconductor diode in a simple circuit with battery.

current flow. When disconnected from the battery, the depletion zone widens, the electrostatic field strength is restored and current flow ceases.

Note that the potential hill or barrier is reduced when connected to the battery as explained but it still exists. A voltage of approximately 0.7 volts is needed to begin the current flow over the potential hill in a silicon semiconductor diode and about 0.3 volts in a germanium semiconductor diode. Thereafter, current flow is linear with the voltage. Caution must be exercised because it is possible to overheat and "burn out" the semiconductor device at the junction with excessive current flow. Also note that temperature has a significant impact of current flow in semiconductors.

REVERSE-BIASED PN JUNCTION

When the battery connections to the PN semiconductor are reversed, as shown in *Figure 1-14*, the diode is said to have reverse bias and current will not flow. The most noticeable effect of reverse bias seen in this illustration is the widened depletion zone.

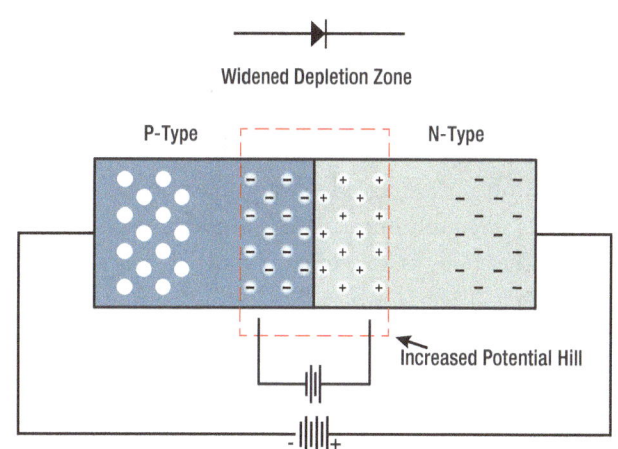

Figure 1-14. Reversed biased PN junction has no current flow.

SEMICONDUCTOR DIODES

Semiconductor diodes are used often in electronic circuits. As discussed in the previous section, PN junction diodes offer very little resistance to electrical current when forward biased and maximum resistance when the diode is reverse biased. When AC current is applied to a diode, current flows during one cycle of the sine wave but not during the other cycle. The diode, therefore, becomes a rectifier and changes the AC current to a pulsating DC current. When the semiconductor diode is forward biased, electrons flow; when the AC cycles, the diode becomes reverse biased and electrons do not flow. This sub-module will go into further detail on diode parameters, symbols, identification and behavior. It will also detail the operation of various types of diodes, and show how they are used in power supplies and other common circuits.

A brief description including the type of diode, the major area of application, and any special features is normally given in the specification sheets. Of particular interest is the specific application for which the diode is suited. The manufacturer will also provide a drawing of the diode, which gives its dimension, weight, and, if appropriate, any identification marks. A static operating table giving spot values of parameters under fixed conditions is often given and sometimes a characteristic curve, similar to the one shown in *Figure 1-15*, is also supplied. The right side of the graph shows the current characteristics of a diode when it is forward biased and the left side of the graph shows the current characteristics of a reverse biased diode.

DIODE PARAMETERS

Semiconductor diodes have properties that enable them to perform many different electronic functions. To do their jobs, engineers and technicians must be supplied with data on these different types of diodes. The information presented for this purpose is called parameters. These parameters are supplied by manufacturers either in their manuals or on specification sheets, also called data sheets. Because of the scores of manufacturers and numerous diode types, it is not practical to present a specification sheet here and call it typical. Aside from the difference between manufacturers, a single manufacturer may supply specification sheets that differ both in format and content. Despite these differences, certain performance and design information is required as follows.

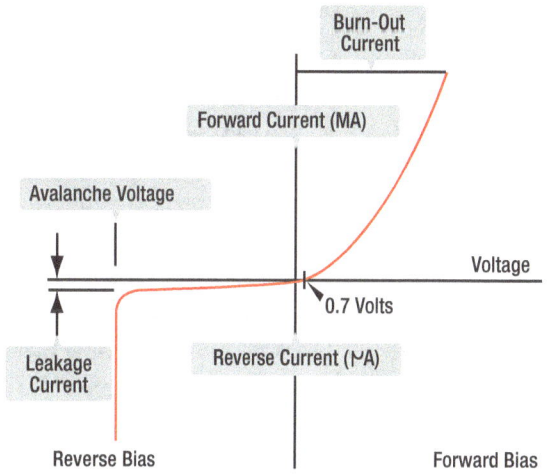

Figure 1-15. Silicon PN junction diode characteristics.

Finally, the specification sheets provide the diode ratings since they are the limiting values of operating conditions outside of which the diode could be damaged. PN junction diodes are generally rated for the following:

1. Maximum (Average) Forward Current (IFAV) – this is the maximum average amount of current that the diode is able to conduct in forward bias, which is directly proportional to the amount of voltage applied. However, there is a thermal limitation regarding how much heat the PN junction can withstand before a structural breakdown can occur. Maximum average forward current is usually given at the maximum power dissipation at a specific temperature, typically at 25 °C. A resistor may be used in series with the diode to limit the forward current.

2. Maximum (Peak or Surge) Forward Current (IFSM) - the maximum peak or surge amount of current that the diode is able to conduct in forward bias in the form of either recurring pulses (peak) or nonrecurring pulses (surge). Again, this rating is limited by the diode's PN junction's thermal capacity, and is usually much higher than the average current rating due to the time it takes to reach maximum junction temperature for a given current. Current should not equal this value for more than a few milliseconds.

3. Maximum Forward Voltage Drop at Indicated Forward Current (VF@IF) - the maximum forward voltage drop across the diode at the indicated forward current.

4. Maximum Reverse Current (IR) - the very small value of direct current that flows when a semiconductor diode is in reverse bias mode and is below the peak inverse voltage applied. This is known as leakage current and is in the micro amperage range.

5. Maximum Reverse Voltage (VR) – also known as the Peak Inverse Voltage (PIV), is the maximum amount of voltage that the diode can withstand continually in the reverse-bias mode without causing a PN junction breakdown. As mentioned, a small amount of current flows through a semiconductor diode when it is reversed biased. However, at a certain voltage, the blockage of current flow in a reversed biased diode breaks down completely. This is known as the avalanche voltage or zener voltage. It is the voltage at which a normal diode can no longer hold back the reverse current, and as a result, it fails.

6. Reverse Recovery Time (Trr) - the time it takes for a diode to "turn off" after it switches from being forward-biased to reverse-biased. For rectifier diodes, recovery time may be in tens of microseconds; whereas signal diodes typically recover in only a few nanoseconds.

7. Total Power Dissipation - the maximum amount of power that the diode can dissipate in the form of heat when it is forward biased (conducting) due to some internal resistance. To find the power dissipation, multiply the voltage drop across the diode time the current flowing through it. This rating, measured in watts, is limited by the diode's thermal capacity.

8. Maximum Operating Temperature – the maximum allowable junction temperature before the structure of the diode deteriorates. It is expressed in units of degrees centigrade per watt.

All of the above ratings are subject to change with temperature variations. If, for example, the operating temperature is above that stated for the ratings, the ratings must be decreased, or heat sinks may need to be attached to the diode to maintain its operation below the rated junction temperature. Since many of these parameters vary with temperature, or some other operating condition, manufacturers typically provide graphs that show the component ratings plotted against other variables, such as temperature, so that the engineer and technician have a better idea of the capabilities of the particular device being used.

DIODE SYMBOLS

Diode symbols used in circuit diagrams are shown in *Figure 1-16*. Different types of diodes have slightly altered symbols for identification. These will be shown as they are discussed.

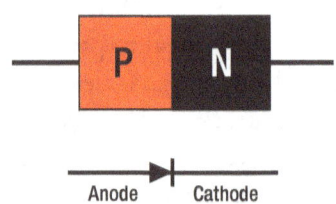

Figure 1-16. Semiconductor diode symbols.

Note that electron flow is typically discussed in this text. The conventional current flow concept where electricity is thought to flow from the positive terminal of the battery through a circuit to the negative terminal is sometimes used in the field. To differential between the two flows in diagrams, the arrows in ***Figure 1-17*** may be used.

DIODE IDENTIFICATION

There are many types of diodes varying in size from the size of a pinhead (used in subminiature circuitry) to large 250-ampere diodes (used in high-power circuits). Because there are so many different types of diodes, some system of identification is needed to distinguish one diode from another. This is accomplished with the semiconductor identification system shown in ***Figure 1-18***. This system is not only used for diodes, but for transistors and many other special semiconductor devices as well.

As illustrated in this ***Figure 1-18***, the system uses numbers and letters to identify different types of semiconductor devices. The first number in the system indicates the number of junctions in the semiconductor device and is a number one less than the number of active elements. Thus 1 designates a diode; 2 designates a transistor (which may be considered as made up of two diodes); and 3 designates a tetrode (a four-element transistor). The letter "N" following the first number indicates a semiconductor. The 2- or 3-digit number following the letter "N" is a serialized identification number. If needed, this number may contain a suffix letter after the last digit. For example, the suffix letter "M" may be used to describe matching pairs of separate semiconductor devices, or the letter "R" may be used to indicate reverse polarity. Other letters are used to indicate modified versions of the device which can be substituted for the basic numbered unit.

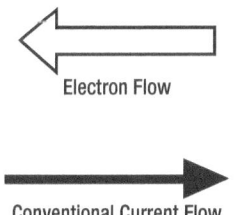

Figure 1-17. Current flow arrows used on diagrams.

XNYYY

XN | YYY

Component | Identification Number

X- Number of Semiconductor Junctions
N - A Semiconductor
YYY - Identification Number (Order or Registration Number) also includes suffix letter (if applicable) to indicate:

1. Matching Devices
2. Reverse Polarity
3. Modification

Example - 1N345A
(An improved version of the semiconductor diode type 345)

Figure 1-18. Semiconductor Identification Codes.

For example, a semiconductor diode designated as type 1N345A signifies a two-element diode (1) of semiconductor material (N) that is an improved version (A) of type 345.

When working with these different types of diodes, it is also necessary to distinguish one end of the diode from the other (anode from cathode). For this reason, manufacturers generally code the cathode end of the diode with a "k," "+," "cath," a color dot or band, or by an unusual shape (raised edge or taper) as shown in ***Figure 1-19***. In some cases, standard color code bands are placed on the cathode end of the diode. This serves two purposes: (1) it identifies the cathode end of the diode, and (2) it also serves to identify the diode by number.

The standard diode color code system is shown in ***Figure 1-20***. Take, for example, a diode with brown, orange, and white bands at one terminal and figure out its identification number. With brown being a "1," orange a "3," and white "9," the device would be identified as a type 139 semiconductor diode, or specifically 1N139.

TYPES OF DIODES

This section will provide a detailed discussion of the operation and characteristics of many common diodes in use today, including the zener diode, silicon diode, photo-conductive diode, light-emitting diode, power rectifier diode, Schottky diode, varistor and varactor diode. A discussion of silicon controller rectifiers (thyristor) will take place in submodule 1.2 since it more closely resembles a transistor.

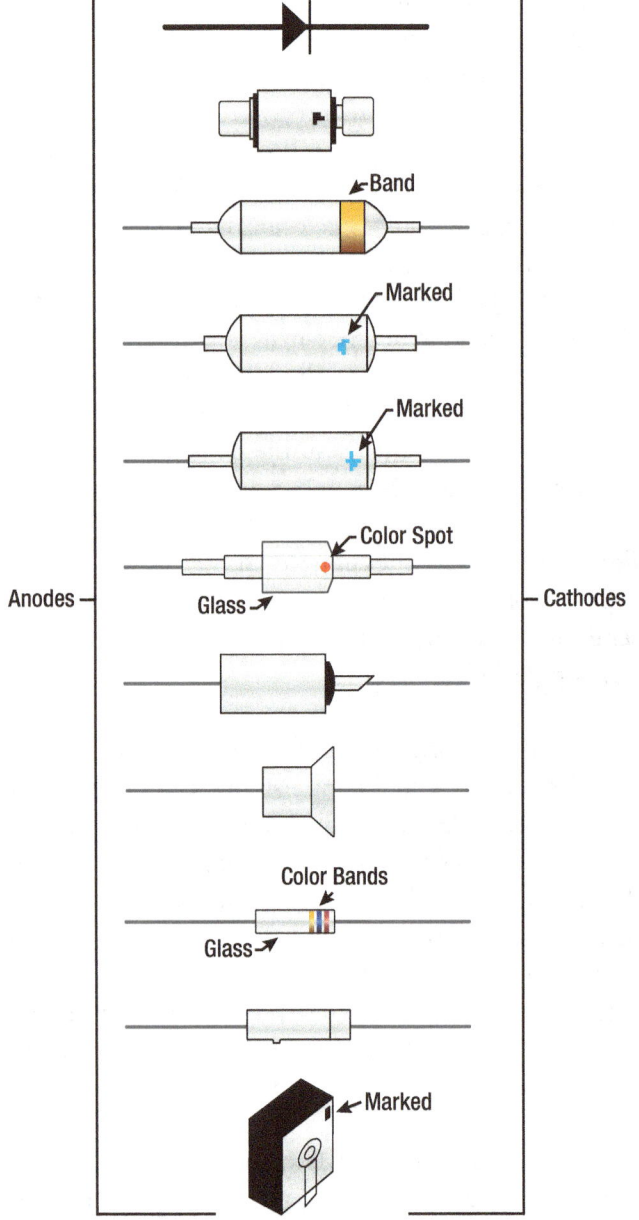

Figure 1-19. Semiconductor Diode Markings.

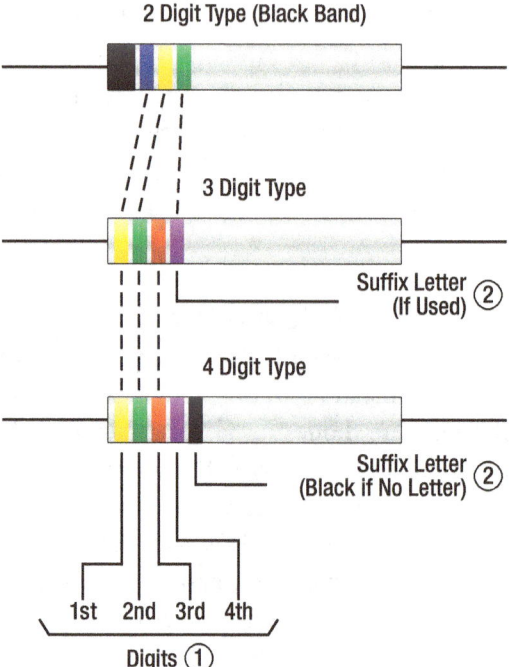

Figure 1-20. Semiconductor diode color code system.

Diodes can be designed with a zener voltage. This is similar to avalanche flow. When reversed biased, only leakage current flows through the diode. However, as the voltage is increased, the zener voltage is reached. The diode lets current flow freely through the diode in the direction in which it is normally blocked. The diode is constructed to be able to handle the zener voltage and the resulting current, whereas avalanche voltage burns out an ordinary diode. A zener diode can be used as means of dropping or regulating voltage. It can be used to step down circuit voltage for a particular application, but only when certain input conditions exist and are constructed to handle a wide range of voltages. *(Figure 1-21)*

SIGNAL DIODES

A signal diode is a small non-linear semiconductor typically found in electronic circuits where high frequencies or small currents are involved, such as television and radio signal processing, and digital logic circuits. The PN junction is usually encapsulated in glass and it has a black or red band at the cathode end. *(Figure 1-22)*

Signal diodes have lower current (i.e., 150mA) and power ratings (i.e., 500mw) than rectifier diodes, but function better in high frequency applications or in clipping or switching circuits that deal with short duration pulse waveforms. Signal diodes can be made of either silicon or germanium diodes. Germanium signal

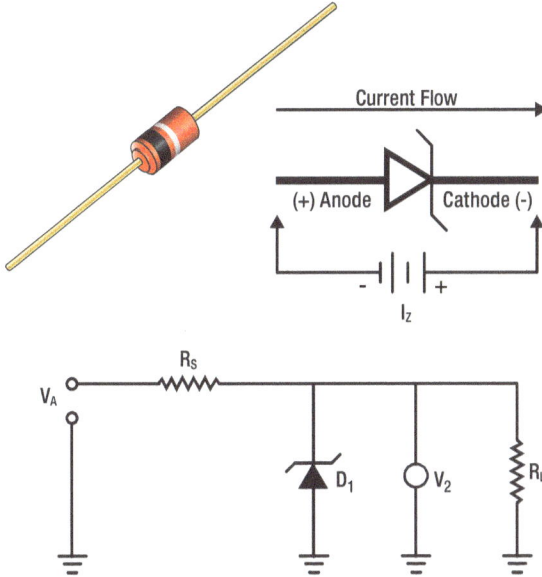

Figure 1-21. A Zener diode, when reversed biased, will breakdown and allow a prescribed voltage (VZ) to flow in the direction normally blocked by the diode.

Figure 1-22. 1N914 signal diode used as a radio frequency signal detector.

diodes have a lower forward voltage drop (0.3v) across the PN junction than silicon signal diodes (0.7v), but have a higher forward resistance. Silicon diodes have higher forward current and higher reverse voltage peak values. The most common sizes for signal diodes are those rated with a maximum reverse voltage of 100v, 120v, 150v and 200v.

PHOTODIODES

Light contains electromagnetic energy that is carried by photons. The amount of energy depends on the frequency of light of the photon. This energy can be very useful in the operation of electronic devices since all semiconductors are affected by light energy. When a photon strikes a semiconductor atom, it raises the energy level above what is needed to hold its electrons in orbit. The extra energy frees an electron enabling it to flow as current. The vacated position of the electron becomes a hole. In light-sensitive diodes, often called photodiodes or photocells, this occurs in the depletion area of the reversed biased PN junction turning "on" the device and allowing current to flow.

Figure 1-23 illustrates a photodiode in a coil circuit. In this case, the light striking the photodiode causes current to flow in the circuit whereas the diode would have otherwise blocked it. The result is the coil energizes and closes another circuit enabling its operation. Thermal energy produces minority carriers in a diode. As the temperature rises, so does the current. Light energy can also produce minority carriers. By using a small window to expose the PN junction, a photodiode can be built. When light fall upon the junction of a reverse-biased photodiode, electrons-hole pairs are created inside the depletion layer. The stronger the light, the greater the number of light-produced carriers, which in turn, causes a greater magnitude of reverse-current. Because of this characteristic, the photodiode can be used in light detecting circuits, such as proximity detectors and fiber optic data bus receivers.

LIGHT EMITTING DIODES

Light Emitting diodes (LEDs) have become so commonly used in electronics that their importance may tend to be overlooked. Numerous avionics displays and indicators use LEDs for indicator lights, digital readouts, and backlighting of liquid crystal display (LCD) screens.

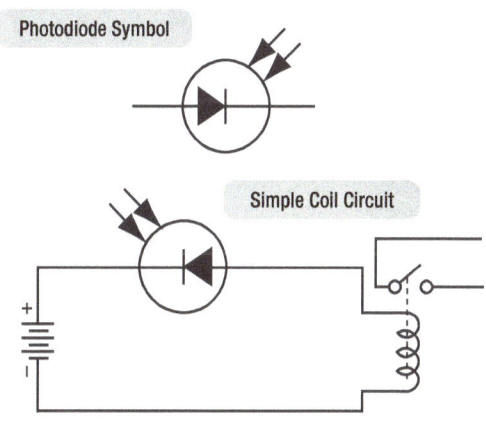

Figure 1-23. Illustrates a photodiode in a coil circuit.

LEDs are simple and reliable. They are constructed of semiconductor material. In a forward biased diode, electrons cross the junction and fall into holes. As the electrons fall into the valence band, they radiate energy. This is true in all semiconductor materials. In most diodes, this energy is dissipated as heat. However, in the light-emitting diode, the energy is dissipated as light. By using elements, such as gallium, arsenic, and phosphorous, an LED can be designed to radiate colors, such as red, green, yellow, blue and infrared light. LEDs that are designed for the visible light portion of the spectrum are useful for instruments, indicators, and even cabin lighting. The advantages of the LED over the incandescent lamps are longer life, lower voltage, faster on and off operations, and less heat. *Figure 1-24* is a table that illustrates common LED colors and the semiconductor material that is used in the construction of the diode.

When the diode is forward biased, the energy given off is visible in the color characteristic for the material being used. *Figure 1-25* illustrates the anatomy of a single LED, the symbol of an LED, and a graphic depiction of the LED process.

LEDs are used widely as "power on" indicators of current and as displays for pocket calculators, digital voltmeters, frequency counters, etc. For use in calculators and similar devices, LEDs are typically placed together in seven-segment displays, as shown in *Figure 1-26* (view A and view B). This display uses seven LED segments, or bars (labeled A through G in the figure), which can be lit in different combinations to form any number from "0" through "9." The schematic, view A, shows a common-anode display. All anodes in a display are internally connected.

Color	Wavelength (nm)	Voltage (V)	Semiconductor Material
Infrared	λ > 760	ΔV < 1.9	Gallium arsenide (GaAs) Aluminium gallium arsenide (AlGaAs)
Red	610 < λ < 760	1.63 < ΔV < 2.03	Aluminium gallium arsenide (AlGaAs) Gallium arsenide phosphide (GaAsP) Aluminium gallium indium phosphide (AlGaInP) Gallium(III) phosphide (GaP)
Orange	590 < λ < 610	2.03 < ΔV < 2.10	Gallium arsenide phosphide (GaAsP) Aluminium gallium indium phosphide (AlGaInP) Gallium(III) phosphide (GaP)
Yellow	570 < λ < 590	2.10 < ΔV < 2.18	Gallium arsenide phosphide (GaAsP) Aluminium gallium indium phosphide (AlGaInP) Gallium(III) phosphide (GaP)
Green	500 < λ < 570	1.9[32] < ΔV < 4.0	Indium gallium nitride (InGaN) / Gallium(III) nitride (GaN) Gallium(III) phosphide (GaP) Aluminium gallium indium phosphide (AlGaInP) Aluminium gallium phosphide (AlGaP)
Blue	450 < λ < 500	2.48 < ΔV < 3.7	Zinc selenide (ZnSe) Indium gallium nitride (InGaN) Silicon carbide (SiC) as substrate Silicon (Si) as substrate — (under development)
Violet	400 < λ < 450	2.76 < ΔV < 4.0	Indium gallium nitride (InGaN)
Purple	Multiple Types	2.48 < ΔV < 3.7	Dual blue/red LEDs, blue with red phosphor, or white with purple plastic
Ultraviolet	λ < 400	3.1 < ΔV < 4.4	diamond (235 nm)[33] Boron nitride (215 nm)[34][35] Aluminium nitride (AlN) (210 nm)[36] Aluminium gallium nitride (AlGaN) Aluminium gallium indium nitride (AlGaInN) — (down to 210 nm)[37]
White	Broad Spectrum	ΔV = 3.5	Blue/UV diode with yellow phosphor

Figure 1-24. Table that illustrates common LED colors and the semiconductor material that is used in the construction of the diode.

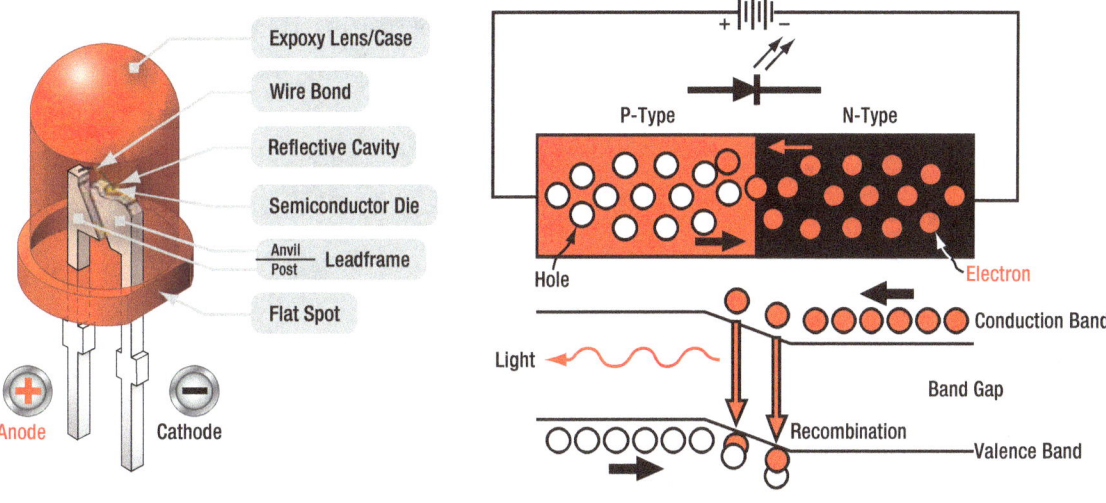

Figure 1-25. Table that illustrates common LED colors and the semiconductor material that is used in the construction of the diode.

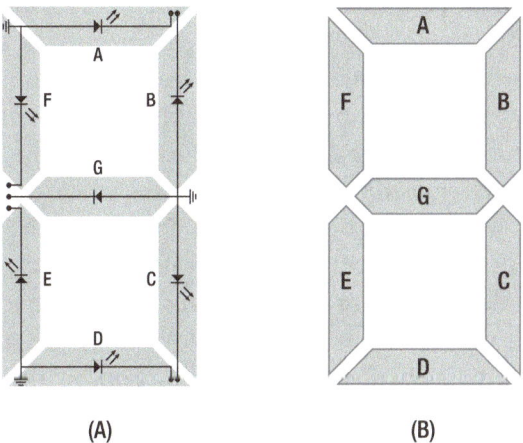

Figure 1-26. Seven-segment LED display.

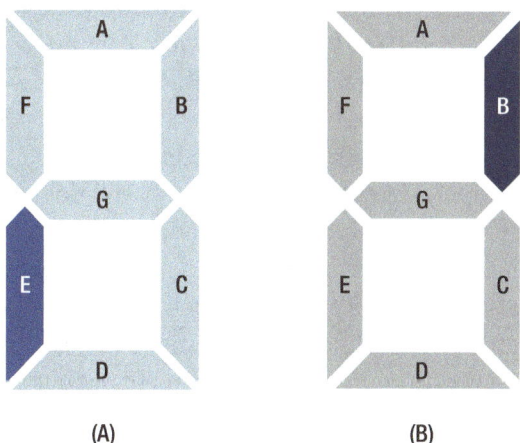

Figure 1-27. Seven-segment LED display examples.

When a negative voltage is applied to the proper cathodes, a number is formed. For example, if negative voltage is applied to all cathodes except that of LED "E," the number "9" is produced, as shown in view A of *Figure 1-27*. If the negative voltage is changed and applied to all cathodes except LED "B," the number "9" changes to "6", as shown in view B.

Seven-segment displays are also available in common-cathode form, in which all cathodes are at the same potential. When replacing LED displays, one must ensure the replacement display is the same type as the faulty display. Since both types look alike, one should always check the manufacturer's number. LED seven-segment displays range from the very small, often not much larger than standard typewritten numbers, to about an inch. Several displays may be combined in a package to show a series of numbers, such as the one shown in *Figure 1-28*.

Figure 1-28. Stacked seven-segment LED display.

POWER RECTIFIER DIODES

The rectifier diode is usually used in applications that require high current, such as power supplies. The range in which the diode can handle current can vary anywhere from one ampere to hundreds of amperes. One common example of a series of power rectifier diodes are those with part numbers 1N4001 to 1N4007. The "1N" indicates that there is only one PN junction, or that the device is a diode. The average current carrying range for these rectifier diodes is one ampere and they

Module 04 B2 - Electronic Fundamentals

1.15

have a peak inverse voltage between 50 volts to 1 000 volts. Larger rectifier diodes can carry currents up to 300 amperes when forward biased and have a peak inverse voltage of 600 volts. A recognizable feature of the larger rectifier diodes is that they are encased in metal in order to provide a heat sink. *Figure 1-29* illustrates a few types of rectifier diodes.

SCHOTTKY DIODES

A Schottky diode is designed to have metal, such as gold, silver, or platinum, on one side of the junction and doped silicon, usually an N-type, on the other side of the junction. In this respect, it is not a pure semiconductor diode. It is a metal-semiconductor diode. A Schottky diode is considered a unipolar device because free electrons are the majority carrier on both sides of the junction. The Schottky diode has no depletion zone or charge storage, which means that the switching time can be as high as 300 MHz. The typical PN semiconductor switches much slower. When an opposite voltage to the voltage supply that forward biases a PN junction diode is applied, current in the diode continues to flow for a brief moment. This time is measurable and is known as reverse recovery time. Schottky diode reverse recovery time is much shorter, which makes it suited for use in high frequency rectification. It also has a very low voltage drop (0.15 volts versus 0.7 volts for a silicon diode).

Figure 1-30 illustrates a Schottky diode with its schematic symbol.

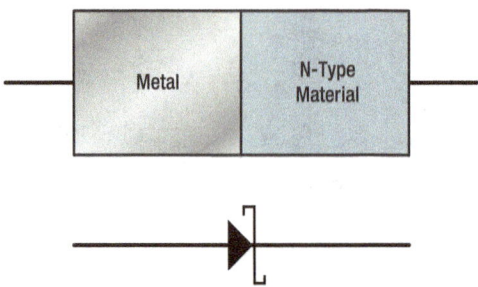

Figure 1-30. Schottky diode construction and schematic symbol.

VARISTOR

A varistor is not exactly a semiconductor diode. It is typically made of a ceramic mass of zinc oxide grains in a matrix of other metal oxides. This material is sandwiched between two metal plates which are the electrodes. *(Figure 1-31)* The numerous grains form diode relationships with other grains so that current flows in one direction only through the device. The current - voltage relationship is non-linear. A small or moderate amount of voltage applied to the varistor causes very little current flow. However, when a large voltage is applied, the effective junction breaks down and large current flow follows. Therefore, the varistor has high resistance at low voltage, and low resistance

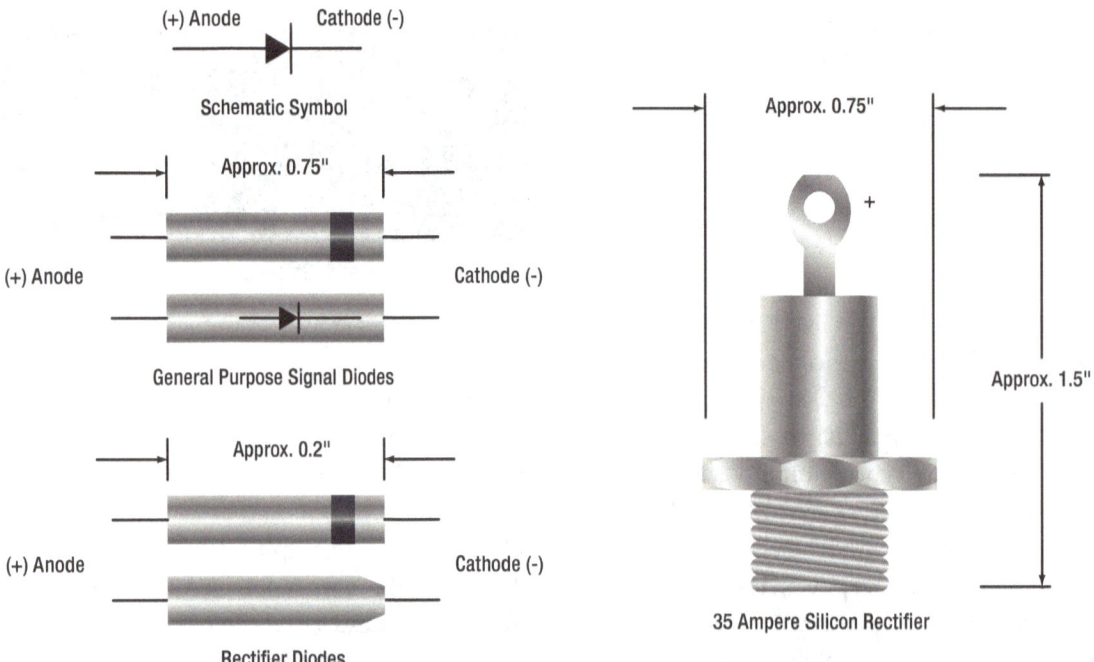

Figure 1-29. Various examples of power rectifier diodes with the one on the right encased in metal to provide a heat sink.

at high voltage. Varistors are often used to protect circuits against excessive transient voltages. They are incorporated so that, when triggered, they shunt the current created by the high voltage away from sensitive components. *Figure 1-32* illustrates the schematic symbol of a varistor. *Figure 1-33* shows the performance graph of a typical varistor.

VARACTOR DIODES

The varactor diode, or varicap, is a diode that behaves like a variable capacitor. Its capacitance is dependent on the applied voltage. The PN junction functions like the dielectric and the N and P materials like the plates of a common capacitor. Understanding how the varactor operates is an important prerequisite to understanding field-effect transistors (FETs), which are covered in this sub-module. The schematic symbol and a varactor drawing are illustrated in *Figure 1-34*.

Figure 1-35 shows a PN junction. Surrounding the junction of the P and N materials is a narrow region void of both positively and negatively charged current carriers. This area is called the depletion region.

The size of the depletion region in a varactor diode is directly related to the bias. Forward biasing makes the region smaller by repelling the current carriers toward the PN junction. If the applied voltage is large enough (about 0.5 volt for silicon material), the negative particles will cross the junction and join with the positive particles, as shown in *Figure 1-36*. This forward biasing causes the

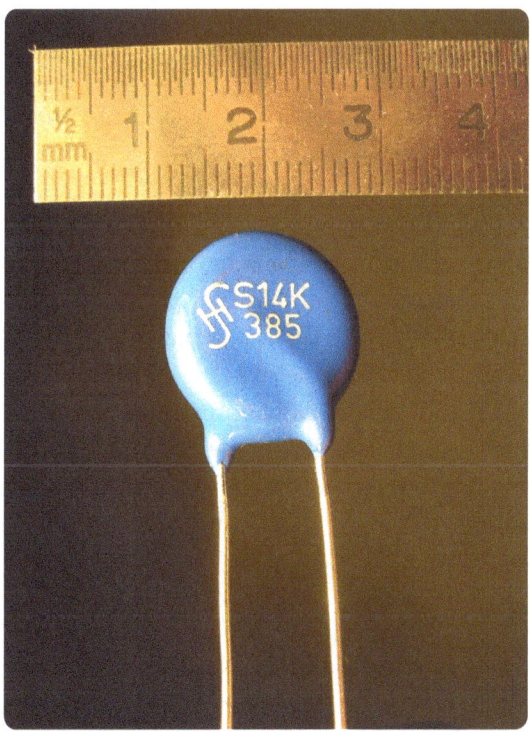

Figure 1-31. A 385-volt metal-oxide varistor.

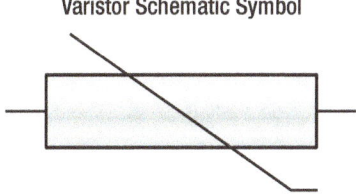

Figure 1-32. A schematic symbol of a varistor.

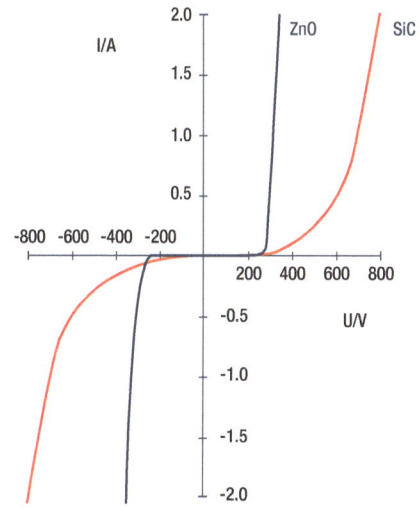

Figure 1-33. Varistor current-voltage characteristics for zinc oxide (ZnO) and silicon carbide (SiC) devices.

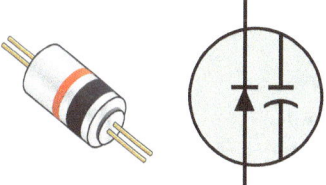

Figure 1-34. A varactor diode and its schematic symbol.

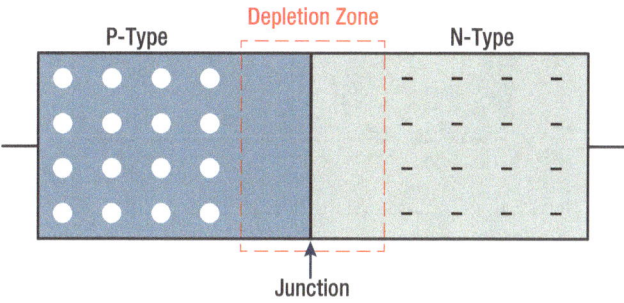

Figure 1-35. Unbiased varactor diode PN junction.

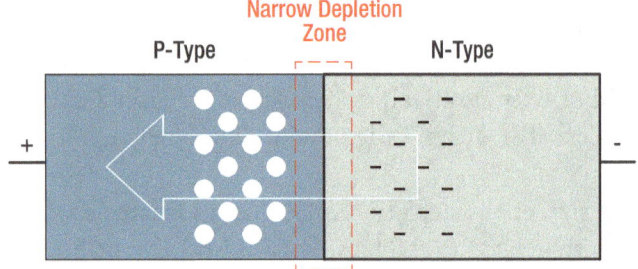

Figure 1-36. Forward-biased PN junction.

depletion region to decrease, producing a low resistance at the PN junction and a large current flow across it. This is the condition for a forward-biased diode.

On the other hand, if reverse-bias voltage is applied to the PN junction, the size of its depletion region increases as the charged particles on both sides move away from the junction. This condition, shown in *Figure 1-37*, produces a high resistance between the terminals and allows little current flow (only in the microampere range). This is the operating condition for the varactor diode, which is nothing more than a special PN junction.

As *Figure 1-37* shows, the insulation gap formed by reverse biasing of the varactor is comparable to the layer of dielectric material between the plates of a common capacitor. Furthermore, the formula used to calculate capacitance (C) can be applied to both the varactor and the capacitor:

$$C = \frac{AK}{d}$$

Where:
  A = plate area
  K = a constant value
  d = distance between plates

In this case, the size of the insulation gap of the varactor, or depletion region, is substituted for the distance between the plates of the capacitor. By varying the reverse-bias voltage applied to the varactor, the width of the "gap" may be varied. An increase in reverse bias increases the width of the gap (d) which reduces the capacitance (C) of the PN junction. Therefore, the capacitance of the varactor is inversely proportional to the applied reverse bias.

The ratio of varactor capacitance to reverse-bias voltage change may be as high as 10 to 1. *Figure 1-38* shows one example of the voltage-to-capacitance ratio. View A shows that a reverse bias of 3 volts produces a capacitance of 20 picofarads in the varactor. If the reverse bias is increased to 6 volts, as shown in view B, the depletion region widens and capacitance drops to 5 picofarads. Each 1-volt increase in bias voltage causes a 5-picofarad decrease in the capacitance of the varactor; the ratio of change is therefore 5 to 1. Of course any decrease in applied bias voltage would cause a proportionate increase in capacitance, as the depletion region narrows. Notice that the value of the capacitance is small in the picofarad range.

In general, varactors are used to replace the old style variable capacitor tuning. They are used in tuning circuits of more sophisticated communication equipment and in other circuits where variable capacitance is required. One advantage of the varactor is that it allows a DC voltage to be used to tune a circuit for simple remote control or automatic tuning functions. One such application of the varactor is as a variable tuning capacitor in a receiver or transmitter tank circuit like that shown in *Figure 1-39*.

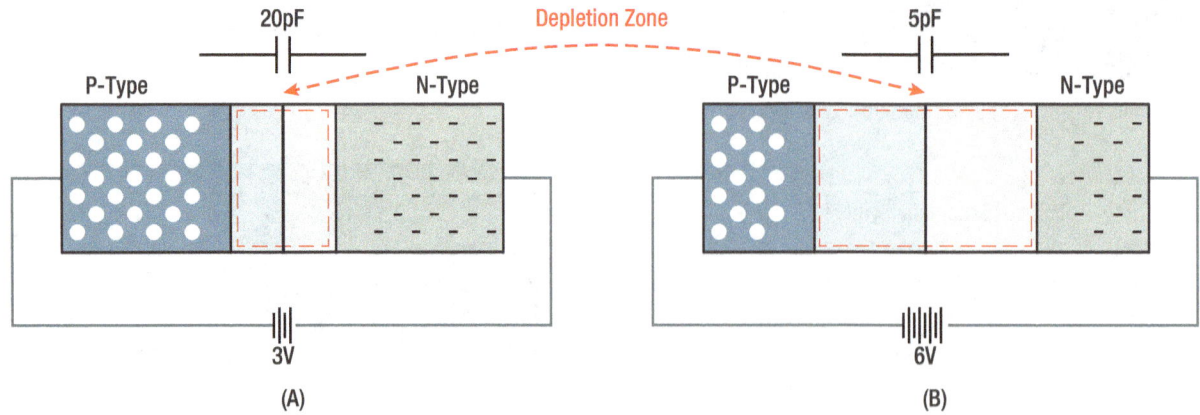

Figure 1-37. Reverse-biased PM junction.

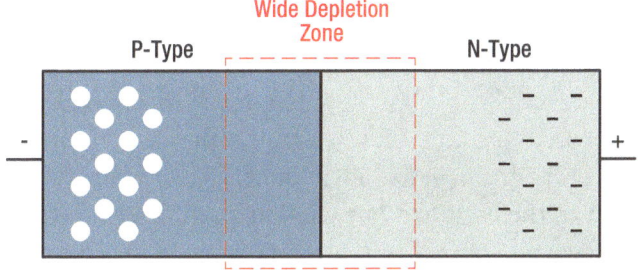

Figure 1-38. Varacter capacitance versus reverse bias voltage.

Figure 1-39 shows a DC voltage felt at the wiper of potentiometer R1 which can be adjusted between +V and –V. The DC voltage, passed through the low resistance of radio frequency choke L2, acts to reverse bias varactor diode C3. The capacitance of C3 is in series with C2, and the equivalent capacitance of C2 and C3 is in parallel with tank circuit L1 and C1. Therefore, any variation in the DC voltage at R1 will vary both the capacitance of C3 and the resonant frequency of the tank circuit. The radio-frequency choke provides high inductive reactance at the tank frequency to prevent tank loading by R1. C2 acts to block DC from the tank, as well as to fix the tuning range of C3.

An ohmmeter can be used to check a varactor diode in a circuit. A high reverse-bias resistance and a low forward-bias resistance with a 10 to 1 ratio in reverse-bias to forward-bias resistance is considered normal.

DIODE MAINTENANCE AND TESTING

Diodes are rugged and efficient. They are also expected to be relatively trouble free. Protective encapsulation processes and special coating techniques have even further increased their life expectancies. In theory, a diode should last indefinitely. However, if diodes are subjected to current overloads, their junctions will be damaged or destroyed. In addition, the application of excessively high operating voltages can damage or destroy junctions through arc-over, or excessive reverse currents. One of the greatest dangers to the diode is heat. Heat causes more electron-hole pairs to be generated, which in turn increases current flow. This increase in current generates more heat and the cycle repeats itself until the diode draws excessive current. This action is referred to as thermal runaway and eventually causes diode destruction. Extreme caution should be used when working with equipment containing diodes to ensure that these problems do not occur and cause irreparable diode damage.

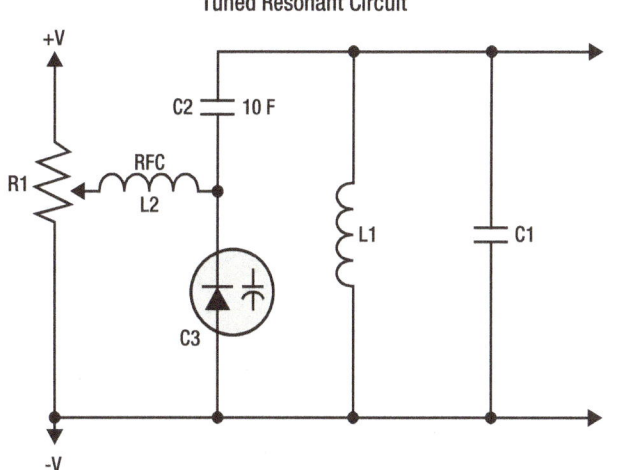

Figure 1-39. Varactor tuned resonant circuit.

The following is a list of some of the special safety precautions that should be observed when working with diodes:

- Never remove or insert a diode into a circuit with voltage applied.
- Never pry diodes to loosen them from their circuits.
- Always be careful when soldering to ensure that excessive heat is not applied to the diode.
- When testing a diode, ensure that the test voltage does not exceed the diode's maximum allowable voltage.
- Never put your fingers across a signal diode because the static charge from your body could short it out.
- Always replace a diode with a direct replacement, or with one of the same type.
- Ensure a replacement diode is put into a circuit in the correct direction.

If a diode has been subjected to excessive voltage or temperature and is suspected of being defective, it can be checked in various ways. The most convenient and quickest way of testing a diode is with an ohmmeter *(Figure 1-40)*. To make the check, simply disconnect one of the diode leads from the circuit wiring, and make resistance measurements across the leads of the diode. The resistance measurements obtained depend upon the test-lead polarity of the ohmmeter; therefore, two measurements must be taken. The first measurement is taken with the test leads connected to either end of the diode and the second measurement is taken with the test leads reversed on the diode.

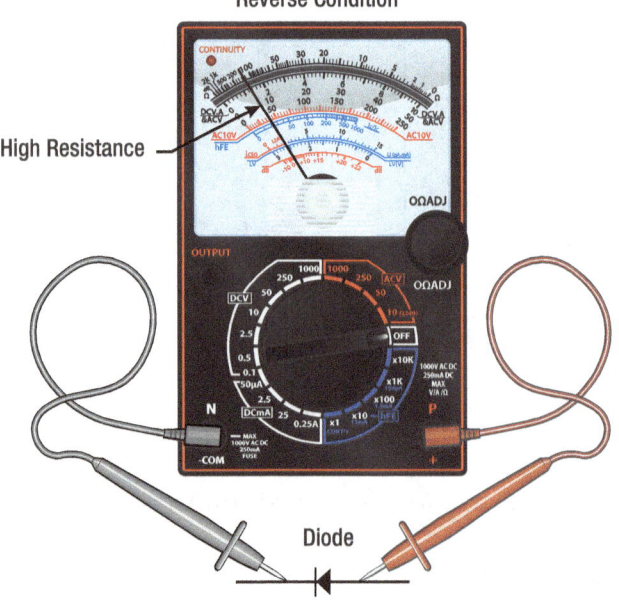

(A) High Resistance Measurement

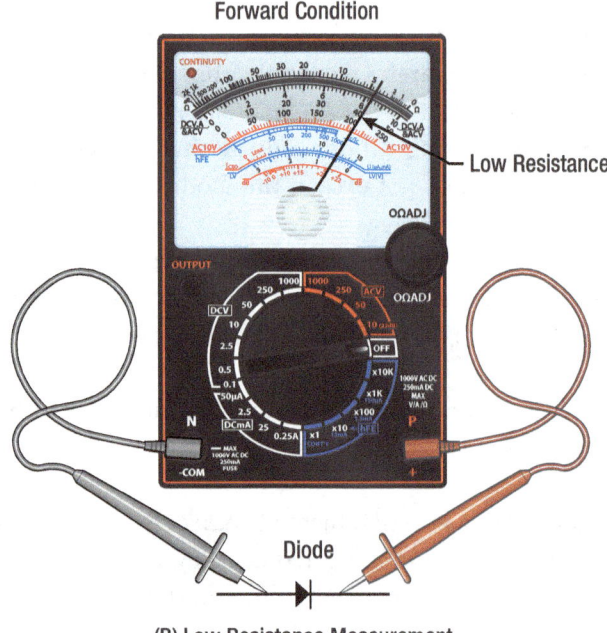

(B) Low Resistance Measurement

Figure 1-40. Checking a diode with an ohmmeter.

The larger resistance value is assumed to be the reverse (back) resistance of the diode, and the smaller resistance (front) value is assumed to be the forward resistance. Measurement can be made for comparison purposes using another identical-type diode (known to be good) as a standard. Two high-value resistance measurements indicate that the diode is open or has a high forward resistance. Two low-value resistance measurements indicate that the diode is shorted or has a low reverse resistance. A normal set of measurements will show a high resistance in the reverse direction and a low resistance in the forward direction. The diode's efficiency is determined by how low the forward resistance is compared with the reverse resistance. That is, it is desirable to have as great a ratio (often known as the front-to-back ratio or the back-to-front ratio) as possible between the reverse and forward resistance measurements. However, as a rule of thumb, a small signal diode will have a ratio of several hundred to one, while a power rectifier can operate satisfactorily with a ratio of 10 to 1.

One thing to keep in mind about the ohmmeter check-it is not conclusive. It is still possible for a diode to check good under this test, but break down when placed back in the circuit. The problem is that the meter used to check the diode uses a lower voltage than the diode usually operates at in the circuit. Another important point to remember is that a diode should not be condemned because two ohmmeters give different readings on the diode. This occurs because of the different internal resistances of the ohmmeters and the different states of charge on the ohmmeter batteries. Because each ohmmeter sends a different current through the diode, the two resistance values read on the meters will not be the same.

Another way of checking a diode is with the substitution method. In this method, a good diode is substituted for a questionable diode. This technique should be used only after you have made voltage and resistance measurements to make certain that there is no circuit defect that might damage the substitution diode. If more than one defective diode is present in the equipment section where trouble has been localized, this method becomes cumbersome, since several diodes may have to be replaced before the trouble is corrected. To determine which stages failed and which diodes are not defective, all of the removed diodes must be tested. This can be accomplished by observing whether the equipment operates correctly as each of the removed diodes is reinserted into the equipment.

In conclusion, the only valid check of a diode is a dynamic electrical test that determines the diode's forward current (resistance) and reverse current (resistance) parameters. This test can be accomplished using various crystal diode test sets that are readily available from many manufacturers.

DIODES IN SERIES AND PARALLEL

A diode offers a slight resistance to current flow in forward bias and, therefore, a voltage drop occurs as current flows through the diode. In a forward biased circuit, the voltage drop is approximately 0.7 volts for a silicon diode, and about 0.3 volts for a germanium diode. The remainder of the voltage is applied to any load in the circuit downstream of the diode.

Diodes connected in series provide a constant DC voltage across the diode combination. The output voltage across the diodes remains constant in spite of changes to the load current or changes to the supply voltage. Thus, series combinations of diodes can be used to create voltage regulator circuits. As shown in *Figure 1-41*, the individual voltage drops across each diode are subtracted from the supply voltage to result in a pre-determined voltage potential across the load resistor. By adding more diodes in series, the voltage is reduced further. The load resistor can also be placed in parallel with the diode stack providing a constant regulated voltage source, as such as shown on the right, where three silicon diodes in series each drop 0.7v which equals an output of 2.1v at R_{LOAD}.

CLIPPER CIRCUIT

A clipper circuit, also known as a diode limiter, has the property that no matter how much the input voltage varies, the output voltage is restricted. As shown in *Figure 1-42*, the diode is reverse biased during one half of the AC sine wave resulting in an open switch, and is forward biased during the other cycle resulting in a closed switch. The output then consists of only the pulses of the applied AC voltage. *Figure 1-42(A)* is called a positive clipper because it removes the positive half cycle. Reversing the direction of the diode will result in a negative clipper. Single-end clipper circuits are used as half-wave rectifiers, to be discussed later.

A circuit that limits the peaks of both half cycles of an AC signal is called a double-end clipper. It consists of two diodes in parallel and two DC voltage sources that determine the output range. As shown in *Figure 1-43*, if the AC input voltage makes excursions outside the range of VB1 and VB2, those portions of the input waveform are clipped off. When the positive input value is greater than the value of VB1, diode D1 conducts, resulting in the output being equal to the voltage of VB1. Likewise, when the negative AC input voltage becomes greater than the voltage of VB2, then D2 conducts, resulting in the output being equal to the voltage of VB2. For values between the upper and lower limits, both diodes are reverse-biased, and therefore, act as open circuits. Please

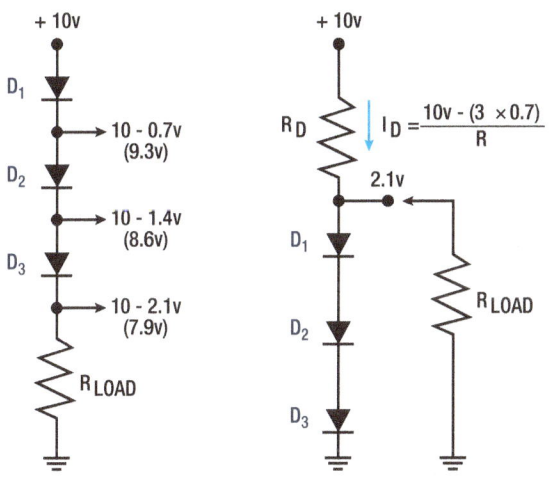

Figure 1-41. Diodes in series create a regulated voltage source.

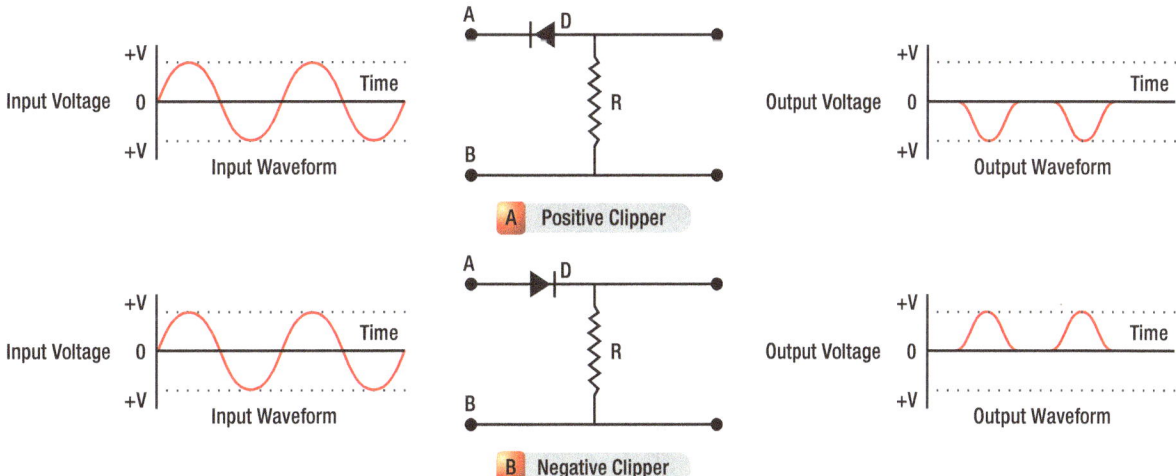

Figure 1-42. Single-end clipper circuits.

Module 04 B2 - Electronic Fundamentals

1.21

note that the battery symbols in this figure indicate that VB1 and VB2 are DC voltages applied to the diodes, not that actual batteries are used in the circuit design.

Diode limiters are typically used to protect circuits against excessive voltage, such as transient voltage spikes. They are also used in signal processing circuits to alter the waveform of the signal input from a sine wave input to an approximate square wave output.

CLAMPER CIRCUIT

A clamper circuit is similar to the single-ended clipper, except that a capacitor is placed in series instead of a resistor. As a result, a clamping circuit places either the positive or negative peak of an AC sine wave at a desired DC level. It other words, it adds a DC component to the output without changing the shape or amplitude of the input AC signal. Diode clampers have a number of useful signal processing applications, and are often used in electronic voltmeters.

Refer to the clamper circuit in *Figure 1-44*. During the negative half of the AC input cycle, the diode is forward biased and current flows through the circuit charging the capacitor to a value equal to the maximum negative peak voltage (Vm). The charge is trapped in the capacitor. It can't discharge because the diode can't conduct in the reverse direction. As a result, the voltage held by the capacitor adds to the output voltage. The output waveform is exactly the same as the input waveform, but the waveform is shifted up by an amount equal to the negative peak value of the input voltage, in this case 2v. Since the output voltage falls to zero when the capacitor voltage has its negative peak value, the circuit is said to clamp the negative peak of the waveform at 0 volts. Signal waveforms can be clamped at levels other than zero by adding a DC voltage source in series with the diode, as shown previously in *Figure 1-43*.

HALF-WAVE RECTIFIER CIRCUIT

With the application of AC voltage to the diode series circuit, the diode allows current to flow in only one direction and blocks it in the opposed direction. The diode in series also rectifies the AC voltage, that is, AC

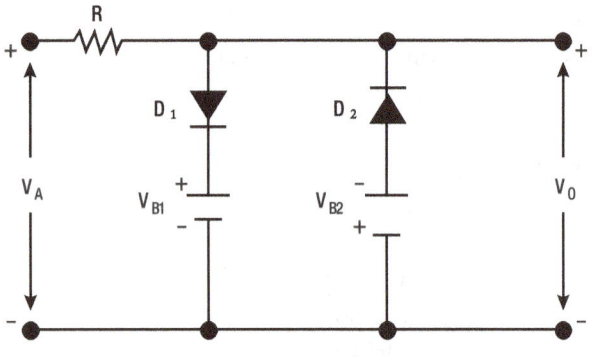

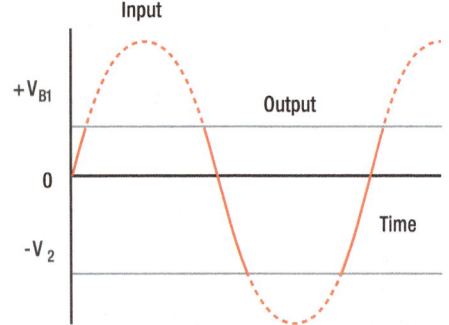

Figure 1-43. Double-end clipper circuit.

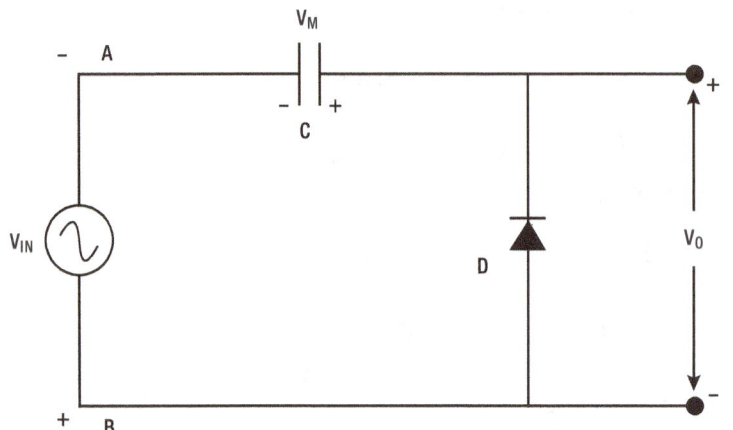

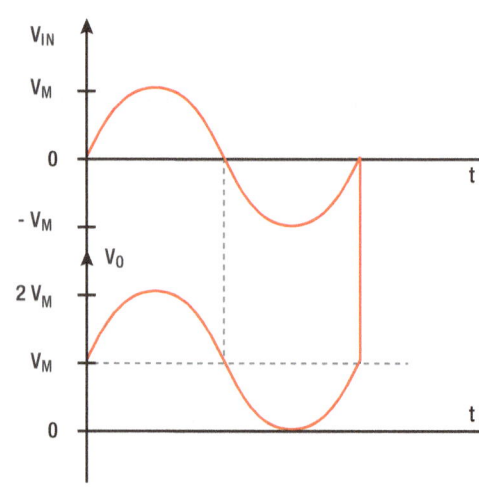

Figure 1-44. Clamper circuit.

voltage is converted to DC voltage. So, in addition to being a clipper, it can also be said that the diode serves as a rectifier. *(Figure 1-45)*

In a half-wave rectifier circuit, the function of the diode is to supply unidirectional current to the load. When the AC sine wave input is positive, the diode acts like a closed circuit since it is forward biased, and as such, produces current in the positive direction. However, when the AC sine wave cycle turns negative, the diode is reverse biased. Here the widened depletion zone acts as an open circuit blocking the current flow. The limitation of the half-wave rectifier is that only half of the AC sine wave voltage is rectified. The other half of the AC voltage is wasted since current cannot flow across the reverse biased diode.

FULL-WAVE RECTIFIER CIRCUIT

AC voltage applied to diodes in a parallel circuit creates similar results, but with greatly improved efficiency. *Figure 1-46* illustrates diodes in a parallel circuit that supplies DC voltage to a load resistor (RL). The AC voltage that is induced into the circuit flows from negative to positive. However, the full wave of the AC voltage is converted to DC, unlike that in the series circuit. As a result, the DC pulses are not separated from each other. The arrows in the diagram show the direction of current flow during the positive and negative cycles of the voltage. Notice that the transformer coil is grounded in the center. This is known as a center-tapped full-wave rectifier circuit. The positive and negative cycles of the AC are used, but the magnitude of the AC voltage is half of what is supplied because of the center tap of the transformer.

BRIDGE RECTIFIER CIRCUIT

A widely used variation of the full-wave rectifier is the bridge rectifier. *(Figure 1-47)* The arrows in the diagram show that current flows in each direction as the AC cycles. With a half-wave rectifier, only have of the AC sine wave is used to produce DC power. With a full-wave rectifier, the positive and negative cycles of the AC are used, but the magnitude of the AC voltage is half of what is supplied because of the center tap of the transformer. With a bridge rectifier, the entire applied AC voltage is rectified resulting in a non-interrupted DC pulse voltage at the output ready to be filtered in to a pure DC voltage.

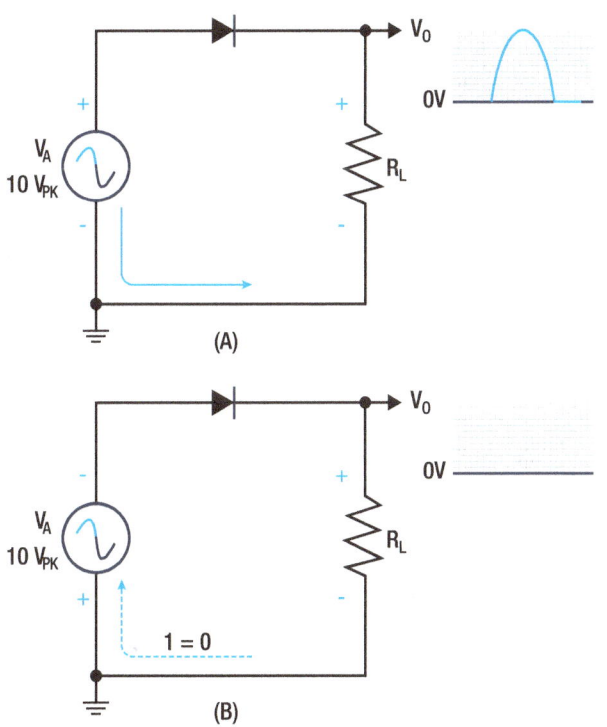

Figure 1-45. Diode and load in a series circuit with AC power applied rectifies the voltage. Only half of the AC voltage is used.

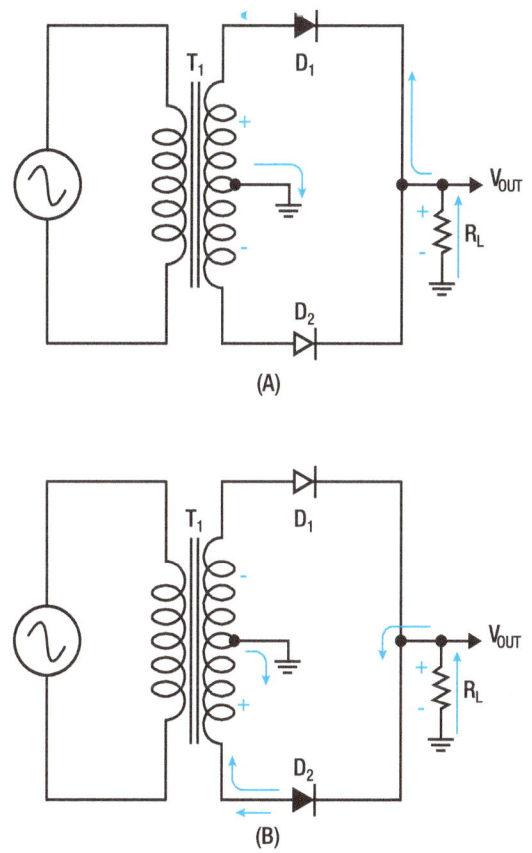

Figure 1-46. Diodes in a parallel circuit create a full-wave rectifier circuit.

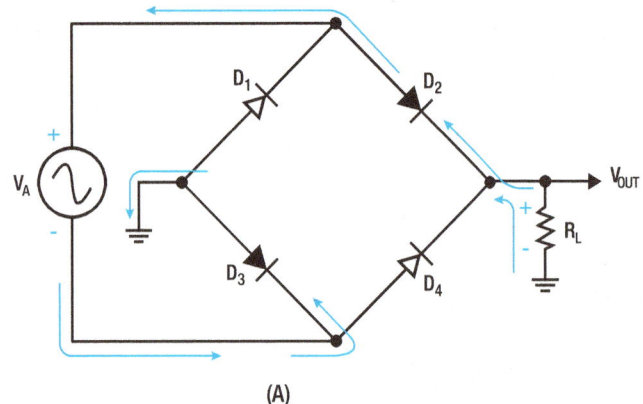

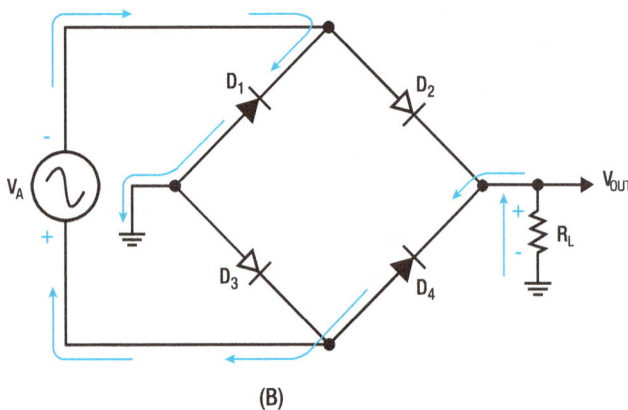

Figure 1-47. A bridge rectifier circuit converts the entire applied AC voltage to a DC voltage.

Power supplies consist of rectifier circuits with smoothing circuits at the output to provide pure DC voltage. A smoothing capacitor (*Figure 1-48*) filters out the pulses from the output waveform. It does this by charging the capacitor during the rise of each pulse, and then discharging the capacitor during the fall of each pulse, resulting in a pure DC output voltage. The time required to charge the capacitor through the resistor to 63% and then discharge it to 37% is called a time constant (T), and is determined multiplying the capacitance (in farads) by the resistance (in ohms): T=RC More elaborate smoothing circuits have RL tank circuits that act as low pass filters.

VOLTAGE DOUBLERS AND TRIPLERS

As shown in *Figure 1-49*, a voltage doubler consists of a clamper circuit (D1 and C1) and a peak rectifier circuit (D2 and C2). The peak rectifier circuit draws current from the clamper circuit and results in a DC output whose value is double the peak-to-peak value of the AC input voltage. During the positive half of the input cycle, clamper diode D1 conducts and peak rectifier diode

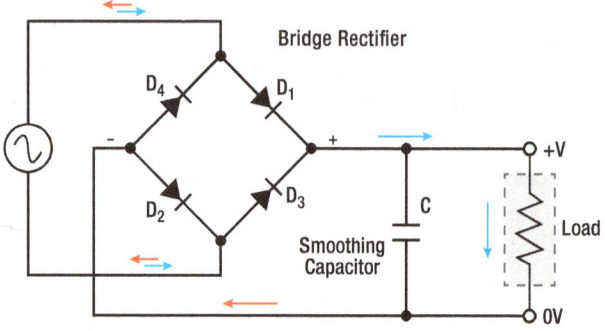

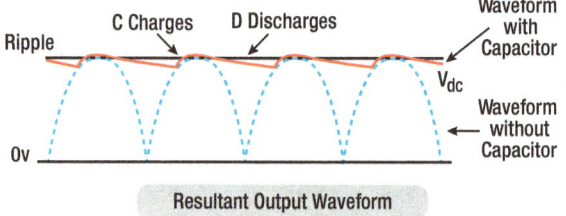

Figure 1-48. A capacitor filters out the pulses providing a pure DC output voltage.

D2 is turned off, allowing the clamper capacitor C1 to charge to the maximum positive peak voltage (Vm). During the negative half of the cycle, diode D1 is turned off and diode D2 conducts charging the peak rectifier capacitor C2 to twice the value of Vm since the voltage across C1 is in series with the input voltage. Over the next positive cycle, D2 is turned off and the voltage at the output appears as 2Vm.

A full-wave voltage doubler is more efficient than a half-wave doubler for the same reason that a full-wave rectifier is more efficient than a half-wave rectifier. As shown in *Figure 1-50*, diode D1 conducts (D2 is turned off) during the positive half cycle charging capacitor C1 to the positive peak input voltage. During the negative half cycle, diode D2 conducts (D1 is turned off) charging capacitor C2 to the negative peak input voltage. The voltage across the output then equals twice the peak input voltage (2Vp).

By extending the basic ideas involved in the voltage doubler, diode circuits can be designed to act as voltage triplers, voltage quadruplers, etc. *(Figure 1-51)* Such circuits are used for developing very high voltage power supplies used for microwave and radar equipment.

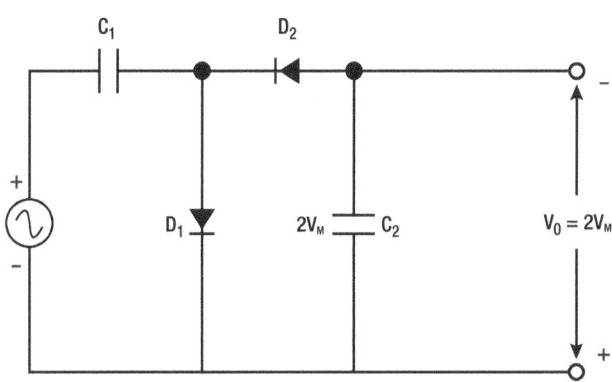

Figure 1-49. Half-wave voltage doubler circuit.

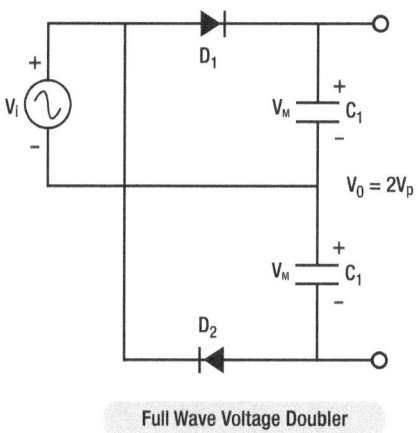

Figure 1-50. Full-wave voltage doubler circuit.

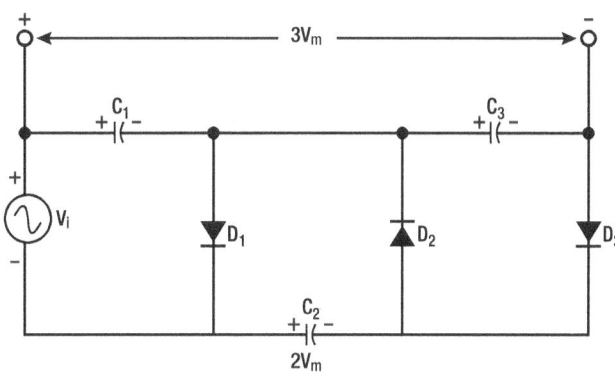

Figure 1-51. Voltage tripler circuit.

TRANSISTORS

While diodes are very useful in electronic circuits, semiconductors can be used to construct true control valves, known as transistors. A transistor is little more than a sandwich of N-type semiconductor material between two pieces of P-type semiconductor material, or vice versa. However, a transistor exhibits some remarkable properties and is the building block of all things electronic. With the application of a small signal voltage, a transistor can act either as a switch in digital electronic applications, or as an amplifier in analog electronic applications.

This sub-module will explain the characteristics and properties of transistors, and shows the schematic symbols used for this device. It will also describe the construction and operation of various transistors, and explain how they are tested. Finally, it will conclude with a section describing how transistors are used in constructing circuits such as amplifiers, cascades, push-pull, oscillators, multivibrators, and flip-flops.

DESCRIPTION, CHARACTERISTICS, PROPERTIES AND SYMBOLS

As with any union of dissimilar types of semiconductor materials, the junctions of the P-type and N-type materials have depletion areas that create potential hills for the flow of electrical charges. Transistors have three electrodes or terminals, one each for the three layers of semiconductor material. The emitter (E) and the collector (C) are on the outside of the sandwiched semiconductor material. The center material is known as the base (B). A change in a relatively small amount of voltage applied to the base of the transistor allows a relatively large amount of current to flow from the collector to the emitter due to the reduction in size of the depletion areas. In this way, when the transistor is fully on, or saturated as it is called, it acts like a switch with a small input voltage controlling a large amount of current. When the transistor is operating in the active region between cut-off and saturation, it behaves more like an amplifier.

Transistors having two junctions of P-type and N-type materials are known as Bipolar Junction Transistors (BJT). BJTs are the most commonly used form of transistor. *Figure 1-52* is a diagram showing the make-up of PNP and NPN Bipolar Junction Transistors with their schematic symbols. The direction of the arrow always points from the positive P-type material to the negative N-type material in both the PNP junction transistor and NPN junction transistor, exactly the same as for the standard diode symbol.

Transistors are categorized by the semiconductor material used in their construction, their PN structure (e.g., unipolar, bipolar, field effect, etc.), electrical polarity (e.g., PNP, NPN, etc.), maximum power rating, maximum operating frequency, and physical packaging. They are also classified by their application, such as general purpose, high-frequency switching, high-voltage, or amplification, and their amplification factor. Thus a particular transistor may be described as a silicon, bipolar junction, NPN, surface mount, low-power, and high-frequency switch.

Transistors are identified as shown in *Figure 1-53*. For a round transistor case, the collector can either be connected to the metal case (example A) or it can be the middle lead with a color dot located on the case next to the collector lead (example B). In example D, the collector lead in this oval case is identified by the wide space between it and the other two leads. The final lead at the far left is the emitter. In many instances, color dots indicate the collector lead, and short leads relative to the other leads indicate the emitter. In a conventional power diode mounted in a TO-5 case, as seen in example E, the collector lead is part of the mounting base, while the emitter and base are leads protruding from the mounting surface.

TESTING OF TRANSISTORS

The previous sub-module discussed how a diode can be tested using an ohmmeter. The same type of test using an ohmmeter can be extended to give a simple and straightforward confidence check for bipolar transistors. Again the test using an ohmmeter only provides a confidence check that the device has not blown, but it is still very useful. The test relies on the fact that the transistor can be considered to comprise of two back-to-back diodes, as shown in *Figure 1-54*. By performing a continuity test, using the middle ohms range, between the base and collector, and the base and emitter, the basic integrity of the transistor can be ascertained.

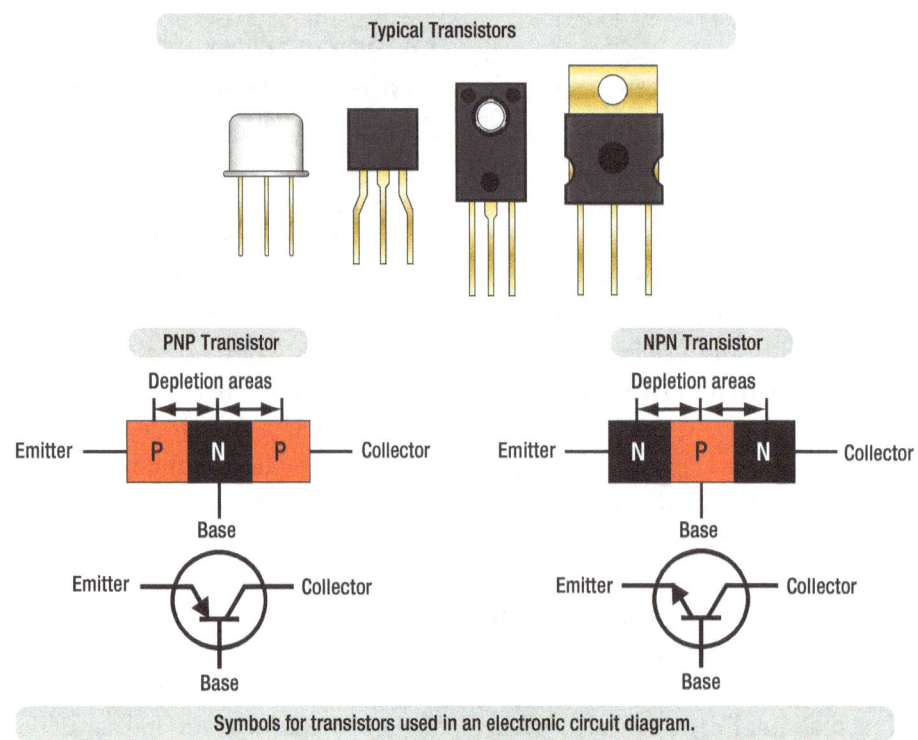

Figure 1-52. Typical transistors, diagrams of a PNP and NPN transistor, and the symbol for those transistors when depicted in an electronic circuit diagram.

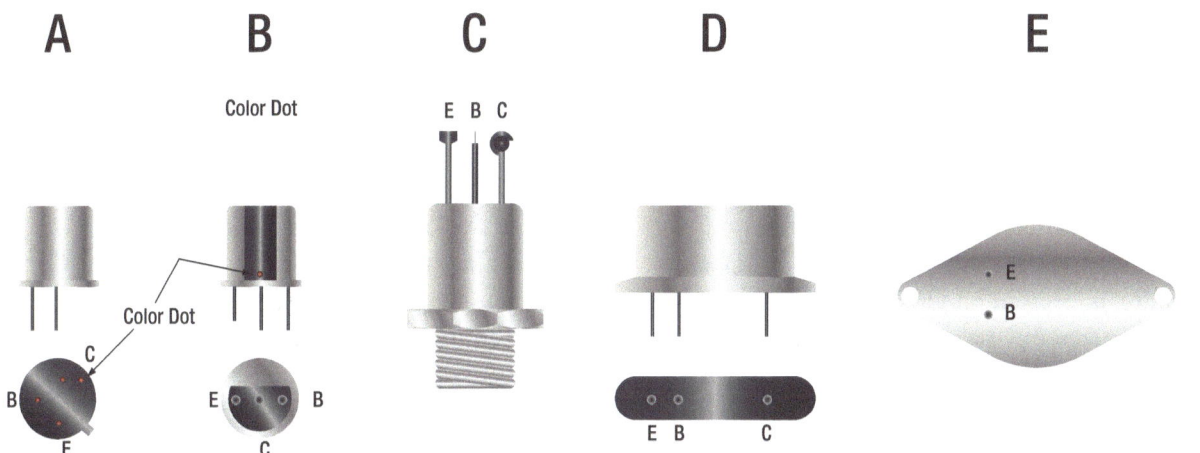

Figure 1-53. Common transistor lead identifications.

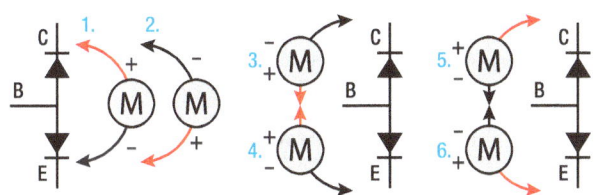

Figure 1-54. Testing a transistor is just like testing two back-to-back diodes.

To make the check, simply disconnect the transistor leads from the circuit wiring, and make resistance measurements across the leads of the transistor. The resistance measurements obtained depend upon the test-lead polarity of the ohmmeter (M); therefore, two measurements must be taken. Begin by connecting the positive lead to the collector and the negative lead to the emitter (1). The ohmmeter should read as an open circuit. Reverse the leads between the collector and emitter (2). Again, the ohmmeter measurement reading should be a high resistance to make certain that the transistor is not short circuited.

The next measurement is taken with the test leads connected to the base and collector (3) and the base and emitter (4), followed by measurements with the test leads reversed between the base and collector (5) and the base and emitter (6), as discussed in the following paragraphs.

Touch the positive (red colored) lead from the ohmmeter to the base of the transistor and connect the negative (black colored) lead to the collector and measure the resistance. The reading should be a low resistance (closed circuit) for an NPN transistor, and a high resistance (open circuit) for a PNP transistor. With the positive lead still connected to the base, repeat the measurement touching the negative lead on to the emitter, Again, it should read as a low resistance for an NPN transistor, and a high resistance for a PNP transistor. The larger resistance value is assumed to be the reverse (back) resistance of the transistor, and the smaller resistance (front) value is assumed to be the forward resistance.

Now reverse the connection to the base of the transistor so that the negative lead is touching the base and the positive lead is touching the collector. In this case, it should read as a high resistance (open circuit) for an NPN transistor, and a low resistance (closed circuit) for a PNP transistor. With the negative lead still connected to the base, repeat the measurement touching the positive lead on to the emitter, Again, the reading should be a high resistance for an NPN transistor, and a low resistance for a PNP transistor.

One thing to keep in mind about the ohmmeter check is that it is not conclusive. It is still possible for a transistor to check "good" under this test, but break down when placed back in the circuit. The problem is that the meter used to check the transistor uses a lower voltage than the transistor usually operates at in the circuit. Another important point to remember is that a transistor should not be condemned because two ohmmeters give different readings on the transistor. This occurs because of the different internal resistances of the ohmmeters and the different states of charge on the ohmmeter batteries. Because each ohmmeter sends a different current through the transistor, the two resistance values read on the meters will not be the same.

As with a transistor, another way of checking a transistor is with the substitution method. In this method, a good transistor is substituted for a questionable diode. This technique should be used only after you have made voltage and resistance measurements to make certain that there is no circuit defect that might damage the substitution transistor. If more than one defective transistor is present in the equipment section where trouble has been localized, this method becomes cumbersome, since several transistors may have to be replaced before the trouble is corrected. To determine which stages failed and which transistors are not defective, all of the removed transistors must be tested. This can be accomplished by observing whether the equipment operates correctly as each removed transistor is reinserted into the equipment.

In conclusion, the only valid check of a transistor is a dynamic electrical test that determines the transistor's forward current (resistance) and reverse current (resistance) parameters. This test can be accomplished using various transistor test sets that are readily available from many manufacturers.

CONSTRUCTION AND OPERATION OF TRANSISTORS

The transistor is a three-terminal device primarily used to amplify signals and control current within a circuit. The basic two-junction PN semiconductor must have one type of region sandwiched between two of the other type. The three regions in a transistor are the collector, which is moderately doped, the emitter, which is heavily doped and the base significantly less doped. The alternating layers of semiconductor material type provide the common commercial name for each type of transistor. The interface between the layers is called a junction. Selenium and germanium diodes previously discussed are examples of junction diodes. Note that the sandwiched layer or base is significantly thinner than the collector or the emitter. In general this permits a "punching through" action for the carriers passing between the collector and emitter terminals.

BIPOLAR JUNCTION TRANSISTORS

As discussed in the section on diodes, the movement of the electrons and holes can be considered current. Electron current moves in one direction, while hole current travels in the opposite direction. In transistors, both electrons and holes act as carriers of current.

If a BJT is put into a simple battery circuit, such as the one shown in *Figure 1-55*, voltage from the battery (EB) forces free electrons and holes toward the junction between the base and the emitter, just as it does in the junction of a semiconductor diode. The emitter-base depletion area becomes narrow as free electrons combine with the holes at the junction. Current (IB), shown as solid arrows, flows through the junction in the emitter-base battery circuit. At the same time, an emitter-collector circuit is constructed with a battery (EC) of much higher voltage in its circuit. Because of the narrow depletion area at the emitter-base junction, current IC is able to cross the collector-base junction, flow through emitter-base junction, and complete the collector-emitter battery circuit (hollow arrows).

To some extent, varying the voltage to the base material can increase or decrease the current flow through the transistor. The emitter-base depletion area changes width in response to the base voltage. If base voltage is removed, the emitter-base depletion area becomes too wide and all current flow through the transistor ceases. Current in the transistor circuit illustrated has a relationship as follows: IE = IB + IC. It should be remembered that it is the voltage applied to the base that turns the collector-emitter current on or off.

Controlling a large amount of current flow with a small independent input voltage is very useful when building electronic circuits. Transistors are the building blocks from which all electronic devices are made, including logic gates that are used to create microprocessor chips. As production techniques have developed, the size of reliable transistors has shrunk. Now, hundreds of millions and even billions of transistors are used to construct a single integrated circuit (IC) used in simple personal computers, as well as complex avionic system computers.

UNIPOLAR JUNCTION TRANSISTORS

Bipolar junction transistors are so named because their operation involves both holes and electrons, which are characteristic of the N-type and P-type semiconductor materials; whereas holes are the majority carrier in P-type materials, and electrons are the majority carriers in N-type materials. In contrast, Unipolar Junction Transistors (UJT) contain only one PN junction, and therefore, have only one type of charge carrier. *(Figure 1-56)*

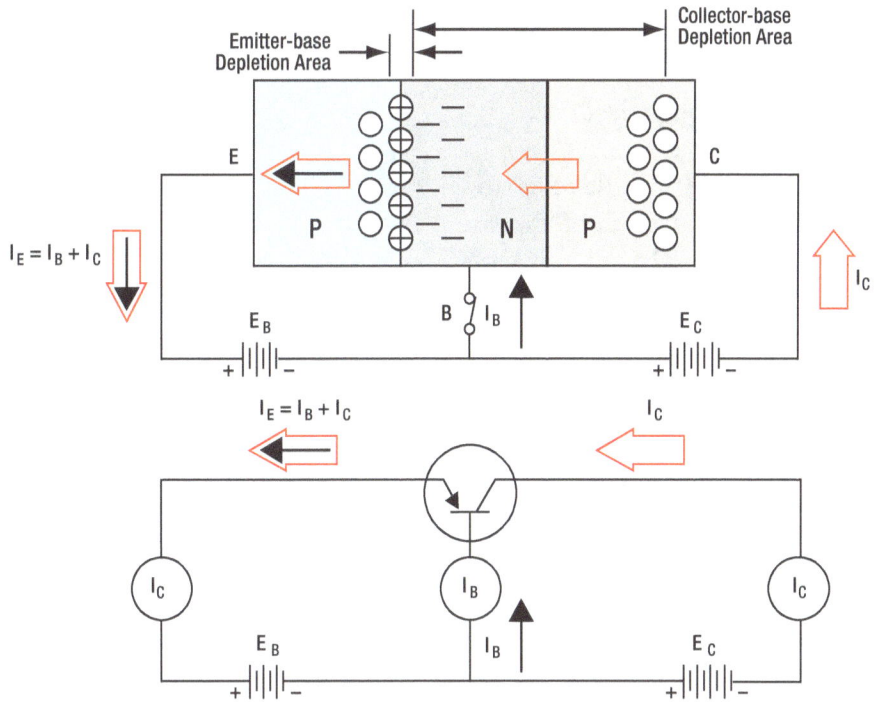

Figure 1-55. The effect of applying a small voltage to bias the emitter-base junction of a transistor (top). A circuit diagram for this same transistor (bottom).

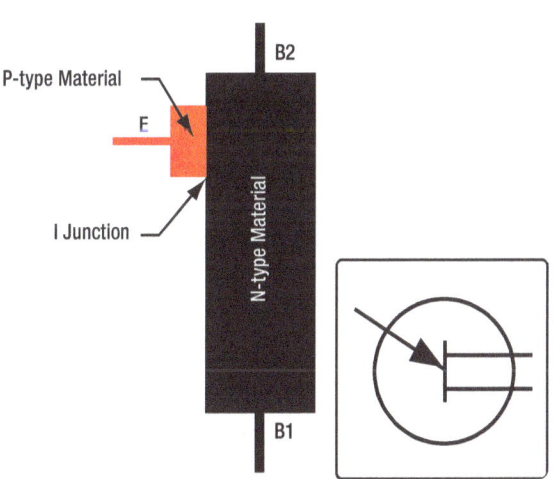

Figure 1-56. A unijunction transistor.

The UJT contains one base semiconductor material and a different type of emitter semiconductor material. There is no collector material. One electrode is attached to the emitter and two electrodes are attached to the base material at opposite ends. These are known as base 1 (B1) and base 2 (B2). The electrode configuration makes the UJT appear physically the same as a bipolar junction transistor. However, there is only one PN junction in the UJT, and as such, it behaves differently.

The base material of a UJT behaves like a resistor between the electrodes. With B2 positive with respect to B1, voltage gradually drops as it flows through the base. *(Figure 1-57)* By placing the emitter at a precise location along the base material gradient, the amount of voltage needed to be applied to the emitter electrode to forward bias the UJT base-emitter junction is determined. When the applied emitter voltage exceeds the voltage at the gradient point where the emitter is attached, the junction is forward biased and current flows freely from the B1 electrode to the E electrode. Otherwise, the junction is reversed biased and no significant current flows although

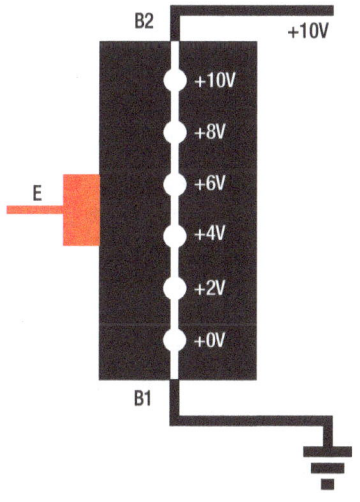

Figure 1-57. The voltage gradient in a UJT.

there is some leakage. By selecting a UJT with the correct bias level for a particular circuit, the applied emitter voltage can control current flow through the device.

UJTs transistors of a wide variety of designs and characteristics exist. A description of all of them is beyond the scope of this discussion. In general, UJTs have some advantages over bipolar transistors. They are stable in a wide range of temperatures. In some circuits, use of UJTs can reduce the overall number of components used, which saves money and potentially increases reliability. They can be found in switching circuits, oscillators, and wave shaping circuits.

FIELD EFFECT TRANSISTORS

The Field Effect Transistor (FET) is a type of unipolar junction transistor device in that it contains only one junction of the P-type and N-type of semiconductor material. The junction is located at the gate where it contacts the main current carrying portion of the device. All FETs have source, drain, and gate terminals that correspond roughly to the emitter, collector, and base of a bipolar junction transistor. All FETs operate by expanding and contracting the depletion area at the junction of the semiconductor materials, and thus are known as depletion mode devices.

The primary difference between the BJT and the FET is that the bipolar transistor has two PN junctions and is a current controlled device, while the FET has only one PN junction and is a voltage controlled device. Within the FET family, there are two general categories of components, the Junction FET (JFET) and the enhancement-mode Metal-Oxide FET (MOSFET).

Figure 1-58 shows the basic construction of the JFET and the schematic symbol. In this figure, it can be seen that the drain (D) and source (S) are connected to an N-type material, and the gate (G) is connected to the P-type material. With gate voltage Vgg set to 0 volts and drain voltage Vdd set to some positive voltage, a current will flow between the source and the drain, through a narrow band of N-material. If then, Vgg is adjusted to some negative voltage, the PN junction will be reverse biased, and a depletion zone (no charge carriers) will be established at the PN junction. By reducing the region of noncarriers, it will have the effect of reducing the dimensions of the N-channel, resulting in a reduction of source to drain current.

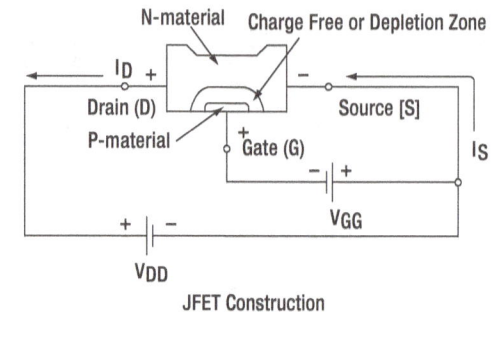
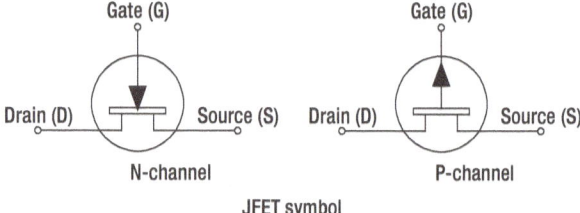

Figure 1-58. General construction and schematic symbol of the MOSFET.

One of the materials in a JFET is called the channel. It is usually the substrate through which the current needing to be controlled flows from a source terminal to a drain terminal. The other type of material intrudes into the channel and acts as the gate. The polarity and amount of voltage applied to the gate can widen or narrow the channel due to expansion or shrinking of the depletion area at the junction of the semiconductors. This increases or decreases the amount of current that can flow through the channel. Enough reversed biased voltage can be applied to the gate to prevent the flow of current through the channel. This allows the JFET to act as a switch. It can also be used as a voltage controlled resistance.

JFETs are exclusively voltage-controlled in that they do not need a biasing current. A JFET is usually on when there is no potential difference between its gate and source terminals. If a potential difference of the proper polarity is applied between its gate and source terminals, the JFET will be more resistive to current flow, which means less current would flow in the channel between the source and drain terminals. Because JFETs are voltage-controlled devices, they have some advantages over the bipolar transistor. One such advantage is that because the gate is reverse biased, the circuit that it is connected to it sees the gate as a very high resistance. This means that the JFET has less of an insertion influence in the circuit. The high resistance also means that less current will be used.

JFETs are easier to manufacture than bipolar transistors and have the advantage of staying on once current flow begins without continuous gate voltage applied. They have higher impedance than bipolar transistors and operate cooler. This makes their use ideal for ICs where millions of JFETs may be in use on the same chip. JFETs come in N-channel and P-channel varieties. Like many other solid-state devices, careless handling and static electricity can damage the JFET. Technicians should take all precautions to prevent such damage.

METAL OXIDE FIELD EFFECT TRANSISTORS

The basic FET has been modified in numerous ways and continues to be at the center of faster and smaller electronic component development. A version of the FET widely used is the Metal Oxide Field Effect Transistor (MOSFET). The MOSFET uses a metal gate with a thin insulating material between the gate and the semiconductor material. This essentially creates a capacitor at the gate and eliminates current leakage in this area.

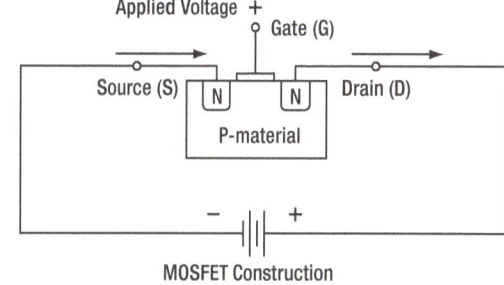

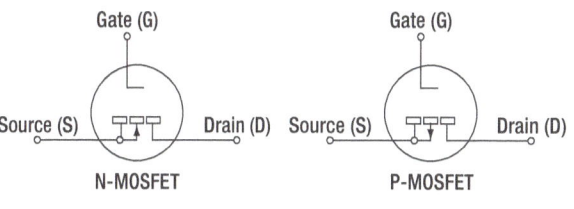

Figure 1-59. General construction and schematic symbol of MOSFET transistor.

Figure 1-59 illustrates the general construction and the schematic symbol of the MOSFET transistor. The biasing arrangement for the MOSFET is essentially the same as that for the JFET. The term "enhancement" comes from the idea that when there is no bias voltage applied to the gate (G), then there is no channel for current conduction between the source (S) and the drain (D). By applying a greater voltage on the gate (G), the P-channel will begin to materialize and grow in size. Once this occurs, the source (S) to drain (D) current Id will increase. The schematic symbol reflects this characteristic by using a broken line to indicate that the channel does not exist without a gate bias.

As with FETs, MOSFETs come with N-channels or P-channels. They can also be constructed as depletion mode or enhancement mode devices. This is analogous to a switch being normally open or normally closed. Depletion mode MOSFETs have an open channel that is restricted or closed when voltage is applied to the gate (i.e., normally open). Enhancement mode MOSFETs allow no current to flow at zero bias, but create a channel for current flow when voltage is applied to the gate (i.e., normally closed). No voltage is used when the MOSFETs are at zero bias. Millions of enhancement mode MOSFETs are used in the construction of integrated circuits. They are installed in complimentary pairs such that when one is open, the other is closed. This basic design is known as Complementary MOSFET (CMOS), which is the basis for integrated circuit design in nearly all modern electronics. Through the use of these transistors, digital logic gates can be formed.

Other more specialized FETs exist. Some of their unique characteristics are owed to design alterations and others to material variations. The transistor devices discussed thus far use silicon-based semiconductors. But the use of other semiconductor materials can yield variations in performance. Metal Semiconductor FETs (MESFETS) for example, are often used in microwave applications. They have a combined metal and semiconductor material at the gate and are typically made from gallium arsenide or indium phosphide. MESFETs are used for their quickness when starting and stopping current flows especially in opposite directions.

High electron mobility transistors (HEMT) and pseudomorphic high electron mobility transistors (PHEMT) are also constructed from gallium arsenide semiconductor material and are used for high frequency applications. Many have poly-crystalline silicon gates rather than metal, but the MOSFET name remains and the basic behavioral characteristic are the same.

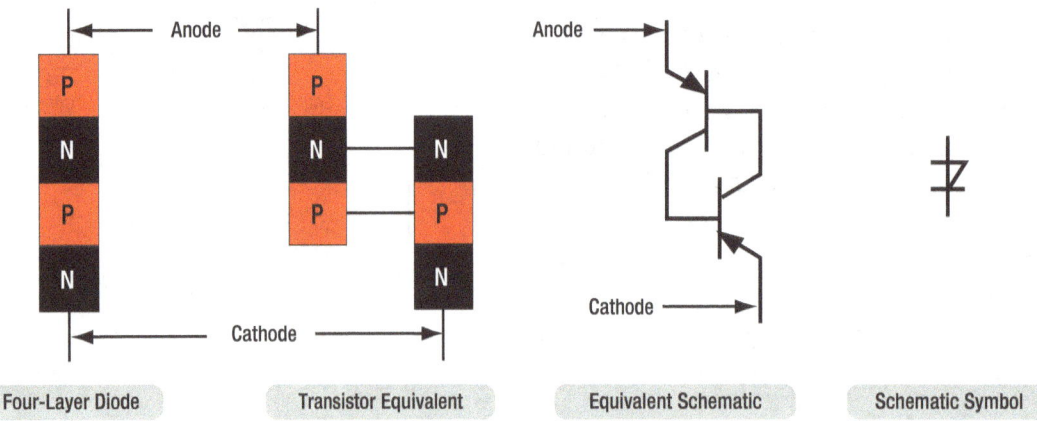

Figure 1-60. A four-layer semiconductor diode behaves like two transistors. When breakover voltage is reached, the device conducts current until the voltage is removed.

MULTI-LAYER SEMICONDUCTOR DEVICES

Combination of semiconductor materials is not limited to a two-layer PN junction diode, or a three-layer PNP or NPN junction transistor. By creating a four-layer sandwich of alternating types of semiconductor material (i.e., PNPN or NPNP), a slightly different semiconductor diode is created. As is the case in a two-layer diode, circuit current is either blocked or permitted to flow through the diode in a single direction.

SHOCKLEY DIODES

Within a four-layer diode, sometimes known as a Shockley diode, there are three junctions. The behavior of the junctions and the entire four-layer diode can be understood by considering it to be two interconnected three-layer transistors. *(Figure 1-60)*

Transistor behavior includes no current flow until the base material receives an applied voltage to narrow the depletion area at the base-emitter junction. The base materials in the four-layer diode transistor model receive charge from the other transistor's collector. With no other means of reducing any of the depletion areas at the junctions, it appears that current does not flow in either direction in this device. However, if a large voltage is applied to forward bias the anode or cathode, at some point the ability to block flow breaks down. Current flows through whichever transistor is charged. Collector current then charges the base of the other transistor and current flows through the entire device.

Some caveats are necessary with this explanation. The transistors that comprise this four-layer diode must be constructed of material similar to that described in a zener diode. That is, it must be able to endure the current flow without burning out. In this case, the voltage that causes the diode to conduct is known as breakover voltage, rather than breakdown voltage. Additionally, this diode has the unique characteristic of allowing current flow to continue until the applied voltage is reduced significantly, in most cases, until it is reduced to zero. In AC circuits, this would occur when the AC sine wave cycles.

SILICON CONTROLLED RECTIFIERS

While the four-layer Shockley diode is useful as a switching device, a slight modification to its design creates a Silicon Controlled Rectifier (SCR), or thyristor. *(Figure 1-61)* To construct a SCR, an additional terminal, known as a gate, is added. It provides more control and utility. In the four-layer semiconductor construction, there are always two junctions forward biased and one junction reversed biased. The added terminal allows the momentary application of voltage to the reversed biased

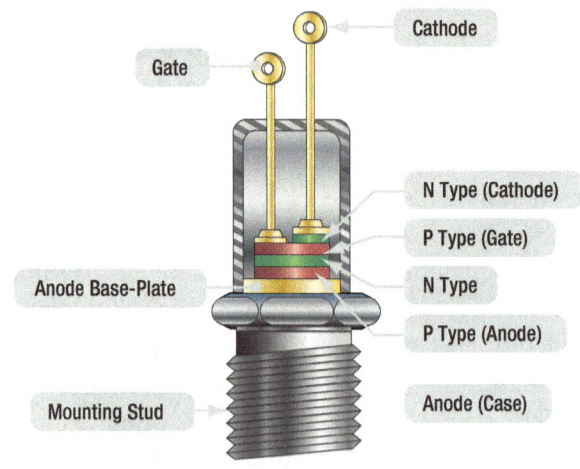

Figure 1-61. Cross-section of a medium power SCR.

junction. All three junctions then become forward biased and current at the anode flows through the device. Once voltage is applied to the gate, the SCR become latched or locked on. Current continues to flow through it until the level drops off significantly, usually to zero. Then, another applied voltage through the gate is needed to reactivate the current flow. *(Figure 1-62)*

SCRs are often used in high voltage situations, such as power switching, phase controls, battery chargers, and inverter circuits. They can be used to produce variable DC voltages for motors and are found in welding power supplies. Often, lighting dimmer systems use SCRs to reduce the average voltage applied to the lights by only allowing current flow during part of the AC cycle. This is done by controlling the pulses to the SCR gate and eliminating the massive heat dissipation caused when using resistors to reduce voltage. *Figure 1-63* graphically depicts the timing of the gate pulse that limits full cycle voltage to the load. By controlling the phase during which time the SCR is latched, a reduced average voltage is applied.

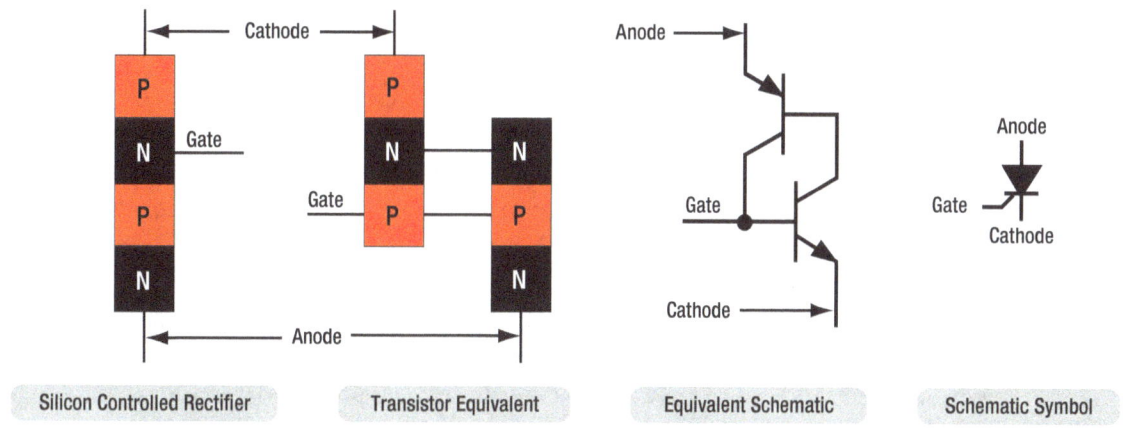

Figure 1-62. A silicon controlled rectifier (SCR) allows current to pass in one direction when the gate receives a positive pulse to latch the device in the on position. Current ceases to flow when it drops below holding current, such as when AC current reverses cycle.

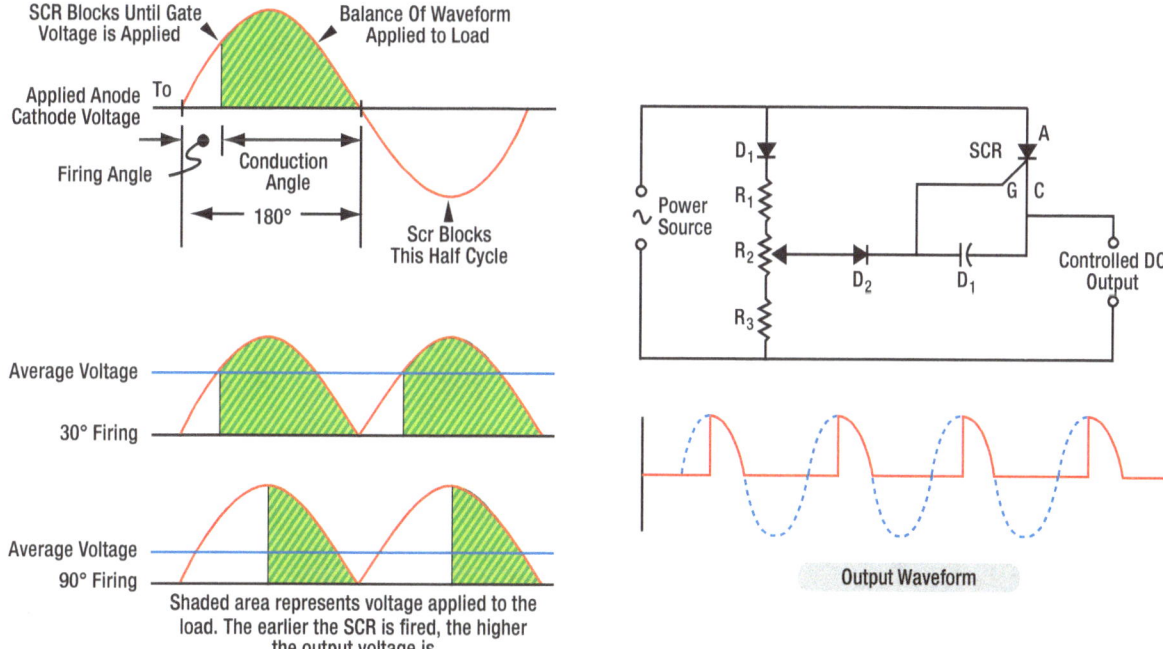

Figure 1-63. Phase control is a key application for SCR. By limiting the percentage of a full cycle of AC voltage that is applied to a load, a reduced voltage results. The firing angle or timing of a positive voltage pulse through the SCR's gate latches the device open allowing current flow until it drops below the holding current, which is usually at or near zero voltage as the AC cycle reverses.

DIACS AND TRIACS

SCRs are limited to allowing current flow in one direction only. In AC circuitry, this means only half of the voltage cycle can be used and controlled. To access the voltage in the reverse cycle from an AC power source, a triac can be used. A triac is also a four-layer semiconductor device similar to a diac, except that it has a gate. *(Figure 1-64)* It differs from an SCR in that it allows current flow in both directions. A positive or negative pulse with respect to the upper terminal allows current to flow through the device in either direction. The gate in the traic works the same way as in a SCR; however, a positive or negative pulse to the gate triggers current flow in a triac. The pulse polarity determines the direction of the current flow through the device.

Figure 1-65 shows a triac used in a simple circuit. It can be triggered with a pulse of either polarity, and remains latched until the voltage declines, such as when the AC sine wave cycles. Then, it needs to be triggered again. In many ways, the triac acts as though it is two SCRs connected side by side only in opposite directions. Like an SCR, the timing of gate pulses determines the amount of the total voltage that is allowed to pass. The output waveform is triggered at 90 degree cycles, as shown in *Figure 1-65*. Because a triac allows current to flow in both directions, the reverse cycle of AC voltage can also be used and controlled.

When used in actual circuits, triacs do not always maintain the same phase firing point in reverse as they do when fired with a positive pulse. This problem can be regulated somewhat through the use of a capacitor in the gate circuit. However, as a result, where precise control is required, two SCRs in reverse of each other are often used instead of the triac.

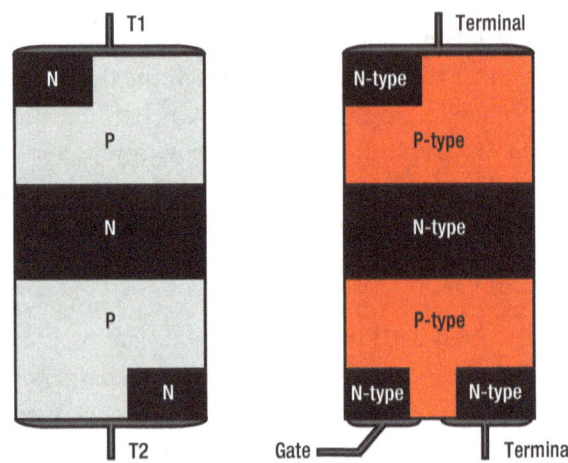

Figure 1-64. A diac (left) and the triac (right) have the same semiconductor layering but the traic also contains a gate.

SIMPLE CIRCUITS

A forward biased PN junction is comparable to a low-resistance circuit element because it passes a high current for a given voltage. On the other hand, a reverse-biased PN junction is comparable to a high resistance circuit element. By using Ohm's law formula for power ($P = I^2R$) and assuming current is held constant through both junctions, it can be concluded that the power developed across the high resistance junction is greater than that developed across a low resistance junction. Therefore, if a semiconductor device were to contain two PN junctions, one forward biased and the other reverse biased, and a low-power signal was injected into the forward biased junction, a high power signal could be produced at the reverse-biased junction.

BIASING

To use the transistor as an amplifier, some sort of external bias voltage must modify each of the junctions. The first PN junction (emitter-base) is biased in the forward direction. This produces a low resistance. The second junction, which is the collector-base junction, is reverse biased to produce a high resistance. *Figure 1-66* illustrates the proper biasing of an NPN transistor.

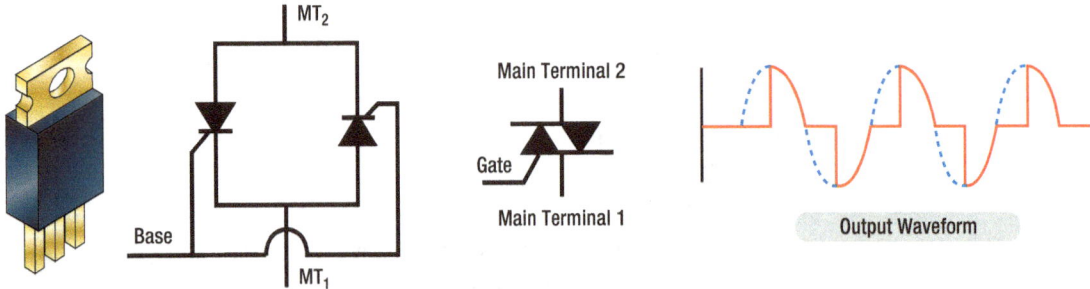

Figure 1-65. A triac is a controlled semiconductor device that allows current flow in both directions.

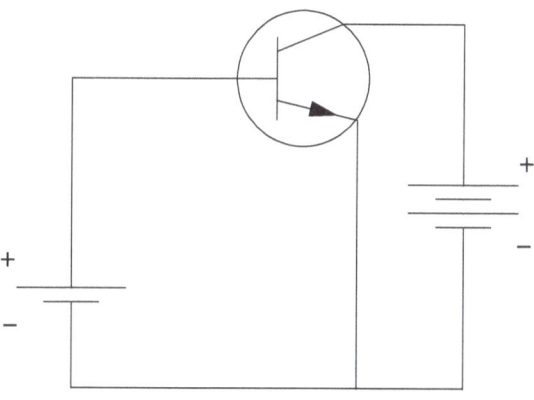

Figure 1-66. NPN Transistor Circuit.

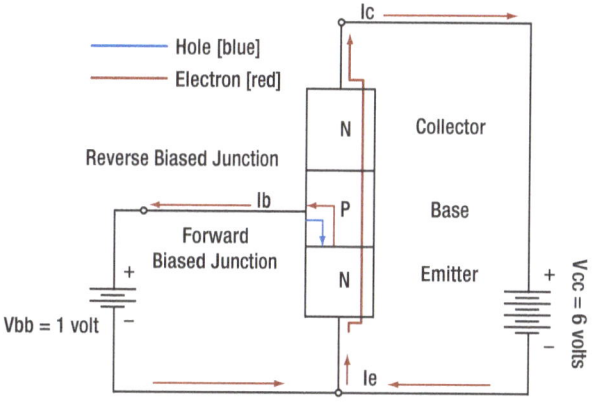

Figure 1-67. NPN Junction.

With the emitter-base junction biased in the forward direction, electrons leave the negative terminal of the battery and enter the N-material. These electrons pass easily through the emitter, cross over the junction, and combine with the hole in the P-material in the base. For each electron that fills a hole in the P-material, another electron will leave the P-material, which creates a new hole and enters the positive terminal of the battery.

The second PN junction, which is the base-collector junction, is reverse biased. This will prevent the majority carriers from crossing the junction, thus creating a high resistance circuit. It is worth noting that there still is a small current passing through the reversed PN junction in the form of minority carriers — that is, electrons in the P-material and holes in the N-material. The minority carriers play a significant part in the operation of the NPN transistor.

Figure 1-67 illustrates the basic interaction of the NPN junction. There are two batteries in the circuit used to bias the NPN transistor. Vbb is considered the base voltage supply, rated in this illustration at 1 volt, and the battery voltage Vcc, rated at 6 volts, is called the collector voltage supply. Current within the external circuit is simply the movement of free electrons originating at the negative terminal of the battery and flowing to the N-material. This is shown as emitter-current (Ie).

As the electrons enter the N-material, they become the majority carrier and move through the N-material to the emitter-base PN junction. This emitter-base junction is forward biased at about 0.65 to 0.7 volts positive with respect to the emitter and presents no resistance to the flow of electrons from the emitter into the base, which is composed of P-material. As these electrons move into the base, they will drop into available holes. For every electron that drops into a hole, another electron exits the base by way of the base lead and becomes the base current or Ib. Of course, when one electron leaves the base, a new hole is formed. From the standpoint of the collector, these electrons that drop into holes are lost and of no use. To reduce this loss of electrons, the transistor is designed so that the base is very thin in relation to the emitter and collector, and the base is lightly doped.

Most of the electrons that move into the base will fall under the influence of the reverse bias of the collector. While collector-base junction is reverse biased with respect to the majority carriers, it behaves as if it is forward biased to the electrons or minority carriers in this case. The electrons are accelerated through the collector-base junction and into the collector. The collector is comprised of the N-type material; therefore, the electrons once again become the majority carrier. Moving easily through the collector, the electrons return to the positive terminal of the collector supply battery Vcc, which is shown in *Figure 1-66* as Ic. Because of the way the transistor operates to transfer current (and its internal resistances) from the original conduction path to another, its name is derived from a combination of the words "transfer" and "resistor".

The PNP transistor generally works the same way as the NPN transistor. The primary difference is that the emitter, base, and collector materials are made of different material than the NPN. The majority and minority current carriers are the opposite in the PNP to that of the NPN. In the case of the PNP, the majority carriers are the holes instead of the electrons in the NPN transistor. To properly bias a PNP transistor, the polarity of the bias network must be reversed.

CONFIGURATIONS

A transistor may be connected in one of three different configurations: common-emitter (CE), common-base (CB), and common-collector (CC). *(Figure 1-68)* The term "common" is used to indicate which element of the transistor is common to both the input and the output. Each configuration has its own characteristics, which makes each configuration suitable for particular applications. A way to determine the configuration is to first find which of the three transistor elements is used for the input signal and which element is used for the output signal. At that point, the remaining element, (base, emitter, or collector) will be the common element to both the input and output, and thus determines the proper configuration.

Common-Emitter Configuration

The CE configuration is most commonly used in amplifier circuits because it provides high gains in voltage, current, and power. The input signal is applied to the base-emitter junction, which is forward biased (low resistance), and the output signal is taken off the collector-emitter junction, which is reverse biased (high resistance). Then the emitter is the common element to both input and output circuits.

When the transistor is connected in a common-emitter configuration, the input signal is injected between the base and emitter, which is a low resistance, low-current circuit. As the input signal goes positive, it causes the base to go positive relative to the emitter. This causes a decrease in the forward bias, which in turn reduces the collector current IC and increases the collector voltage (EC being more negative). During the negative portion of the input signal, the voltage on the base is driven more negative relative to the emitter. This increases the forward bias and allows an increase in collector current IC and a decrease in collector voltage (EC being less negative and going positive). The collector current, which flows through the reverse-biased junction, also flows through a high resistance load resulting in a high level of amplification. Because the input signal to the common-emitter goes positive when the output goes negative, the two signals are 180° out of phase. This is the only configuration that provides a phase reversal. The common-emitter is the most popular of the three configurations because it has the best combination of current and voltage gain. Gain is a term used to indicate the magnitude of amplification. Each transistor configuration has its unique gain characteristics even though the same transistors are used.

Common-Collector Configuration

This transistor configuration is usually used for impedance matching. It is also used as a current driver, due to its high current gain, and is very useful in switching circuits, since it has the ability to pass signals in either direction. In the common-collector circuit, the input signal is applied to the base, and the output signal is taken from the emitter, leaving the collector as the common point between the input and the output. The input resistance of the CC circuit is high, while the output resistance is low. The current gain is higher than that in the common-emitter, but it has a lower power gain than either the common-emitter or common-base configuration. Just like the common-base configuration, the output signal of the common-collector circuit is in phase with the input signal. The common-collector is typically referred to as an emitter-follower because the output developed on the emitter follows the input signal that is applied to the base.

Common-Base Configuration

The primary use of this configuration is for impedance matching because it has a low input impedance and a high output resistance. Two factors, however, limit the usefulness of this circuit application. First is the low input resistance and second is its lack of current, which

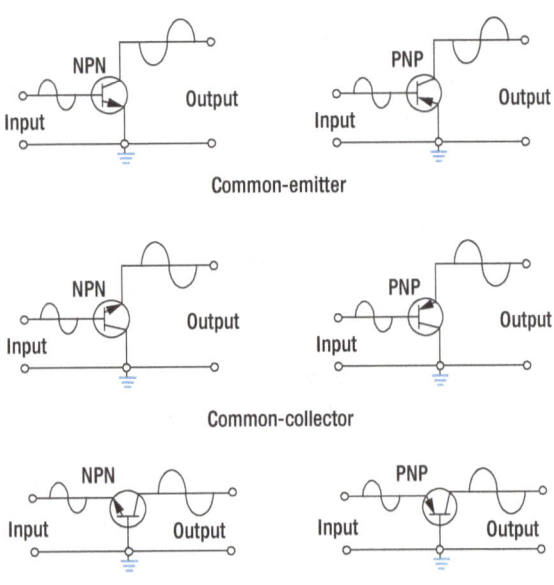

Figure 1-68. Transistor configurations (common-emitter, common-collector, common-base).

is always below 1. Since the CB configuration will give voltage amplification, there are some applications for this circuit, such as microphone amplifiers. In the common-base circuit, the input signal is applied to the emitter and the output signal is taken from the collector. In this case, both the input and the output have the base as a common element. When an input signal is applied to the emitter, it causes the emitter-base junction to react in the same manner as that in the common-emitter circuit. When an input adds to the bias, it will increase the transistor current; conversely, when the signal opposes the bias, the current in the transistor decreases. The signal adds to the forward bias, since it is applied to the emitter, causing the collector current to increase. This increase in IC results in a greater voltage drop across the load resistor, thus lowering the collector voltage EC. The collector voltage, in becoming less negative, will swing in a positive direction and is therefore in phase with the incoming positive signal.

BASIC AMPLIFIER CIRCUITS

An amplifier is a device that enables an input signal to control an output signal. The output signal will have some or all of the characteristics of the input signal, but will generally be a greater magnitude than the input signal in terms of voltage, current, or power. Gain is the basic function of all amplifiers. Because of this gain, one can expect the output signal to be greater than the input signal. If for example there is an input signal of 1 volt and an output signal of 10 volts, then the gain factor can be determined by:

$$\text{Gain} = \text{Signal out} / \text{Signal in}$$
$$\text{Gain} = 10V/1V = 10$$

Voltage gain is usually used to describe the operation of a small gain amplifier. In this type of an amplifier, the output signal voltage is larger than the input signal voltage. Power gain, on the other hand, is usually used to describe the operation of large signal amplifiers. In the case of power gain amplifiers, the gain is not based on voltage, but on watts. A power amplifier is an amplifier in which the output signal power is greater than the input signal power. Most power amplifiers are used as the final stage of amplification and drive the output device. The output device could be a cockpit or cabin speaker, an indicator, or antenna. Whatever the device, the power to make it work comes from the final stage of amplification.

Drivers for autopilot servos are sometimes contained in Line Replaceable Units (LRUs), or "black boxes", called autopilot amplifiers. These units take the low signal commands from the flight guidance system and amplify the signals to a level usable for driving the servo motors.

The classification of a transistor amplifier circuit is determined by the percentage of the time that the current flows through the output circuit in relation to the input signal. There are four classifications of operation: A, AB, B, and C. Each class of operation has a certain use and characteristic. No individual class of amplifier is considered the "best." The best use of an amplifier is a matter of proper selection for the particular operation desired.

Class A Amplifiers

Figure 1-69, shows a simplified Class A amplifier circuit. In the Class A operation, the current in the transistor flows for 100 percent or 360° of the input signal. Class A operation is the least efficient class of operation, but provides the best fidelity. Fidelity simply means that the output signal is a good reproduction of the input signal in all respects other than the amplitude, which is increased. In some cases, there may be some phase shifting between the input signal and the output signal. Typically, the phase difference is 180°. If the output signal is not a good reproduction of the input signal, then the signal is said to be distorted. Distortion is any undesired change to the signal from the input to the output.

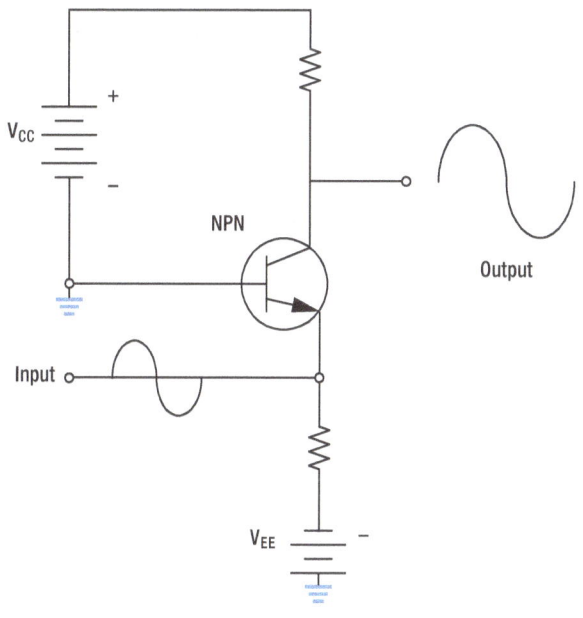

Figure 1-69. Simplified Class A amplifier circuit.

The efficiency of an amplifier refers to the amount of power delivered to the output compared to the power supplied to the circuit. Every device in the circuit consumes power in order to operate. If the amplifier operates for 360° of input signal, then it is using more power than if it was using only 180° of input signal. The more power consumed by the amplifier, the less there is available for the output signal. Usually the Class A amplifier is used where efficiency is of little concern and where fidelity in reproduction is desired.

Class AB Amplifiers

Figure 1-70 shows a simplified Class AB amplifier circuit. In the Class AB operations, the transistor current flows for more than 50 percent but less than 100 percent of the input signal. Unlike the Class A amplifier, the output signal is distorted. A portion of the output circuit appears to be truncated. This is due to the lack of current through the transistor during this point of operation. When the emitter in this case becomes positive enough, the transistor cannot conduct because the base to emitter junction is no longer forward biased. The input signal going positive beyond this point will not produce any further output and the output will remain level. The Class AB amplifier has a better efficiency and a poorer fidelity than the Class A amplifier. These amplifiers are used when an exact reproduction of the input is not required, but both the positive and negative portions of the input signals need to be available on the output.

Class B Amplifier

Figure 1-71 shows a simplified Class B amplifier circuit. In Class B operations, the transistor current flows for only 50 percent of the input signal. In this illustration, the base-emitter bias will not allow the transistor to conduct whenever the input signal is greater than zero. In this case, only the negative portion of the input signal will be reproduced. Unlike the rectifier, the Class B amplifier will not only reproduce half of the input signal, but it will also amplify it. Class B amplifiers are twice as efficient as the Class A amplifier because the amplifying device only uses power for half of the input signal.

Class C Amplifier

Figure 1-72 shows a simplified Class C amplifier circuit. In Class C operations, the transistor current flows for only 50 percent of the input signal. Because the transistor does not conduct except during a small portion of the input signal, this is the most efficient class of amplifier.

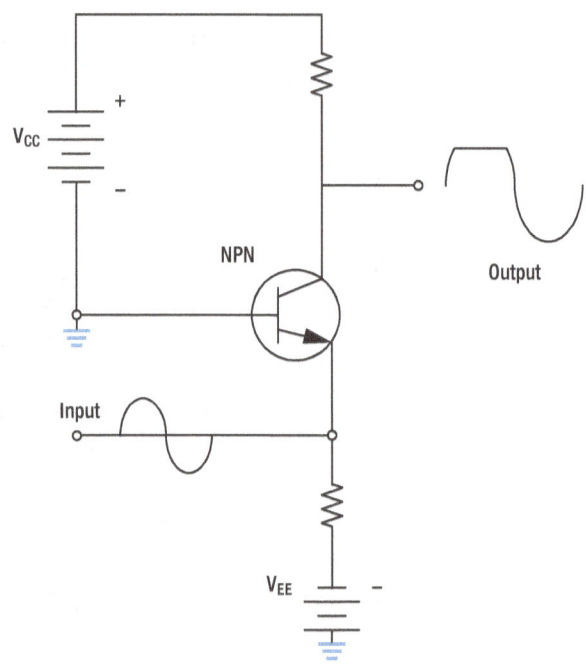

Figure 1-70. Simplified Class A amplifier circuit.

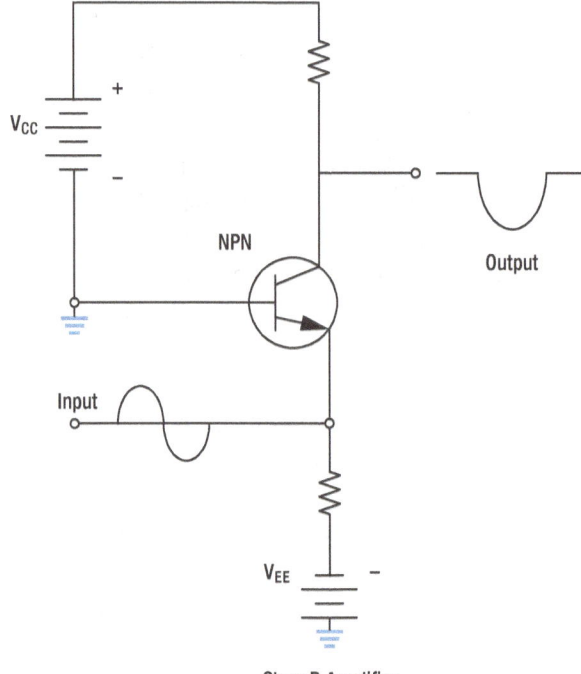

Figure 1-71. Simplified Class B amplifier circuit.

The distortion of the Class C amplifier is greater (poor fidelity) than the Class A, AB, and B amplifiers because a small portion of the input signal is reproduced on the output. Class C amplifiers are used when the output signal is used for only small portions of time.

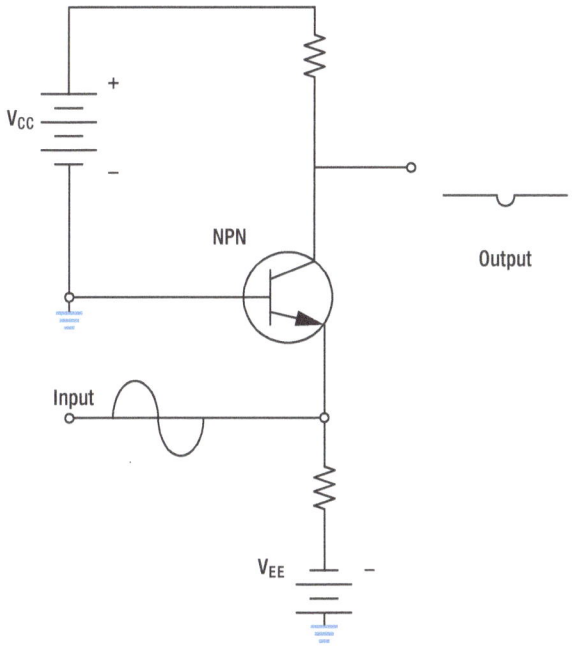

Figure 1-72. Simplified Class C amplifier circuit.

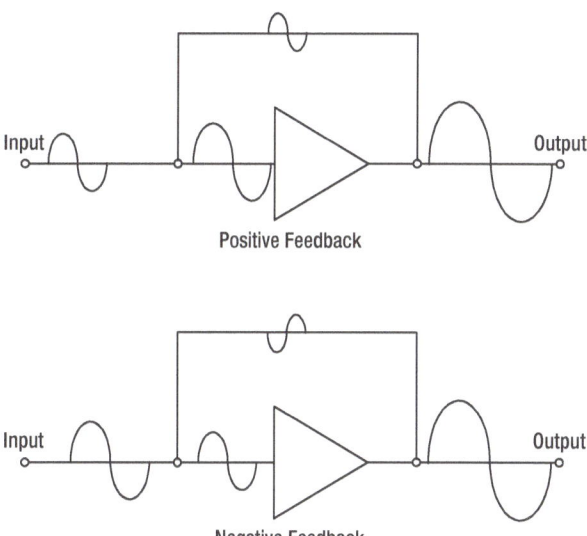

Figure 1-73. Positive and negative feedback.

CASCADE AMPLIFIERS

The maximum voltage gain obtainable from a single transistor amplifier circuit such as those just described is usually between 10 and 100. Since many applications require much more amplification gain, it is common practice to connect two or three amplifiers in a cascade, such that each amplifier increases the voltage gain in succession. The total gain is then that product of the gains of each stage of amplification. Multistage amplifiers use a common practice called positive feedback to obtain good performance.

Feedback And Stabilization

Feedback occurs when a small portion of the amplifier's output signal is sent back to the input signal. There are two types of feedback that can be present in any amplifier: positive or regenerative feedback, and negative or degenerative feedback. The main difference between these two is whether the feedback signal adds to the input signal, or if the feedback diminishes the input signal. When the feedback is positive, the signal being returned to the input is in phase with the input signal and thus interferes constructively.

Figure 1-73 illustrates this concept applied in an amplifier circuit using a block diagram. (The amplifier is shown as a triangle, its schematic symbol.) Notice that the feedback signal is in phase with the input signal, which will regenerate the input signal. This results in an output signal with amplitude greater than would have been without the constructive, positive feedback. Having too much positive feedback is what causes an audio system to squeal.

Figure 1-73 also illustrates with a block diagram how negative or degenerative feedback occurs. Negative feedback tends to stabilize the amplifier so that it can function in its normal operating range without oscillation. In this case, the feedback signal is out of phase with the input signal. This causes destructive interference and degenerates the input signal. The result is a lower amplitude output signal than would have occurred without the feedback.

There is particular attention paid to effects of feedback on quiescent point stability and on the gains and impedances of each iterated stage of a cascaded amplifier. The quiescent operating point, or Q-point, is the steady-state voltage or current at a specified terminal of a transistor with no input signal applied. An amplifier that is instable will function as an oscillator. Following is a discussion regarding various methods used to couple amplifier stages, beginning with the simplest method, direct coupling.

Direct Coupling

Coupling is used to transfer a signal from one stage of an amplifier to another stage. Regardless of whether an amplifier is a single stage or one in a series of stages, there must be a method for the signal to enter and leave the circuit. Coupling is the process of transferring the energy between circuits. Direct coupling is the connection of the output of one stage directly to the input of the next stage. Direct coupled amplifiers typically use one transistor for voltage gain and the other for impedance matching. Direct coupling uses fewer components and provides a higher gain than other methods of coupling.

The cascaded two-stage amplifier, shown in *Figure 1-74*, is of particular interest because the common-emitter design provides the maximum gain obtainable in direct-coupled circuits. Here the collector of Q1 couples the signal directly to the base of Q2 where it is inverted and amplified. R1 and R2 form a voltage divider bias resistor network, which is provided to the base of Q1. In addition, two collector feedback resistors, RC and R2, limit the overall current gain. Known as a current-feedback amplifier, this circuit offers flexibility in design and good Q-point tracking when the DC supply voltage (Vcc) varies.

Direct coupling provides a good frequency response because frequency-sensitive components, such as capacitors, inductors and transformers, are not used. However, they can be issues with impedance matching and supply voltage fluctuations. Direct coupling amplifiers are used in pulse amplifiers, differential amplifiers, and regulator circuits.

Resistive-Capacitive Coupling
Resistive-Capacitive coupling, or RC coupling, is the most common method of coupling because it eliminates impedance matching issues that can occur with direct coupling. It uses a coupling capacitor and signal developing resistors. *Figure 1-75*, shows a simplified RC coupling circuit. In this circuit, R1 acts as a load resistor for Q1 and develops the output signal for that stage. The capacitor C1 blocks the DC bias signal and passes the AC output signal. R2 then becomes the load over which the AC signal is developed as an input to the base of Q2. This arrangement allows for the bias voltage of each stage to be blocked, while the AC signal is passed to the next stage.

Impedance Coupling
Impedance coupling uses a coil as a load for the first stage, but otherwise functions just as an RC coupling. *Figure 1-76* shows a simplified impedance coupling circuit. This method is similar to the RC coupling method. The difference is that R1 is replaced with

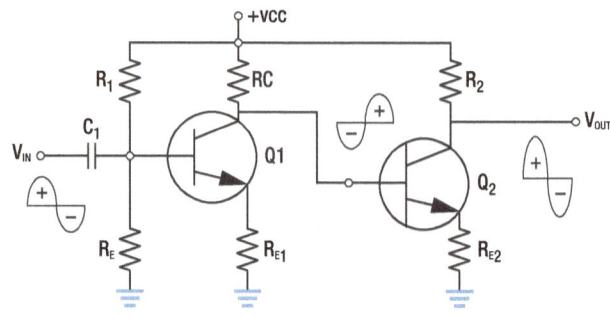
Figure 1-74. Direct coupled amplifier circuit.

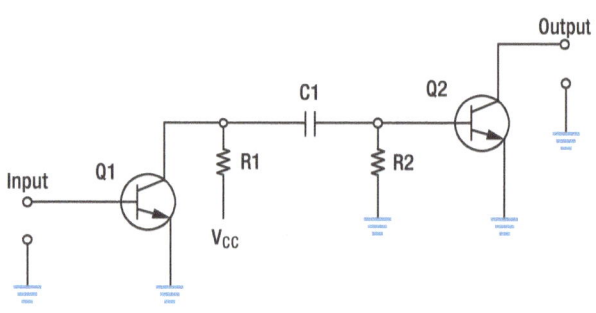
Figure 1-75. RC coupled amplifier circuit.

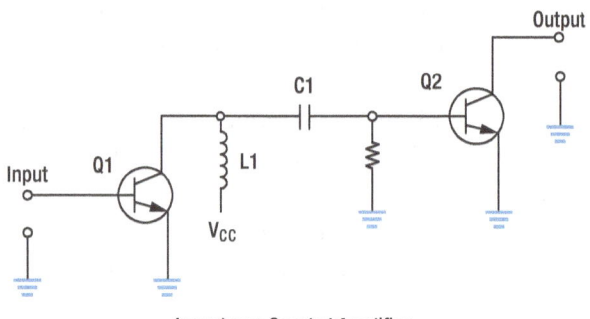
Figure 1-76. Impedance coupled amplifier circuit.

inductor L1 as the output load. The amount of signal developed on the output load depends on the inductive reactance of the coil. In order for the inductive reactance to be high, the inductance must be large, the frequency must be high, or both. Therefore, load inductors should have relatively large amounts of inductance and are most effective at high frequencies.

Transformer Coupling
Transformer coupling uses a transformer to couple the signal from one stage to the next. *Figure 1-77* shows a simplified transformer coupling circuit. The transformer action of T1 couples the signal from the first stage to the second stage. The primary coil of T1 acts as a load

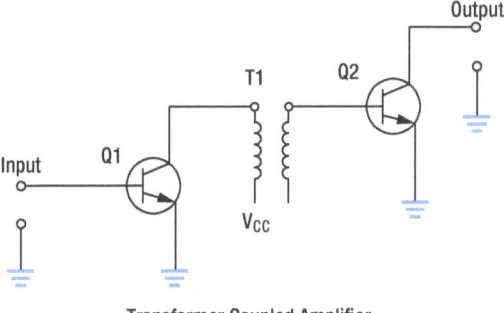

Figure 1-77. Transformer coupled amplifier circuit.

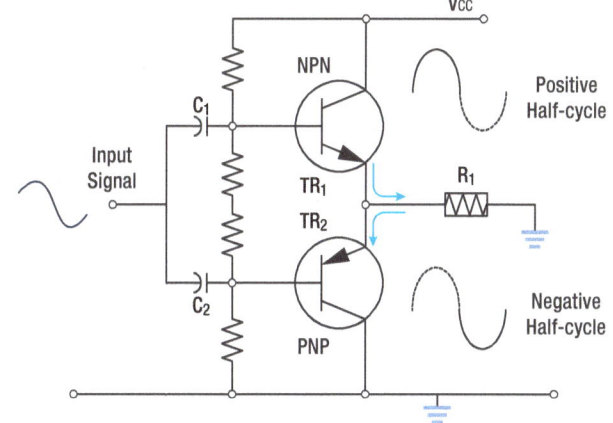

Figure 1-78. Push-pull power amplifier circuit.

for the output of the first stage while the secondary coil acts as the developing impedance for the second stage Q2. Transformer coupling is very costly, but efficient and the transformer can aid greatly in impedance matching between stages.

PUSH-PULL AMPLIFIERS

Electronic systems are often called upon to deliver substantial amounts of power to a device that serves as the load for the system. Examples of such devices are loudspeakers for sound reproduction and servomotors for automatic flight control systems. The amount of power that a transistor can deliver depends on its maximum current, voltage, and power dissipation ratings. Power amplifiers are designed specifically for obtaining large amount of power with the fewest transistors, while keeping the signal distortion at a low level.

Power output can be increased by using two transistors instead of one in the output stage. One way of connecting two transistors is by paralleling all three leads so that the currents are doubled. However, the transistors will share the load only if equalizing resistors are used, but these resistors consume valuable power. A more efficient design is the push-pull amplifier *(Figure 1-78)* whereby the transistors are phased is such a manner that they carry the load peaks alternately, and are not required to divide the load equally as with parallel transistors. Because the transistors carry the load alternatively, it is possible to bias the amplifier so that the transistor power flows only when there is a signal present.

All though not shown on this figure, the input signal is typically supplied from a center-tapped secondary of an input transformer that develops two signals which are identical, but opposite in phase, such that when TR1 is conducting current, TR2 is turned off, and vice versa. The positive half-cycle output of TR1 and negative half cycle output of TR2 is then combined in an output transformer to reproduce the original, but amplified, sine wave input signal.

As previously discussed, amplifiers that operate with the power at a fixed continuous value such that the current in the transistor flows for 100 percent or 360° of the input signal are known as Class A Amplifiers, and those that operate such that the current flows for only 50 percent of the input signal are known as Class B amplifiers. The push-pull amplifier is a classic example of a Class B amplifier. It is biased just at the cutoff point so it uses very little DC source power under standby conditions, and under operating conditions, has a higher power conversion efficiency (78.5%) as compared to a Class A amplifier with a 50% efficiency. In addition, with a 50% duty cycle for each power transistor, a smaller heat sink is required for cooling. The only disadvantages of the push-pull amplifier are that the harmonic distortion is higher, self-bias can't be used, and the supply voltage must have very good regulation.

OSCILLATORS

The preceding sections were concerned with amplifier designs providing the greatest amount of fidelity. Fidelity is defined as the ability of an amplifier to produce as exact a replica of the input signal during amplification with the least amount of distortion. As discussed, positive feedback is used to control amplifier gain. However, too much positive feedback can result is an unstable operation, whereby the amplifier produces oscillations that degrade the performance of the amplifier; and therefore, must be avoided. However, oscillations of this kind are used to an advantage in the design of unstable feedback amplifiers found in radio frequency transceivers, signal generators, and oscilloscopes.

A typical oscillator circuit design could have direct coupling between the output and the input providing the maximum positive feedback. The problem with this design is that there is no means of controlling the amplitude of the oscillations, and it is difficult to tune it to a desired frequency. Likewise, if the feedback is too strong, the oscillations would continue to increase in amplitude producing signal distortions. Therefore, oscillator designs incorporate an automatic bias control to provide the correct amount of voltage for constant amplitude oscillations. Automatic bias control assures that if oscillations increase in amplitude, the bias will also increase, thereby reducing the gain of the amplifier.

The popular Hartley oscillator *(Figure 1-79 left)* has an automatic bias control feedback circuit using a tuned inductor-capacitor (LC) tank circuit connected between the collector and the base of the transistor. The emitter is connected to the tapping point on the inductor coil. The feedback loop of the tank circuit is taken from the center tap of the inductor to feed a fraction of the output signal back to the emitter. Since the output of the emitter is always in phase with the output of the collector, the feedback signal is positive. The frequency range of the oscillator is determined by the resonant frequency (fR) of the tank circuit, which can be adjusted by varying the capacitance of the tuning capacitor.

For example, if the inductor (L) is 1mH and the capacitor (C) can be adjusted between 100pf and 500pf, the frequency range of the oscillator can be determined using the following formula:

$$f_R = \frac{1}{2\Pi\sqrt{L \times C}} = \frac{1}{2\Pi\sqrt{1mh \times 100pf}} = 503khz$$

$$f_R = \frac{1}{2\Pi\sqrt{L \times C}} = \frac{1}{2\Pi\sqrt{1mh \times 500pf}} = 225khz$$

Frequency Range = 503khz - 225khz = 278 khz

Another popular oscillator circuit is the Colpitts oscillator as shown on *Figure 1-79 right*. The distinguishing feature of the Colpitts oscillator is that the feedback is taken from a voltage divider made up of two capacitors in series across the inductor in the tank circuit. Resistors R1 and R2 provide the usual stabilizing DC bias for the transistor, while the additional capacitors act as DC-blocking bypass capacitors. A Radio-Frequency Choke (RFC) is used in the collector circuit to provide a high reactance at the frequency of oscillation, and a low resistance at DC to help start the oscillations. The advantage of the Colpitts oscillator over the Hartley oscillator is improved frequency stability.

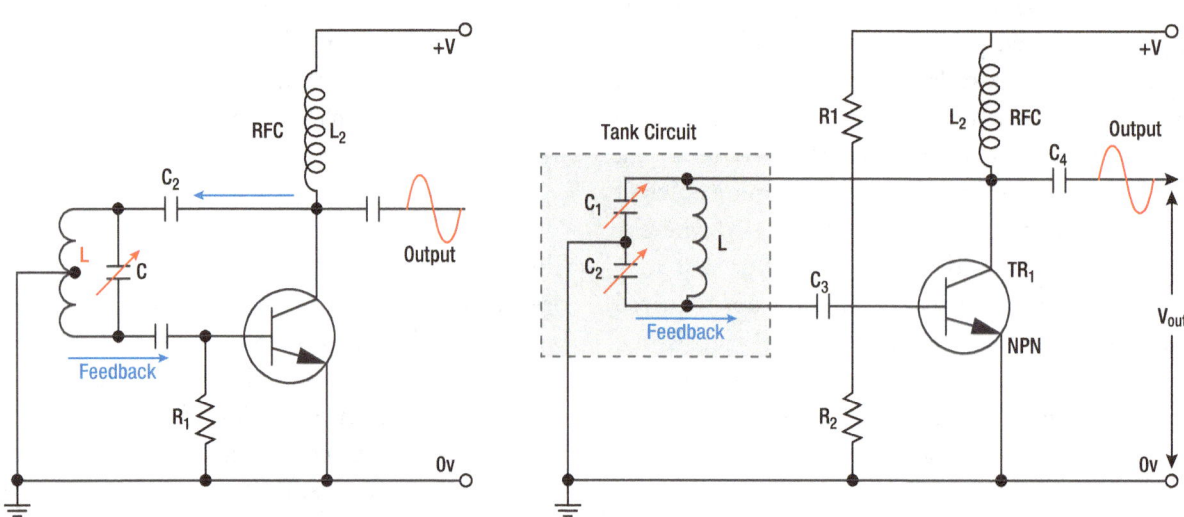

Figure 1-79. Hartley oscillator (left) and Colpitts oscillator (right).

MULTIVIBRATORS

An astable multivibrator is a Class B amplifier that has been designed to oscillate such that it functions as a square wave generator. It is called an astable multivibrator, because unlike a monostable multivibrator, that requires an external trigger pulse to generate an output, the astable multivibrator is free-running. In other words, it has automatic built-in triggering that allows it to switch continuously between its two unstable states.

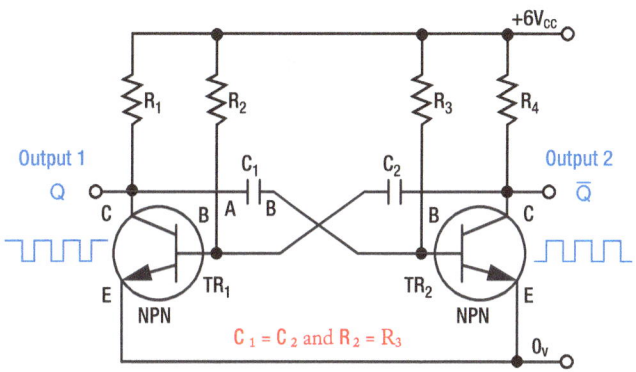

Figure 1-80. Free-running multivibrator circuit.

As shown in *Figure 1-80*, it consists of two cross-coupled common-emitter amplifier circuits, with a feedback network, and two time delay capacitors that permit alternate on and off states producing two square wave outputs with one output inverted from the other. One stage of the amplifier is saturated "on" while the other cuts "off". The amplitude of the square wave output is approximately the same as the supply voltage (Vcc). The time period of each switching state is determined by the RC time constant of the resistor-capacitor networks at the base of each transistor. The values of the resistors and capacitors for both networks must be identical.

Let's assume that transistor TR2 is turned "off", and TR1 is turned "on", such that all the current flowing through TR1 offers almost no resistance causing the capacitor C1 to charge through resistor R3 (at an RC time constant determined by R3 × C1). The right hand side of capacitor C1 (plate B) is connected to the base of transistor TR2, which is now at cutoff. However, as plate B becomes increasing negative, it turns on TR2 allowing it to conduct. Almost instantaneously, TR2 becomes saturated and the voltage at Output 2 changes from –Vcc to approximately 0 volts. This change in voltage is coupled through capacitor C2 to the base of transistor TR1, forcing TR1 to turn "off", while TR2 is turned "on". The process will continue to repeat itself as long as the supply voltage is present.

FLIP-FLOP CIRCUITS

Flip-flops are bi-stable multi-vibrator circuits that form basic storage units of sequential logic used in shift registers and counters. They have the ability to maintain their state without further application of a signal allowing them to store a bit of data or one place of a larger binary number. Their ability to set one condition and reset or change to an alternate condition results in a latch, also known as a flip-flop. They will be discussed in detail in the next sub-module.

INTEGRATED CIRCUITS

TTL (Transistor-Transistor Logic) circuit elements are primarily bipolar semi-conductor components connected together to produce a consistent output. This output may be combined with the output of other TTL logic elements and logic circuits to perform a task. TTL circuits operate with +5-volts power source. It uses positive logic, meaning it is ON with +5 volts and is OFF with 0 volts.

CMOS (Complementary Metal Oxide Semiconductor) logic circuits are constructed with metal oxide semiconductor transistors, rather than the bipolar junction transistors used in TTL. CMOS logic circuits use less power because of the construction of the logic gates and, therefore, the digital circuits that are comprised of CMOS components use fewer elements. The output of the CMOS transistor is triggered by a lower voltage and does not rely on current flowing through the base-emitter junction. CMOS logic circuits are less susceptible to electrical interference and operate with a wider range of voltages (ON between +3 and +18 volts). CMOS technology is predominant in modern integrated circuits used in aircraft systems.

Integrated Circuits (ICs) are miniaturized electronic circuits that contain anywhere from a few to over a billion tiny electronic components. ICs are complete, digital electronic circuits contained in a single device, known as a chip. TTL and CMOS circuits are miniaturized and manufactured on tiny, thin, silicon semiconductor wafers. Assemblies with billions of transistors can fit on a chip the size of a fingernail. *(Figure 1-81)* With so many transistors and logic gates, computer systems with increasingly computational power are achieved.

Integrated circuits are used in nearly every modern computing and electronic device, including the many electronic devices found on aircraft. The microscopic circuits are constructed directly on the silicon chip during manufacture and cannot be removed or separated. A microprocessor contains one (or more) integrated circuit microchips at the core of the processing unit. It responds to inputs in accordance with instructions contained in its own memory. Due to the physical limitations of placing integrated circuits on a single chip, electronic developers have created microprocessors that combine the use of more than one chip in an architecture. These enable extremely fast processing due to the proximity of the integrated circuits to each on the tiny chip assemblies.

To facilitate the use of integrated circuits and other electronic components, standards have been developed. The Dual In-line Package (DIP) standard allows the installation of micro-components onto printed circuit boards. It basically calls for two rows of connecting terminals, equal-spaced along each edge of the IC housing as shown in *Figure 1-82*. The dimensions of the terminals are standardized as is their use (e.g., power, ground, output, etc.). The come in a variety of sizes with various numbers of terminals. Inside a DIP element there can be transistor circuits, logic circuits and even complete integrated circuits and microprocessors.

Chips are manufactured from a wafer of a thin substrate of semiconductor material, such as silicon, gallium nitride, gallium arsenide, etc. The process begins with growing the crystal material. As shown in *Figure 1-83*, the material is then processed in to the shape of thin, round wafers up to 12 inches in diameter. The electronic circuits are etched into the wafers using photo lithographic and chemical processing steps to form hundreds of chips. The wafers are then polished, cleaned, and inspected. The individual chips are cut from the wafers and mounted in plastic or ceramic packages. Tiny wires are soldered from the chip to the connecter pins and it undergoes a final test. *(Figure 1-84)*

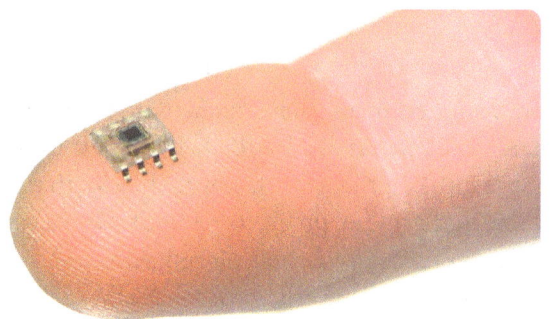

Figure 1-81. Integrated Circuits.

Figure 1-82. A DIP element containing a microprocessor and connection terminals for installation on a printed circuit board.

All of the discrete components, such as resistors, transistors, diodes, and capacitors, are constructed on these small pieces of semiconductor material and are an integral part of the chip. They come in a variety of sizes with various numbers of terminals. Inside there can be transistor logic circuits or a complete microprocessor with cache memory and a bus interface.

Diodes and transistors are arranged to form logic gates in digital circuits. These logic circuits operate based on the binary numbering system, rather than the decimal numbering system that we use in everyday life. The following sections will discuss the binary numbering system, explain the function of logic gates, and demonstrate the use binary numbers in logic circuits.

BINARY NUMBERING SYSTEM

Numbers are used to describe the quantity of something. A numbering system is a written system for expressing numbers as symbols. All numbering systems have bases to understand how the numbering system works. For example, the symbol "10" could mean "ten" in decimal form (base-10) or it could mean "two" in binary form (base-2).

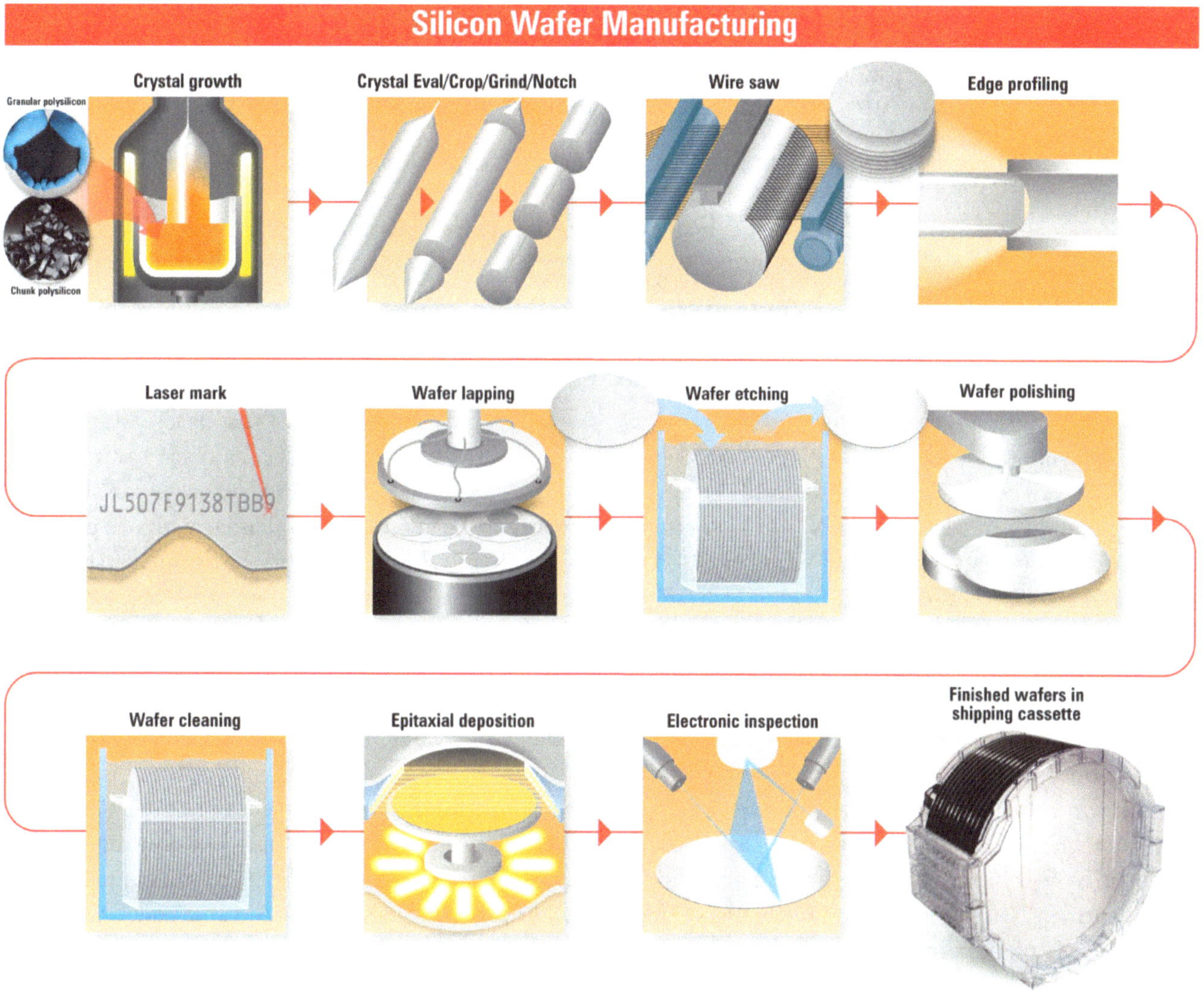

Silicon Wafer Manufacturing

Figure 1-83. IC's are manufactured on thin Semiconductor Wafers.

The most common numbering system that used in everyday life is the decimal system. The prefix in the word "decimal" is a Latin root for the word "ten". Thus, the decimal system uses ten different symbols (0, 1, 2, 3, 4, 5, 6, 7, 8, and 9) and is referred to as a base-10 numbering system. To represent a number higher than 9, go to the next digit placement, such that 10 means zero units of one and one unit of ten. At the last symbol, a new placement is created to the left and counted up, so that 100 appears after 99, and so on. Each additional placement is an additional power of 10. Knowing this will help in understanding the other bases.

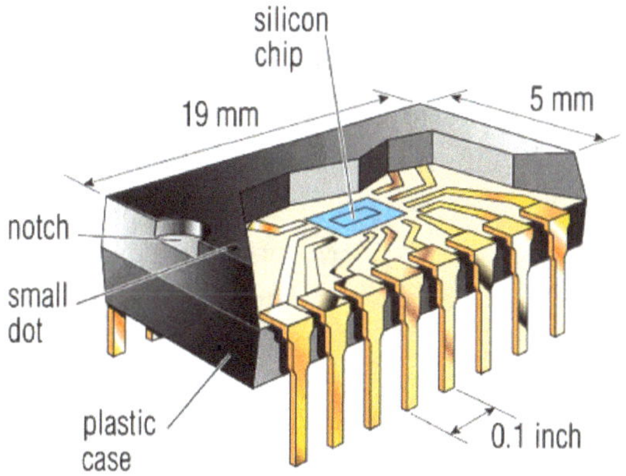

The binary number system has only two symbols: 0 and 1. The prefix in the word "binary" is a Latin root for the word "two", and as such, is referred to as a base-2 numbering system. The use of the binary numbering system is based on the fact that switches (or valves) have two states: ON or OFF (OPEN or CLOSED).

Primary uses of the binary number system include computers and digital electronics. In computers, information is stored as a series of 0's and 1's, forming strings of binary numbers known as machine language.

Figure 1-84. Silicon Chip Mounted in a Dual-Inline Package.

DECIMAL PLACE VALUE CHART

10^7	10^6	10^5	10^4	10^3	10^2	10^1	10^0
= 10 000 000	= 1 000 000	= 100 000	= 10 000	= 1 000	= 100	= 10	= 1

Figure 1-85. Place values of the decimal number system.

BINARY PLACE VALUE CHART

2^7	2^6	2^5	2^4	2^3	2^2	2^1	2^0
= 128	= 64	= 32	= 16	= 8	= 4	= 2	= 1

Figure 1-86. Derivation of the place values of the binary number system.

Similarly, the binary number system is used in digital electronics because the two basic conditions of electricity, ON and OFF, can represent the two digits of the binary number system. When a switch is ON, it represents the digit 1, and when it is OFF, it represents the digit 0. Millions and even billions of tiny switches are arranged so that digital devices can perform the functions they do with a binary number system.

It is easy to recognize a binary number when written because it only uses 1's and 0's. To ensure it is not mistaken for another number system expression, a binary number system numeral may be written with a prefix or suffix that indicates it is binary. Binary number system identifiers are shown in the following example. The value of all of the binary numbers shown in this example is the same (11 in the decimal number system).

1011_2 $1011base_2$ bin 1011   0b1011   1011b

When reading or pronouncing a binary number, it is common to simply say "1" or "0" moving from left to right until all the digits are pronounced.

To read 1011_2, say, "one, zero, one, one"

PLACE VALUES

As stated previously, the decimal number system used in everyday life is the base-10 system. There are 10 symbols available for use as place value holders; 0, 1, 2, 3, 4, 5, 6, 7, 8, and 9. When positioned in a number, they are also positioned to represent a place value. If 9 is exceeded, the place value resets to 0 and a 1 must be placed in the next place value column to the left. *Figure 1-85* illustrates the decimal number system place values. They are derived by sequentially raising 10 to a higher power moving from right to left. Thus, each position has a value 10 times that of the position to its right.

The binary number system is a base-2 system. There are 2 digits available for use as place value holders; 0 and 1. Each place value in the binary number system represents 2 raised to a sequentially higher power from right to left. This is similar to the decimal system used in everyday life. *Figure 1-86* illustrates the place values of the binary number system. It shows to what power 2 is raised to establish value and the decimal number system equivalent of each place. Each place value position has a value 2 times that of the position to its right.

Remember, when writing binary numbers and placing digits in positions of place value, the only digits available are 0 and 1. To exceed 1, the place value is reset to 0 and a 1 is placed in the next place value column to the left. Place values are used to convert our everyday decimal numbers to binary numbers.

Figure 1-87 illustrates how binary numbers are formed by placing a 1 or a 0 in the binary place value positions. Binary digits are called "bits". The Least Significant Bit (LSB) is the bit with the smallest weight. The LSB on the far right of the binary place value position table is 20, which equals 1. In this last column, alternate every other time going down the column inserting 1s and 0s. Likewise, the next LSB is 21, or 2, which means alternate every 2 times down the column inserting 1s and 0s, and so forth. The Most Significant Bit (MSB) is the bit with the largest weight. The MSB is on the far left side of the binary place value position table. Here the bits alternate every 8 times between 1s and 0s. Together all four bits across each row form the binary equivalent of the decimal number shown in the far left column.

BINARY NUMBER SYSTEM CONVERSION

Each binary number column has a decimal value. To convert from a decimal number to a binary number, find the binary column that has the largest value but is equal

to or smaller than the decimal number being converted. Place a 1 in that column and subtract the column value from the decimal number being converted. Look at the difference. Place a 1 in the column that has the largest value but is equal to or smaller than the decimal number difference of what was just subtracted. Now subtract this column value from the difference of the decimal number being converted and the previous column difference. If a column is not used, place a zero in it. Continue this operation until all of the binary place value columns with 1's, when added together, have the same value as the decimal number being converted. Write the number in binary form including a 1 or a 0 for each column.

Example:

Convert the number 100_{10} to a binary number. Use the binary place value chart in *Figure 1-88* to assist in remembering the decimal equivalent value for each binary place value holder. The largest decimal number system value in a binary number system place holder that is less than or equal to 100 is 64. Thus, a 1 is paced in the 64 column (2^6) of the binary place value chart. Subtract 64 from 100 for a difference of 36. The binary place value holder that is less than or equal to 36 is 32. Place a 1 in the 32 column (2^5) of the binary place value chart. Subtract 32 from 36 for a difference of 4. The binary place value holder that is less than or equal to 4 is 4. Place a 1 in the 4 column (2^2) of the binary place value chart. Subtract 4 from 4 for a difference of 0. Since there is nothing left to be converted, place a 0 in all place value columns that do not contain a 1. Write the number using all the 1's and 0's recorded in the chart from right to left; $1100100_2 = 100_{10}$

To convert a binary number to a decimal number, simply add the column values of the binary place holders with a 1.

Example:

Convert the binary number 10010111 to a decimal number. From left to right, the base-2 values represented by each 1 in this binary number are added together: 128 + 16 + 4 + 2 + 1 = 151. $10010111_2 = 151_{10}$.

DECIMAL	BINARY PLACE VALUE POSITIONS			
	8	4	2	1
0	0	0	0	0
1	0	0	0	1
2	0	0	1	0
3	0	0	1	1
4	0	1	0	0
5	0	1	0	1
6	0	1	1	0
7	0	1	1	1
8	1	0	0	0
9	1	0	0	1
10	1	0	1	0
11	1	0	1	1
12	1	1	0	0
13	1	1	0	1
14	1	1	1	0
15	1	1	1	1

Figure 1-87. Decimal to binary number conversion table.

As can be seen, a binary number is typically much longer that its decimal equivalent. However, modern circuits have very fast switching speeds so that the length of binary numbers can be tolerated. This is especially true because of the reliability that is gained from a system that is built from components that are either ON (1) or OFF (0), that is, either have voltage or do not have voltage.

BINARY CODED DECIMALS

Computers instructions are formed by groupings binary digits (bits) to form words. A series of four binary digits will form a 4-bit word. These 4-bit words are represented by Binary-Coded Decimals (BCD). As shown in *Figure 1-88*, binary 1000 represents decimal 8 and binary 0010 represents decimal 2. BCD coding uses the binary equivalent of the decimal number; however, BCD numbers and binary numbers are not the same. A BCD number must be between decimal number 0 and 9 since each BCD number is expressed in units, tens, hundreds, thousands, etc. For example, the binary number equivalent of decimal 82 is 01010010. However, the BCD expression would be two 4-bit words consisting of 1000 representing number 8, and 0010 representing number 2, as two separate decimals.

Example:

Convert the number 264_{10} to a BCD number by first separating each decimal number in to its place value and then converting each decimal in to 4-bit BCD words.

$$2 = 0010 \quad 6 = 0110 \quad 4 = 0100$$

Module 04 B2 - Electronic Fundamentals

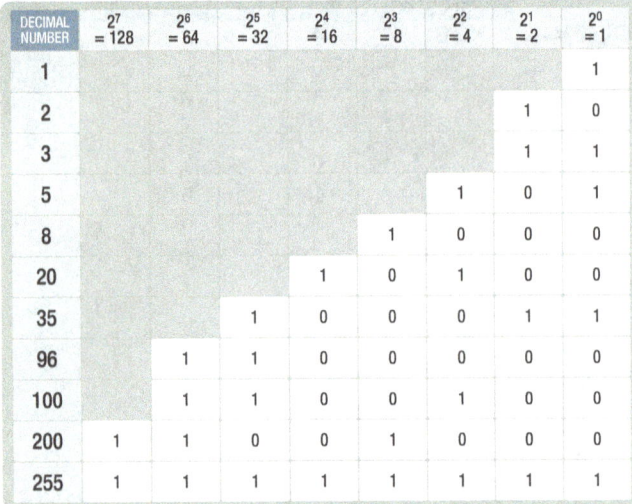

Figure 1-88. Use of binary number system place values to write various decimal numbers in binary (base2).

LOGIC GATES

A gate is a special type of circuit designed to accept and generate voltage signals corresponding to binary 1's and 0's. Transistors are used in digital electronics to construct circuits that act as digital logic gates. The purpose and task of the device is achieved by manipulating electric signals through the logic gates. Thousands, and even millions, of tiny transistors can be placed on a chip to create the digital logic landscape through which a component's signals are processed.

As explained previously, digital logic is based on the binary number system. There are two conditions than may exist, 1 or 0. In a digital circuit, these are equivalent to voltage or no voltage. Within the binary system, these two conditions are called Logic 1 and Logic 0. Using just these two conditions, gates can be constructed to manipulate information. There are a handful of common logic gates that are used. By combining any number of these tiny solid-state gates, significant memorization, manipulation, and calculation of information can be performed. A brief discussion of logic gates, their symbols, and truth tables follow.

NOT GATE

The NOT gate, also known as an "inverter", is the simplest of all gates. If the input to the gate is Logic 1, then the output is NOT Logic 1. This means that it is Logic 0, since there are only two conditions in the binary world. In an electronic circuit, a NOT gate would invert the input signal. In other words, if there was voltage at the input to the gate, there would be no output voltage. The gate can be constructed with transistors and resistors to yield this electrical logic every time. (The gate or circuit would also have to invert an input of Logic 0 into an output of Logic 1.)

To understand logic gates, truth tables are often used. A truth table gives all of the possibilities in binary terms for each gate containing a characteristic logic function. For example, a truth table for a NOT gate is illustrated in *Figure 1-89*. Any input (A) is NOT present at the output (B). This is simple, but it defines this logic situation. A tiny NOT gate circuit can be built using transistors that produce these results. In other words, a circuit can be built such that if voltage arrives at the gate, no voltage is output or vice-versa.

When using transistors to build logic gates, the primary concern is to operate them within the circuits so the transistors are either OFF (not conducting) or fully ON (saturated). In this manner, reliable logic functions can be performed. The variable voltage and current situations present during the active mode of the transistor are of less importance.

Figure 1-90 illustrates an electronic circuit schematic diagram that performs the logic NOT gate function. Any input, either a no voltage or voltage condition, yields the opposite output. This gate is built with bipolar junction transistors, resistors, and a few diodes. Other designs exist that may have different components. When examining and discussing digital electronic circuits, the electronic circuit design of a gate is usually not presented. The symbol for the logic gate is most often used. The technician can then concentrate on the configuration of the logic gates in relation to each other.

BUFFER GATE

Another logic gate with only one input and one output is the buffer. It is a gate with the same output as the input. While this may seem redundant or useless, an operational amplifier may be considered a buffer in a

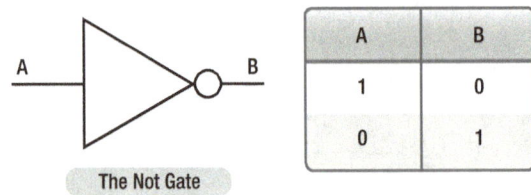

Figure 1-89. A NOT logic gate symbol and a NOT gate truth table.

digital circuit because if there is voltage present at the input, there is an output voltage. If there is no voltage at the input, there is no output voltage. When used as an operational amplifier, the buffer can change the values of a signal. This is often done to stabilize a weak or varying signal. All gates are amplifiers subject to output fluctuations. The buffer steadies the output of the upstream device while maintaining its basic characteristic. Another application of a buffer, using two NOT gates in series, is to use it to isolate a portion of a circuit. *(Figure 1-91)*

AND GATE

Most common logic gates have two inputs. Three or more inputs are possible on some gates. When considering the characteristics of any logic gate, an output of Logic 1 is sought and a condition for the inputs is stated or examined. For example, *Figure 1-92* illustrates an AND gate.

For an AND gate to have a Logic 1 output, both inputs have to be Logic 1. In an actual electronic circuit, this means that for a voltage to be present at the output, the AND gate circuit has to receive voltage at both of its inputs. As pointed out, there are different arrangements of electronic components that yield this result. Whichever is used is summarized and presented as the AND gate symbol. The truth table in *Figure 1-92* illustrates that there is only one way to have an output of Logic 1 or voltage when using an AND gate.

An example of AND logic could possibly be engage logic, found in an autopilot. In this case, the autopilot would not be allowed to be engaged unless certain conditions are first met. Such conditions could be: Vertical gyro is valid AND directional gyro is valid AND all autopilot control knobs are in detents AND servo circuits are operational. Only when these conditions are met will the autopilot be engaged. *Figure 1-93* shows the logic of this system found in the aircraft wiring diagrams.

OR GATE

Another useful and common logic gate is the OR gate. In an OR gate, to have an output of Logic 1 (voltage present), one of the inputs must be Logic 1. As seen in *Figure 1-94*, only one of the inputs needs to be Logic 1 for there to be an output of Logic 1. When both inputs are Logic 1, the OR gate has a Logic 1 output because it still meets the condition of one of the inputs being Logic 1.

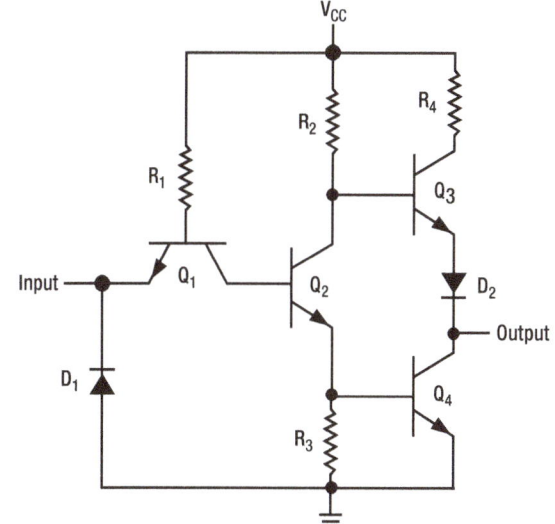

Figure 1-90. An electronic circuit that reliably performs the NOT logic function.

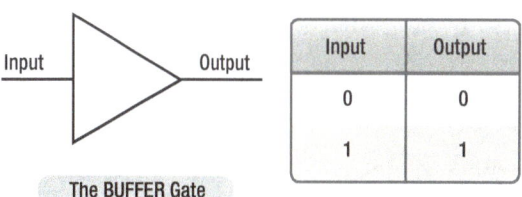

Figure 1-91. A buffer or amplifier symbol and the truth table of the buffer, which is actually two consecutive NOT gates.

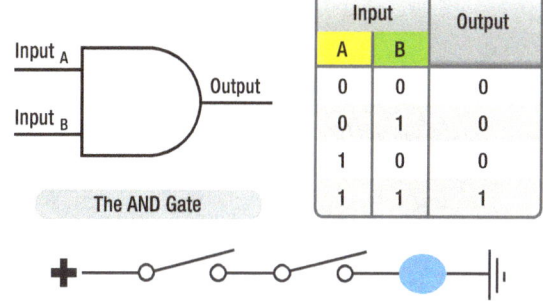

Figure 1-92. An AND gate symbol and its truth table.

Figure 1-95 is a simplified circuit that illustrates the OR logic. The example used is a "DOOR UNSAFE" annunciator. Let's say in this case that the plane has one cabin door and a baggage door. In order for the annunciator light on the master warning panel to extinguish, both doors must be closed and locked. If any one of the doors is not secured properly, the baggage door OR the cabin door, then the "DOOR UNSAFE" annunciator will illuminate. In this case, two switches are in parallel with each other. If either one of the two switches is closed, the light bulb will light up. The lamp will be off only when both switches are open.

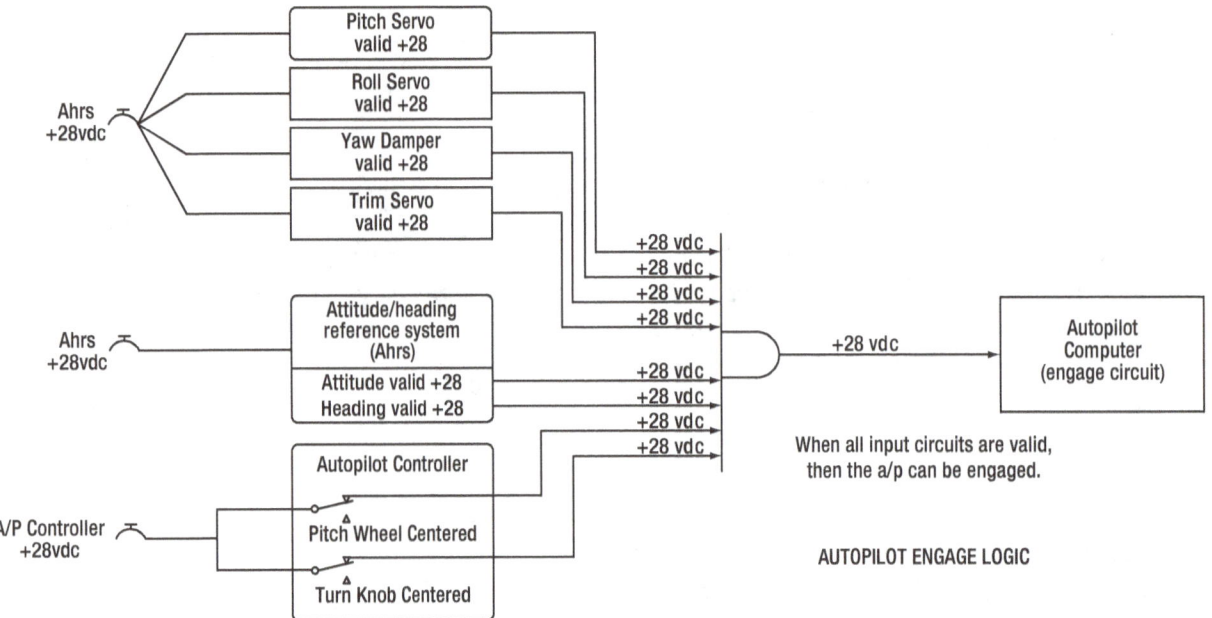

Figure 1-93. AND logic of system found in the aircraft wiring diagrams.

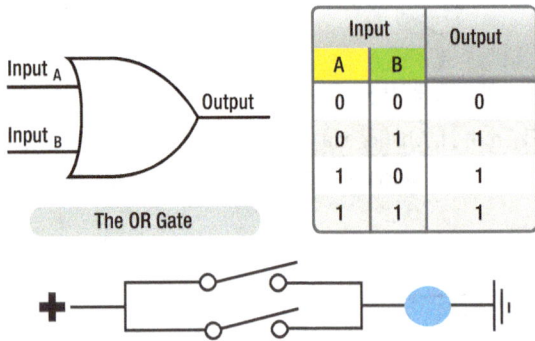

Figure 1-94. An OR gate symbol and its truth table.

Figure 1-95. Simplified circuit that illustrates OR logic.

NAND GATE

The AND, OR, and NOT gates are the basic logic gates. A few other logic gates are also useful. They can be derived from combining the AND, OR, and NOT gates. The NAND gate is a combination of an AND gate and a NOT gate. This means that AND gate conditions must be met and then inverted. So, the NAND gate is an AND gate followed by a NOT gate. The truth table for a NAND gate is shown in *Figure 1-96* along with its symbol.

If a Logic 1 output is to exist from a NAND gate, inputs A and B must not both be Logic 1. Or, if a NAND gate has both inputs Logic 1, the output is Logic 0. Stated in electronic terms, if there is to be an output voltage, then the inputs cannot both have voltage or, if both inputs have voltage, there is no output voltage.

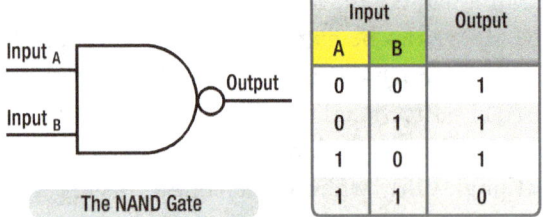

Figure 1-96. A NAND gate symbol and its truth table illustrating that the NAND gate is an inverted AND gate.

NOTE: The values in the output column of the NAND gate table are exactly the opposite of the output values in the AND gate truth table.

NOR GATE

A NOR gate is similarly arranged except that it is an inverted OR gate. If there is to be a Logic 1 output, or output voltage, then neither input can be Logic 1 or have input voltage. This is the same as satisfying the OR gate conditions and then putting the output through a NOT gate. The NOR gate truth table in *Figure 1-97* shows that the NOR gate output values are exactly the opposite of the OR gate output values.

EXCLUSIVE OR GATE

Another common logic gate is the EXCLUSIVE OR (XOR) gate. It is the same as an OR gate except for the condition where both inputs are Logic 1. In an OR gate, there would be a Logic 1 when both inputs are Logic 1. This is not allowed in an EXCLUSIVE OR gate. When either of the inputs is Logic 1, the output is Logic 1. However, with an EXCLUSIVE OR gate, if both inputs are Logic 1, the Logic 1 output is excluded and results in Logic 0. *(Figure 1-98)*

EXCLUSIVE NOR GATE

The Exclusive NOR (X-NOR) gate is nothing more than an XOR gate with an inverted output. It produces a 1 output when all inputs are 1s and also when all inputs are 0s. The standard symbol and truth table is shown in *Figure 1-99*.

NEGATIVE LOGIC GATES

There are also negative input logic gates. The negative OR and the negative AND gates are gates wherein the inputs are inverted rather than inverting the output. Negative logic gates are used when the inputs need to be buffered or isolated. This creates a unique set of outputs as seen in the truth tables in *Figure 1-100*.

The negative OR gate is not the same as the NOR gate as is sometimes misunderstood. Neither is the negative AND gate the same as the NAND gate. However, as the truth tables reveal, the output of a negative AND gate is the same as a NOR gate, and the output of a negative OR gate is the same as a NAND gate.

AIRCRAFT LOGIC GATE APPLICATIONS

One example of logic gates applied to aircraft applications would be illuminating display segments of numbers on a radio control head. The circuit shown in *Figure 1-101* uses a NOT gate and three OR gates. Feeding patterns of binary numbers into the four inputs on the left will turn the segment "ON" and "OFF".

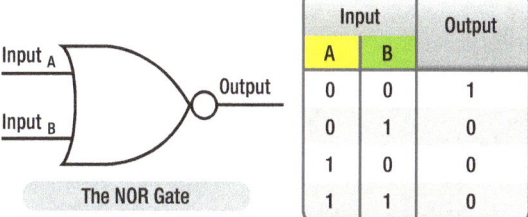

Figure 1-97. A NOR gate symbol and its truth table illustrating that the NOR gate is an inverted OR gate.which is an EXCLUSIVE OR gate with the output inverted.

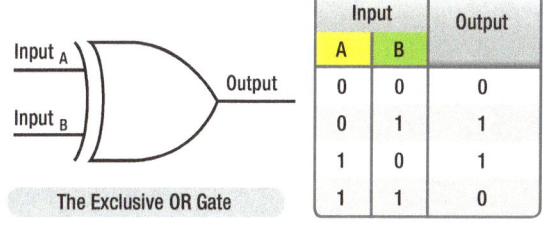

Figure 1-98. An EXCLUSIVE NOR gate symbol and its truth table, which is an EXCLUSIVE OR gate with the output inverted.

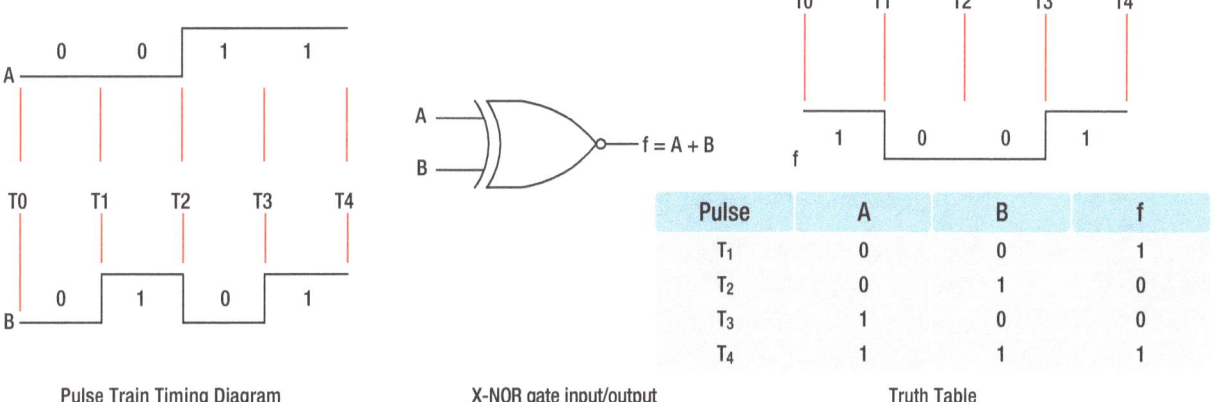

Figure 1-99. Standard Symbol for X-NOR gate and its truth table.

For example, feed in the number 7 as four binary inputs of "0111" and the gates will trigger as shown, switching "ON" the lower right display segment.

Another aircraft logic gate circuit application is the Landing Gear Warning Indicator. It consists of a 3-input NOR gate and a 3-Input AND gate, as shown in *Figure 1-102*. As can be seen from the truth tables, when all 3 landing gear are extended and locked they each activate a limit switch which provides a voltage (1) to the 3 inputs of both gates thereby turning "OFF" (0) the red LED (light-emitting diode) and turning "ON" (1) the green LED. The opposite occurs when all three landing gear are retracted turning "ON" (1) the red LED and turning "OFF" (0) the green LED indicator.

The following sections will discuss how these gates are formed into more complex logic circuits and will go into further detail regarding linear circuits, such as buffer gates employed as operational amplifiers (op amp). It will also discuss the operation and function of an op amp in integrator, differentiator, voltage follower, and comparator circuits. Finally, there will be a discussion on various levels or scales of chip integration and what type of circuits are contained in each level.

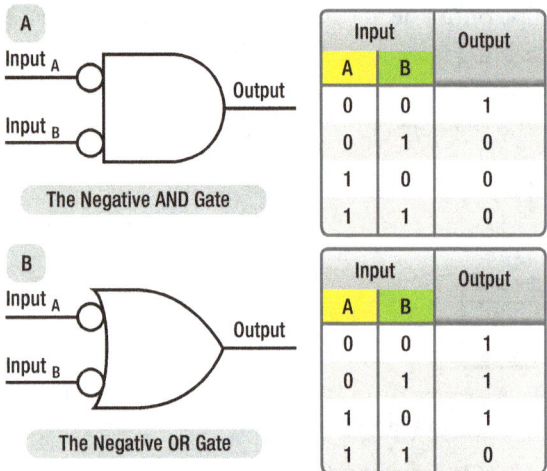

Figure 1-100. The NEGATIVE AND gate symbol and its truth table (A) and the NEGATIVE OR gate symbol and truth table (B). The inputs are inverted in the NEGATIVE gates.

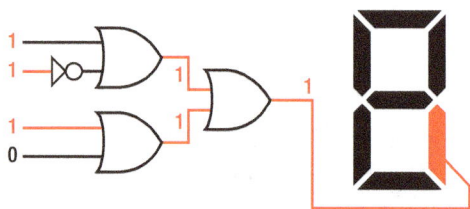

Figure 1-101. Logic circuit used on a radio control head display.

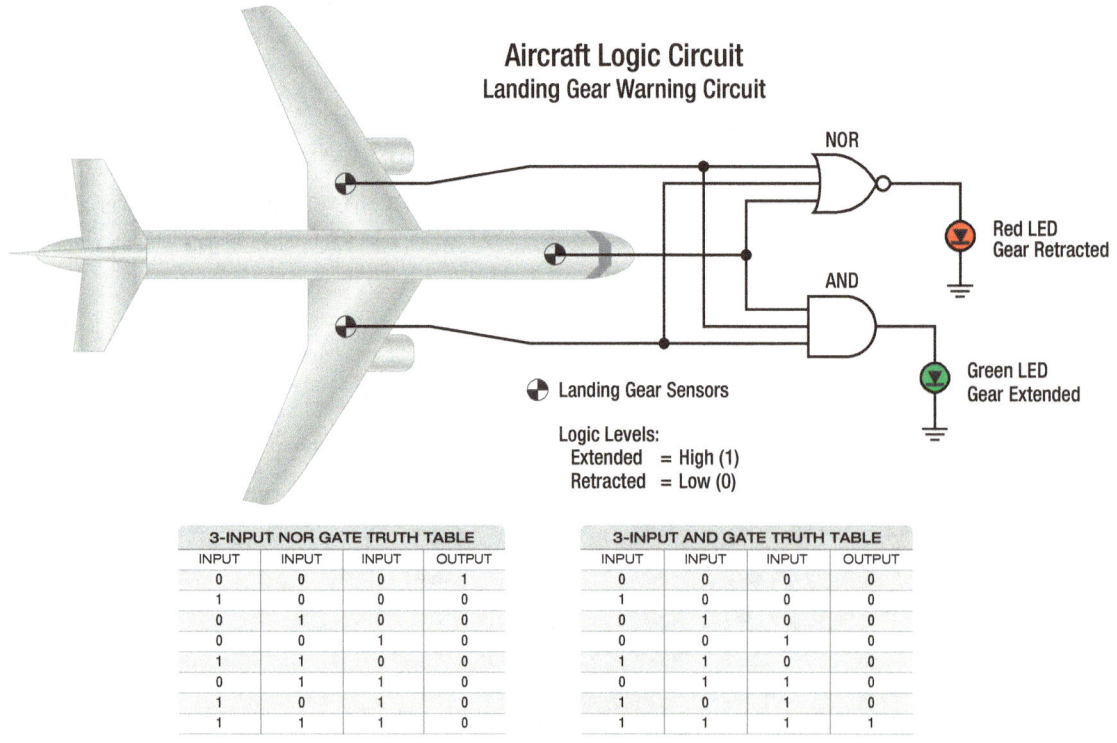

Figure 1-102. Typical aircraft logic circuit for landing gear warning.

1.52 Module 04 B2 - Electronic Fundamentals

LOGIC CIRCUITS

Electronic circuits use transistors in ICs to construct logic gates that produce outputs related to the inputs shown in the truth tables for each kind of gate. The gates are then assembled with other components to manipulate data in digital circuits. The electronic digital signals used are voltage or no-voltage representations of Logic 1 or Logic 0 conditions. By using a series of voltage and/or no-voltage outputs, a logic circuit manipulates, computes, and stores data.

ADDER LOGIC CIRCUITS

An example of this is the half-adder logic circuit, shown in *Figure 1-103*, consisting of an Exclusive OR (XOR) gate and an AND gate. As seen from the truth table, voltage applied to either input A or B will cause the sum (S) to be 1. Voltage applied to both A and B will cause S to be 0 and the carry (C) to be 1 forming the binary number 10, which is the decimal number 2. Half-adders can only add two digits. A full-adder becomes necessary when a carry input (C in) must be added to the two binary digits to obtain a decimal sum of 3. In this case, a full-adder logic circuit can be constructed from two half-adders and an OR gate, as shown in *Figure 1-104*.

It is worth noting again that an advantage of digital components and circuits is that voltage and current flow does not need to be exact. Using TTL devices, positive voltage between 2.6 and 5.0 volts at the input of a gate is considered an input signal of Logic 1. Any voltage less than 2.5 volts at the gate input is considered no voltage or an input of Logic 0.

FLIP-FLOP LOGIC CIRCUITS

Flip-flops are bi-stable multi-vibrator circuits that form basic storage units of sequential logic used in shift registers and counters. They have the ability to maintain their state without further application of a signal allowing them to store a bit of data or one place of a larger binary number. Their ability to set one condition and reset or change to an alternate condition results in a latch, also known as a flip-flop. Either cross-coupled NAND gates or cross-coupled NOR gates *(Figure 1-105)* are used to form Reset-Set (RS) flip-flop circuits. Each gate has two inputs and two outputs. The outputs Q and Q (not Q) are always in opposite states, so if Q is set to logic 1 then Q is reset to logic 0, and vice versa.

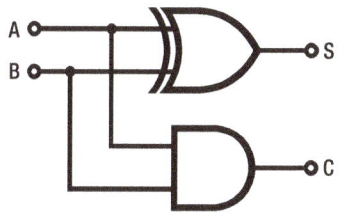

HALF-ADDER TRUTH TABLE

A	B	C	S
0	0	0	0
1	0	0	1
0	1	0	1
1	1	1	0

Figure 1-103. Half-adder logic circuit used for adding two numbers.

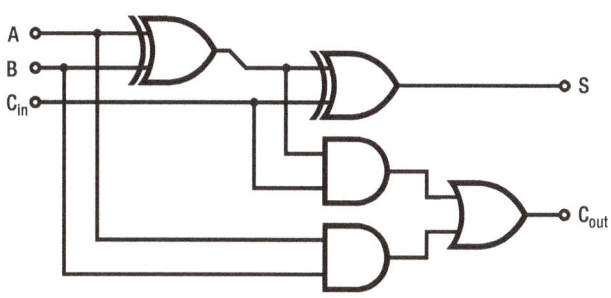

FULL-ADDER TRUTH TABLE

A	B	Cin	Cout	Sout
0	0	0	0	0
0	1	0	0	1
1	0	0	0	1
1	1	0	1	1
0	0	1	0	0
0	1	1	1	0
1	0	1	1	0
1	1	1	1	1

Figure 5-14. Full-adder logic circuit for adding three numbers.

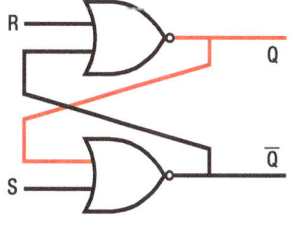

S	R	Q	Q̄
0	0	No Change	
0	1	0	1
1	0	1	0
1	1	disallowed	

Figure 1-105. RS Flip-flop using Cross-Coupled NOR gates and its truth table.

To turn on the flip-flop circuit, the Set (S) gate receives a +5v signal which is inverted to a logic 0 and sent to the input of the Reset (R) gate. Since both inputs to the R gate are logic 0, the Q̄ output is inverted to a logic 1 (red) which is fed to the alternate input of the S gate causing its Q output to be logic 0 (black). When both inputs are logic 0, the flip-flop remains in an unchanged (remember) state until a +5v signal is applied to either gate to reset the flip-flop. The disallowed (unused) state is when inputs to both the R and S gates are logic 1.

The truth table for the cross-coupled NAND RS flip-flop is exactly the same as the NOR RS flip-flop, except that if both inputs are logic 1, the flip-flop is in a remember state, and having both inputs as logic 0 is disallowed. *Figure 1-106* is a picture of a 7400 chip in a DIP package containing four NAND gates, which is sufficient to form two RS flip-flop circuits. The two additional pins, VCC and GND, are for +5v power and ground respectively.

When using flip-flops, it is often desirable to establish the logic level outputs at a time other than when the signals are initially applied. This is accomplished using a flip-flop circuit that is triggered by a clock input. The clock pulse acts as the control to allow the signals that appears at inputs of the S and R gates to pass to the cross-coupled flip-flop. Depending on the design, either the rising edge or the trailing edge of the clock pulse can trigger the flip-flop. *Figure 1-107* illustrates a clocked RS flip-flop using NAND gates and its associated timing diagram where C is the clock timing pulse, S and R are the inputs and Q and Q̄ are the outputs.

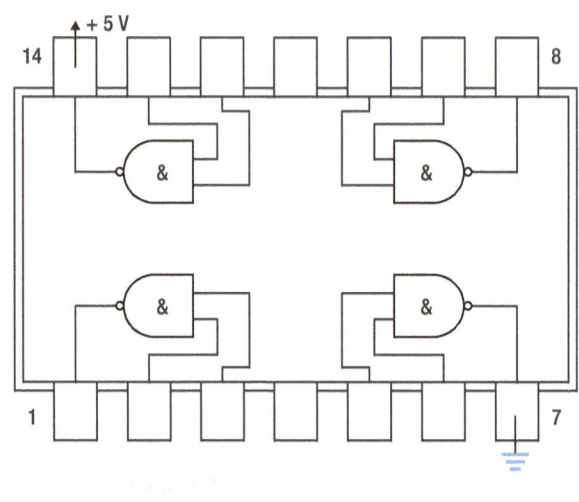

Figure 1-106. 7400 NAND chip.

The timing diagram shows that the rising edge of the first clock pulse sets Q to logic 1 because S is set to logic 1. Later, S changes to logic 0 and R changes to logic 1. However, Q remains set at logic 1 until the second clock pulse is detected, which resets Q to logic 0 and Q̄ to logic 1.

A very popular logic circuit is the clocked JK flip-flop, shown in *Figure 1-108*. The JK flip flop has the distinct advantage that they are no disallowed combinations as with the RS flip flops. When J and K are both at logic 1, the outputs Q and Q̄ will toggle on and off with the

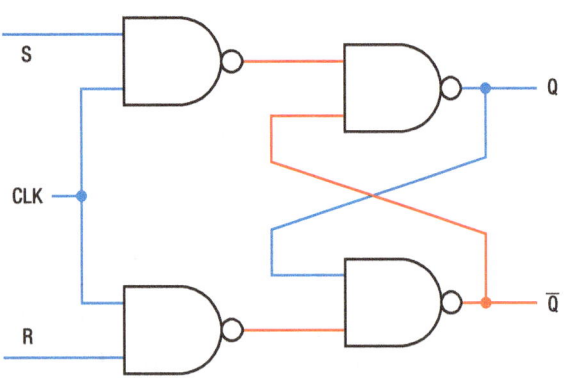
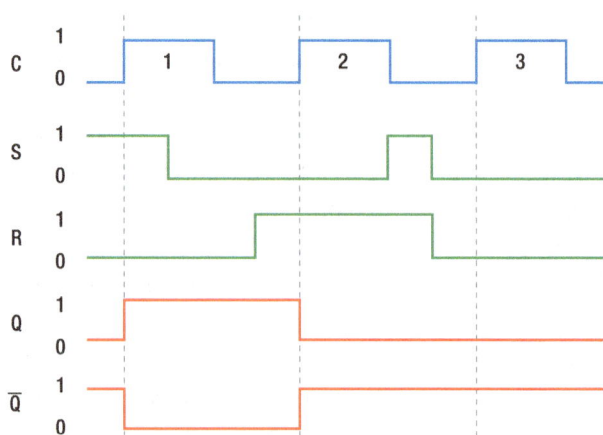

Figure 1-107. Clocked RS Flip-Flop using NAND gates and timing diagram.

rising edge of every clock pulse. When J = 1 and K = 0, the flip-flop will set Q to 1 and Q̄ to 0 on the first clock pulse, if not already set to this state. When J = 0 and K = 1, Q will reset to 0 and Q̄ will reset to 1 on the next clock pulse. When both J and K are set to 0, all clock pulses will be blocked from turning on the first two NAND gates resulting in no change occurring in either of the outputs.

COMPARATOR LOGIC CIRCUITS

Unlike a flip-flop that counts and stores binary numbers, the function of a comparator is to compare sets of binary numbers. Comparators are often used as parity checkers. An example of a comparator is the 7484 chip *(Figure 1-109)* that compares the 4 bits that are input to A to the 4 bits that are input to B and provides a signal on one of three comparison outputs depending on whether A is less (<) than B, A is equal (=) to B, or A is greater (>) than B. For example, if the binary input to A is 1010 (decimal number 10) and the binary input to B is 1101 (decimal number 13), there would be a logic 1 signal present on the output labeled A<B.

The 7485 chip has three additional inputs for cascading comparators when comparing larger binary numbers. For example, the first comparator can be used to compare units, a second comparator added to compare tens, a third comparator used to compare hundreds, etc. In the diagram shown in *Figure 1-110*, the left 7485 chip, used for comparing tens, is cascaded to the right 7585 chip, used for comparing units. To compare 32 versus 24, the Binary Coded Decimal (BCD) of 3 (0011) is applied to terminals A0 through A3 with A3 being the Most Significant Bit (MSB), which is 0, and A0 being the Least Significant Bit (LSB), which is 1; the BCD of 2 (0010) is applied to A4 through A7, with A7 being the MSB, and A4 being the LSB. Likewise, for the decimal 24, the BCD of 2 (0010) would be applied to B0 through B3 and the BCD of 4 (0100) would be applied to B4 through B7. In this example, the tens comparator (on the left) would output A>B to the units comparator (on the right), thereby passing the result directly through the units comparator since it is not needed to perform a comparison. However, if the BCD input to the A terminals is decimal 18 and the BCD input to the B terminals is decimal 14, the tens comparator would allow the units comparator to perform the comparison since the difference between the two decimals is in the units place, not in the tens place.

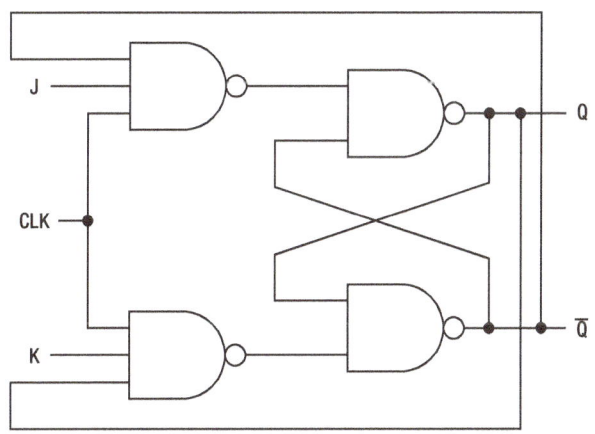

Figure 1-108. JK Flip-Flop using NAND gates.

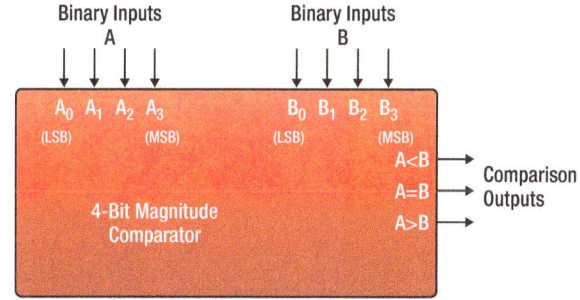

Figure 1-109. 7485 chip (4-bit magnitude comparator).

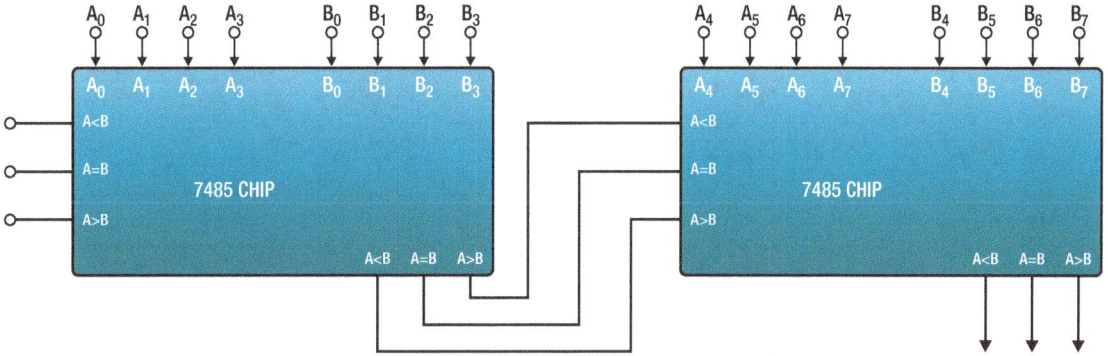

Figure 1-110. 7485 comparator cascading diagram.

Module 04 B2 - Electronic Fundamentals

1.55

ENCODER LOGIC CIRCUITS

The function of an encoder is to convert decimal numbers to binary numbers or binary-coded decimals. ***Figure 1-111*** illustrates the functional equivalent of an encoder that generates a 3-bit binary code corresponding to a switch position. In the example shown, switch position 4 results in a binary coded output of 4 = 1, 2 = 0, and 1 = 0, or binary 100, which corresponds to decimal number 4. Likewise, in ***Figure 1-112***, the compass needle pointing east provides a +5v input to D2 of the 74148 chip, an 8-line decimal to 3-line BCD encoder, which results in a binary code of 010 corresponding to an angular position of decimal number 2 or octal number 8.

In systems where two or more inputs may go HIGH (logic 1) simultaneously, a priority encoder is used to establish which input will be used. A priority encoder produces an output signal in accordance with a priority scheme based on the magnitude of the decimal numbers appearing at the input of the encoder.

Figure 1-113 is an illustration of the pin connections and truth table of the 74147, a 10-line decimal to 4-line BCD priority encoder. The 74147 chip is classified as an "active LOW" encoder since there are inverters present at the inputs and outputs such that these inputs and outputs become active at the LOW (logic 0) level. The outputs at A, B, C and D correspond to the highest-order LOW input with decimal 9 having the highest priority and decimal 1 having the lowest priority. All other inputs are irrelevant (as denoted by the "X" in the truth table). Note that the zero condition does not require any LOW inputs since zero is automatically encoded when all of the 9 inputs are set to HIGH.

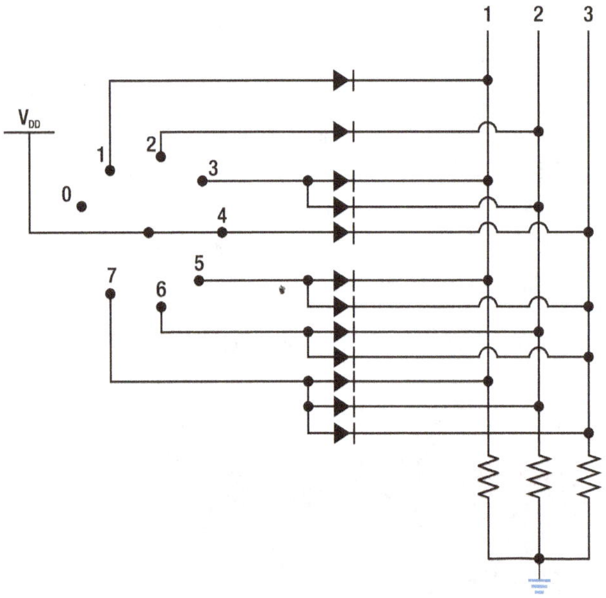

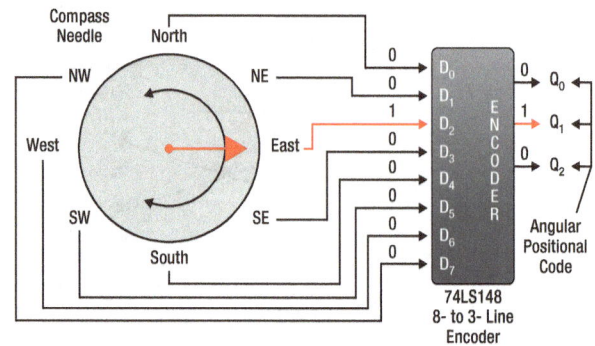

Figure 1-111. Simple digital encoder circuit.

Figure 1-112. 74148 chip (8-line to 3-line encoder).

SN54/74LS147 FUNCTIONAL TABLE

1	2	3	4	5	6	7	8	9	D	C	B	A
H	H	H	H	H	H	H	H	H	H	H	H	H
X	X	X	X	X	X	X	X	L	L	H	H	L
X	X	X	X	X	X	X	L	H	L	H	H	H
X	X	X	X	X	X	L	H	H	H	L	L	L
X	X	X	X	X	L	H	H	H	H	L	L	H
X	X	X	X	L	H	H	H	H	H	L	H	L
X	X	X	L	H	H	H	H	H	H	L	H	H
X	X	L	H	H	H	H	H	H	H	H	L	L
X	L	H	H	H	H	H	H	H	H	H	L	H
L	H	H	H	H	H	H	H	H	H	H	H	L

H = HIGH LOGIC LEVEL   L = LOW LOGIC LEVEL   X = IRRELEVANT

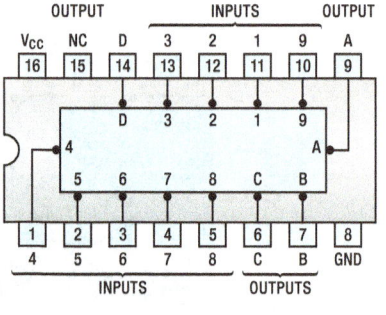

Figure 1-113. 74147 chip (10-line to 4-line priority encoder) with truth table.

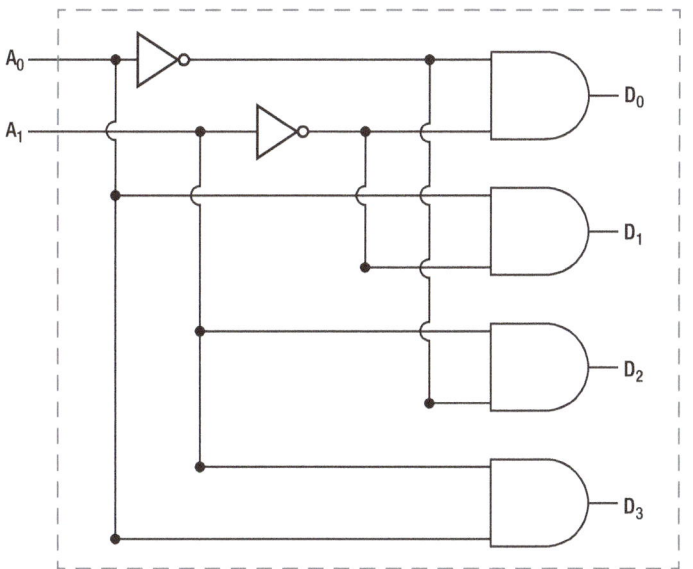

Figure 1-114. 2-line to 4-line decoder.

DECODER LOGIC CIRCUITS

Decoders perform the opposite function of encoders in that they convert binary numbers in to decimal numbers. For example, the 2-bit decoder, shown in *Figure 1-114*, contains 2 inputs denoted by A1 and A0 (with A1 being the most significant bit), and four outputs denoted by D0, D1, D2, and D3. The decoder enables one and only one of the four AND gates for each possible binary input. The two inverters provide the opposite logic inputs in the proper order to enable each gate based on the binary number input resulting in HIGH outputs from either D0, D1, D2, or D3 representing decimal numbers 0, 1, 2, or 3 respectively. For example, if the inputs are binary 00, then the output will be decimal 0; however, if the inputs are binary 11, then the output will be decimal 3.

Increasing the binary number input from 2 bits to 3 bits increases the number of outputs to 23 or 8 bits, resulting in a 3-Line to 8-Line decoder. *Figure 1-115* depicts the truth table (A), logic diagram (B), and pin-out (C) of the 74138 chip, a 3-Line to 8-Line decoder with an enable line. The enable input performs no logical operation but is only responsible for making the decoder either active or inactive. As shown in the truth table, if the enable line is LOW, then all the outputs will be LOW regardless of the A0, A1 and A2 input values (shown as "X" for don't care). However, if the enable line is HIGH, then the decoder will perform its normal operation. The 74138 chip actually has three enable inputs, two of which are inverted, meaning the enable code must be binary 001 in order for the encoder to produce an output. In the example shown, the first two enable pins are assumed to be grounded (logic 0) so that only one enable line is used for making the decoder active or inactive.

What would be a practical application of a decoder? Consider *Figure 1-116*, which uses a 7447 chip, a 4-line to 7 line decoder, to illuminate individual segments of a 7-segment liquid crystal display (LCD) based on the BCD input presented to the decoder. Such displays are commonly found on aircraft communication, navigation and surveillance radio control panels.

Larger decoders can be built by using combinations of smaller ones. For example, an 8-line to 64-line decoder can be made by using four 4-line to 16-line decoders and one 2-line to 4-line decoder. Often, decoders and encoders are used together to decode binary data into decimals for a particular application and then encoded back for a different application *(Figure 1-117)*.

LINEAR CIRCUITS AND OPERATIONAL AMPLIFIERS

A linear circuit is one in which the output is directly proportional to the input. If graphed, the performance of the circuit would be drawn as a straight line. An electronic circuit made up of linear components that maintain their values regardless of the level of voltage or current in the circuit is linear. Circuits that are composed exclusively of ideal resistors, capacitors, inductors, transformers and other linear circuit

10-LINE TO 4-LINE TRUTH TABLE

E	A_2	A_1	A_0	Y_7	Y_6	Y_5	Y_4	Y_3	Y_2	Y_1	Y_0
0	×	×	×	0	0	0	0	0	0	0	0
1	0	0	0	0	0	0	0	0	0	0	1
1	0	0	1	0	0	0	0	0	0	1	0
1	0	1	0	0	0	0	0	0	1	0	0
1	0	1	1	0	0	0	0	1	0	0	0
1	1	0	0	0	0	0	1	0	0	0	0
1	1	0	1	0	0	1	0	0	0	0	0
1	1	1	0	0	1	0	0	0	0	0	0
1	1	1	1	1	0	0	0	0	0	0	0

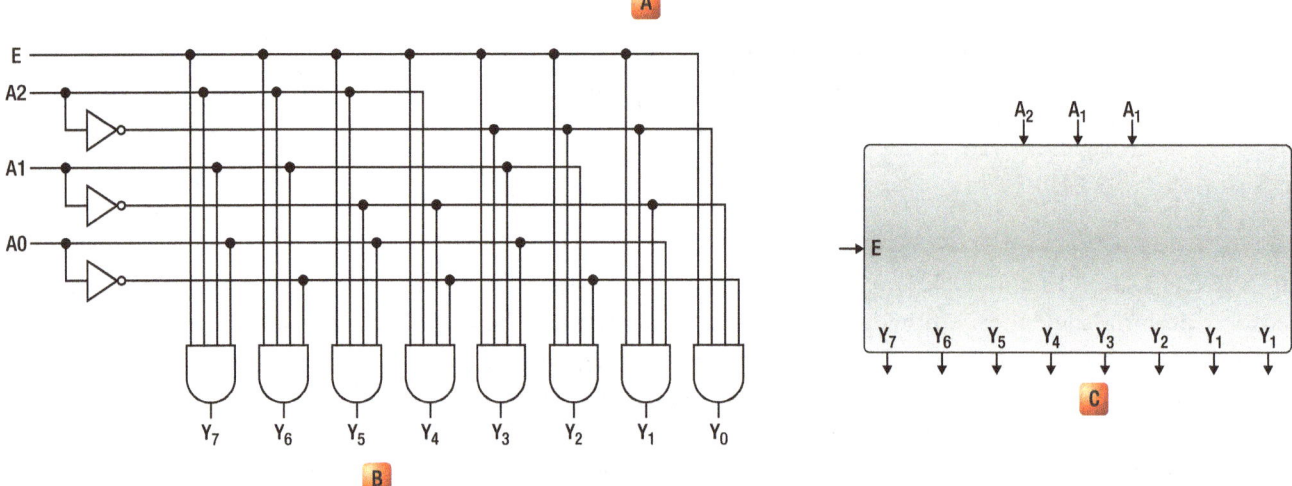

Figure 1-115. 74138 chip (3-line to 8-line decoder).

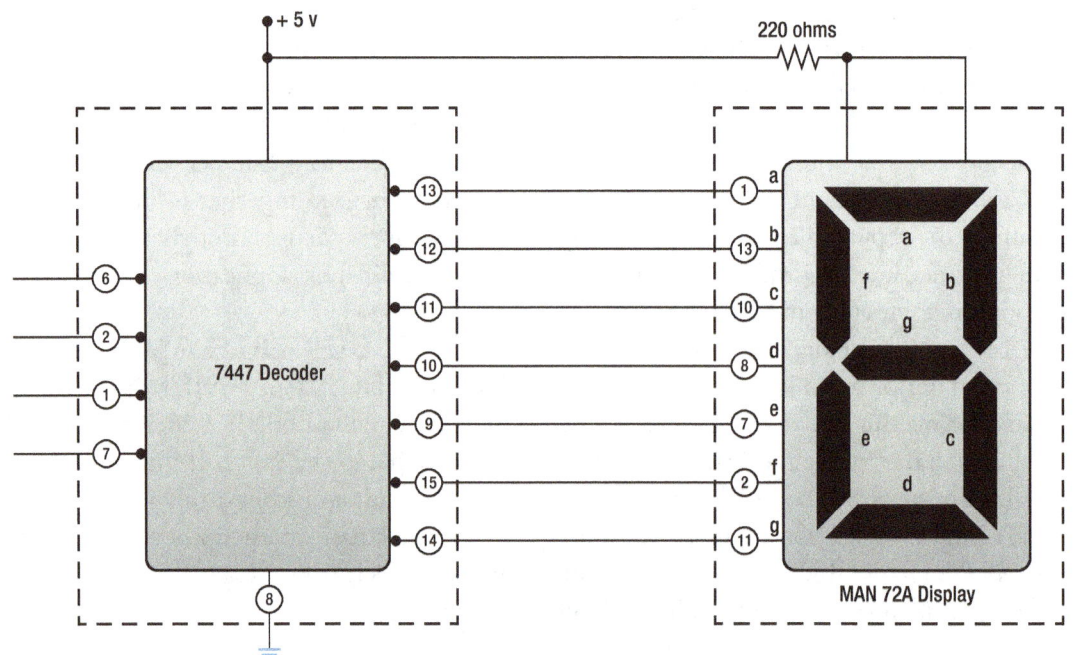

Figure 1-116. 7447 Chip (4-Line to 7-Line decoder).

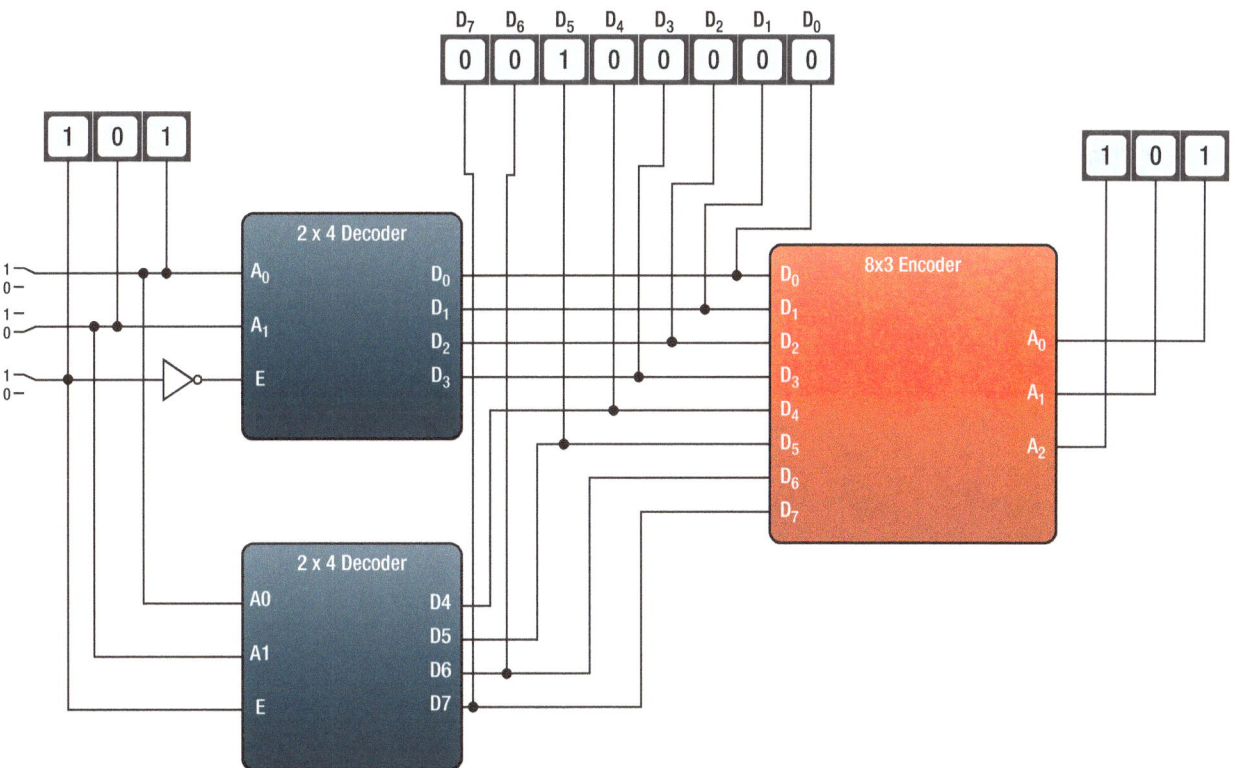

Figure 1-117. Decoder-Encoder interconnect circuit.

elements are linear. A linear component is one in which a linear relationship exists between the input current and the output voltage.

Linear circuits are easy to analyze mathematically. The sum of the inputs to a linear circuit is equal to the output. Linear circuits are used in small signal amplifiers, differentiators, and integrators. Diodes and transistors are non-linear. However, nonlinear components are often used to assemble circuits that are approximately linear.

The most commonly used linear integrated circuit is an operational amplifier, or commonly known as an "op amp". It is a high-gain differential amplifier where the output is proportional to the difference between the two input signals. An op amp has two inputs, an inverting input (-) and a non-inverting input (+) and one output. The polarity of the signal applied to the inverting input will be reversed at the output. A signal applied to the non-inverting input will retain its polarity on the output. To be classified as an operational amplifier, the device must have a very high gain, very high input impedance, and very low output impedance.

Op amps are used in a wide variety of electronic circuits, including signal processing circuits, control circuits, and instrumentation. The very popular 741 op-amp chip, shown in *Figure 1-118*, contains 20 transistors, 11 resistors, and one capacitor, as shown schematically in *Figure 1-119*. It requires dual power supplies with a positive voltage at pin 7 and a negative voltage at pin 4. The offset null inputs, used to correct for noise, will not be covered in this discussion.

The 741 op amp, when operated with a +/-15 volts power supply, has a typical open-loop gain of 200 000. Open loop simply means operating without a feedback circuit to limit its gain. The op amp provides an amplified output voltage that is proportional to the difference between the inverting input signal and the non-inverting input signal. As shown in *Figure 1-120*, the output voltage (Vo) = Ao (V2–V1), where Ao is the amplifier gain. When Vo reaches the supply voltage (Vs), the op-amp is said to be saturated and will produce no further gain. For example, if Vs is +/- 15v and the gain is 200 000, the op-amp will saturate at 15v/200 000 = 75µv. If the difference between the two input signals is more than 150µv, the output will be +15v if V1 is less than V2, or -15v if V1 is greater than V2.

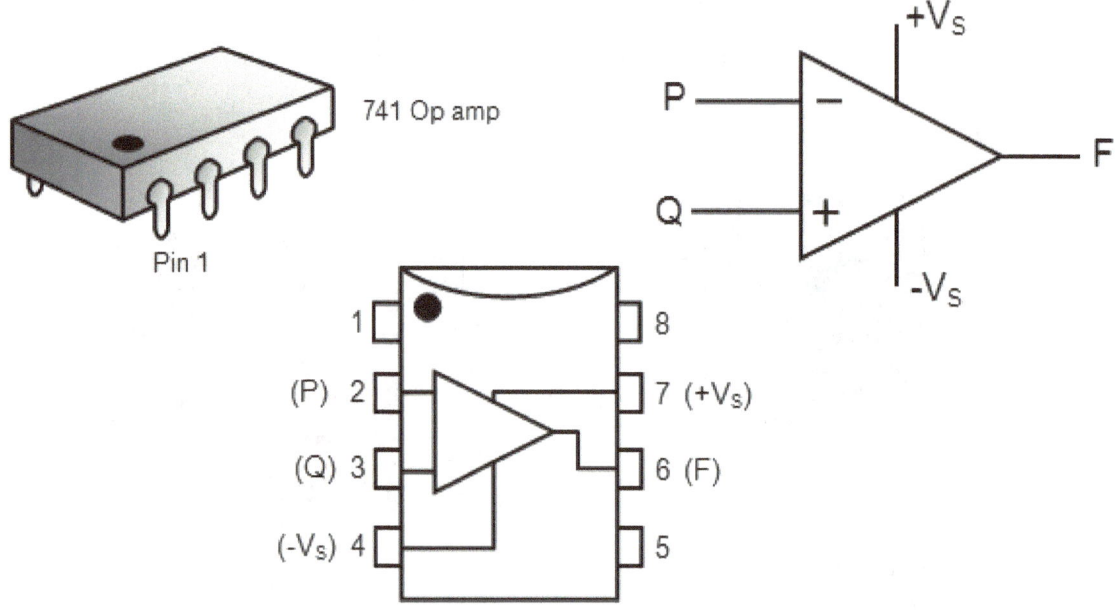

Figure 1-118. 741 op amp chip in a DIP package.

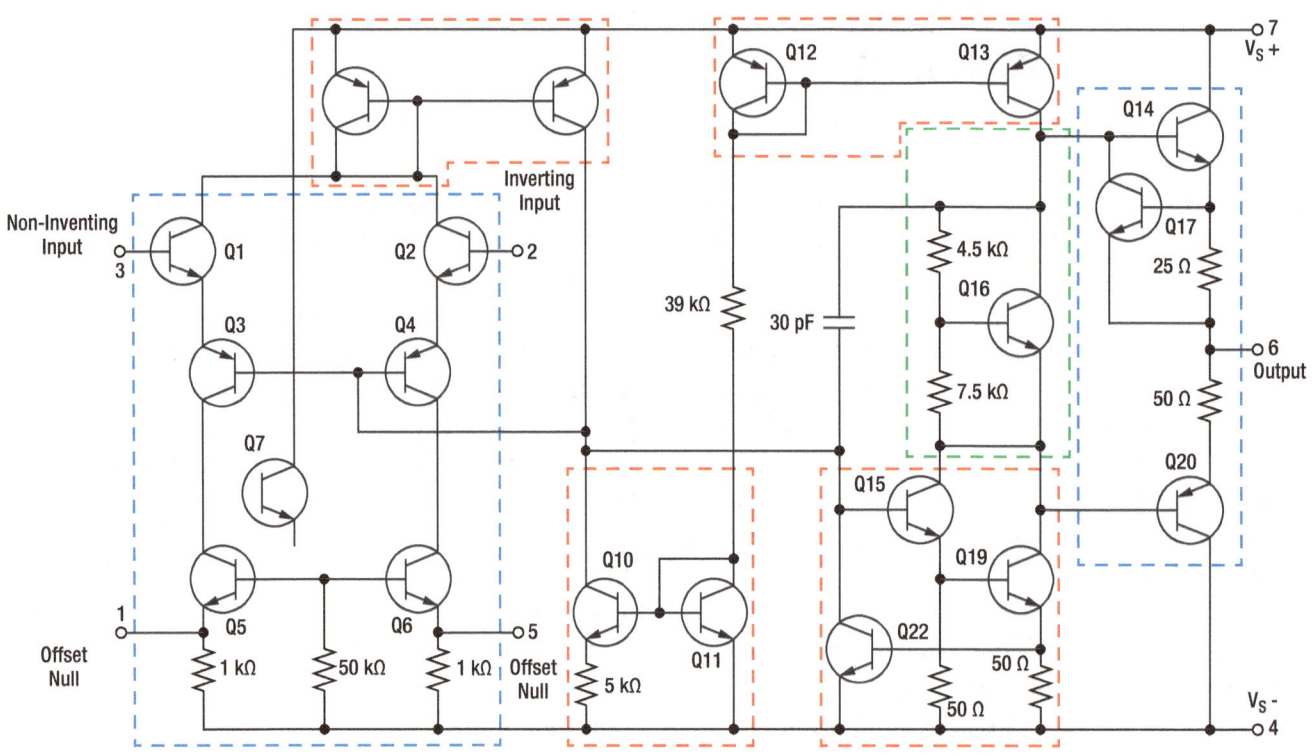

Figure 1-119. 741 Op amp schematic diagram.

The following paragraphs will provide a description of the operation of various linear circuits using op amps, such as comparators, voltage followers, integrators and differentiators. It will also discuss positive and negative feedback used to control amplifier gain. The various coupling methods used for op amps are the same as those used for transistors discussed previously.

COMPARATOR CIRCUIT

A comparator compares a signal voltage on one input with a reference voltage on the other input. If an AC sine wave is applied to one of the inputs, the op amp will act like a switch turning on when the AC voltage exceeds the DC reference voltage and turning off when falls below the DC reference voltage. As shown in *Figure 1-121*, R2 and R3 forms a voltage divider providing a

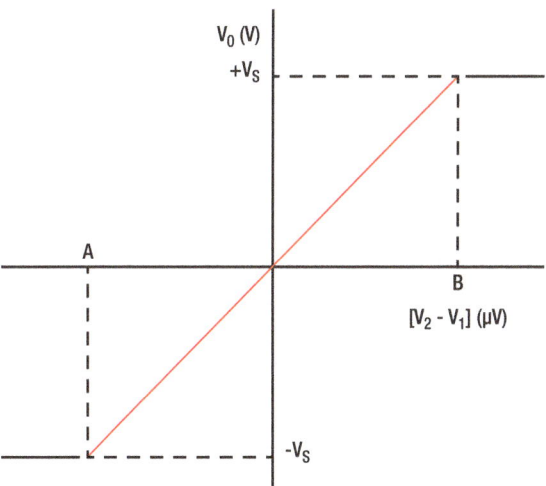

Figure 1-120. Output voltage (V_0) = A_0 ($V_2 - V_1$), where A_0 is the amplifier gain.

fixed DC reference voltage (Vref) at pin 3. Assume that the source voltage (Vs) is +/-15v. When the AC voltage applied to the inverted input (pin 2) rises above Vref, the op amp becomes saturated and provides an output of -15v until such time that the AC voltage falls below Vref where the output is 0v.

POSITIVE AND NEGATIVE FEEDBACK

Feedback is a term used to describe a condition when a portion of the output is fed back into the input of a device. Most people have experienced the loud squeal heard from a speaker when the microphone is too close to the speaker. This is called positive feedback because it tends to increase the output. Negative feedback has the opposite effect of reducing the output to prevent the op amp from going into saturation, which typically occurs around +/- 65μv.

In the previous comparator circuit, the op amp was operating in an open loop mode, which provides the maximum gain that an op amp will exhibit without a feedback network. *Figure 1-122* illustrates the op amp with a closed-loop negative feedback network with the addition of a resistor (Rf). In this example, the amplifier gain (Ao) is equivalent to Rf / Rin = 10 000Ω / 1 000Ω = 10. If the voltage at the inverted input (pin 2) is 0.2v, the output voltage (Vo) would be equal to Ao ($V_2 - V_1$) = -2.0v. Positive feedback can be achieved by inserting the feedback on the positive input (pin 3) of the op amp, instead of the negative input. Positive or negative gain can be adjusted by changing the ratio of the two feedback resistors in the network.

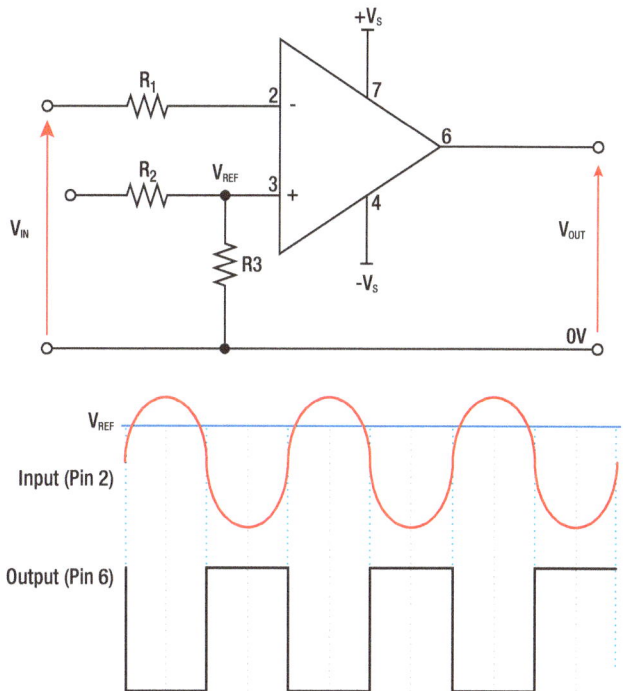

Figure 1-121. Op amp used as comparator.

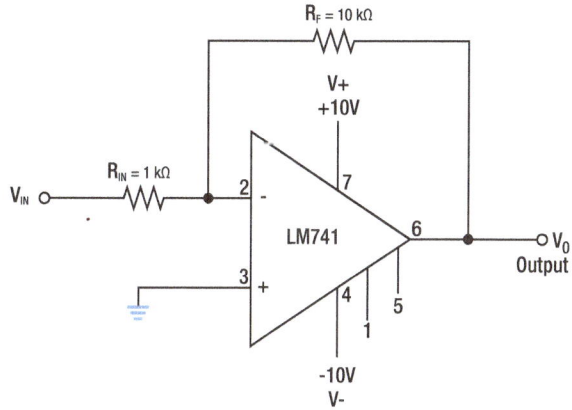

Figure 1-122. Negative feedback network is used to control op-amp gain.

The op amp in this example is called an inverting amplifier because the signal is applied to the inverted input providing a negative amplified output. A non-inverting amplifier provides a positive amplified output by simply routing the input signal to pin 3 and grounding pin 2. In this case, the closed-loop feedback network would appear between pins 6 and 3, instead of between pins 6 and 2.

VOLTAGE FOLLOWER CIRCUIT

The op amp that exhibits the highest input impedance is the voltage follower. Full negative feedback is achieved in a voltage follower circuit *(Figure 1-123)* with direct coupling of the output to the input causing a voltage

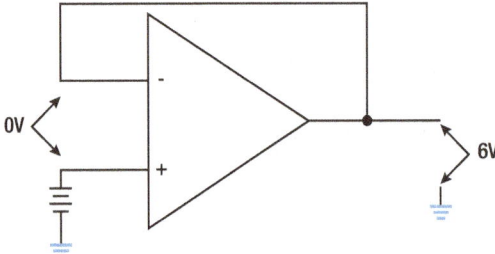

Figure 1-123. A voltage follower uses direct coupling negative feedback.

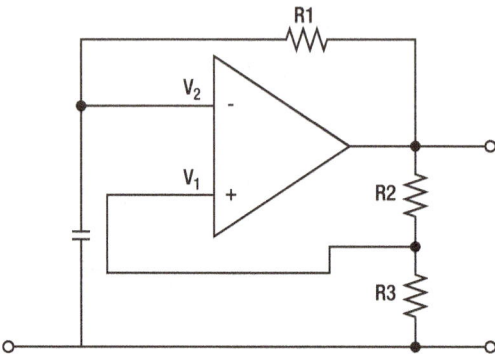

Figure 1-124. Positive feedback network used in a multivibrator circuit.

gain of 1. This is known as unity amplification, since the output voltage equals the input voltage in both magnitude and sign. Thus, as the name implies, the output voltage follows the input voltage.

This type of an op-amp is also known as a buffer amplifier or isolation amplifier. Its input resistance is high (many mega ohms), and therefore it draws negligible current from the signal source, providing a high degree of isolation between the source and the amplifier output. In addition, a very low output impedance allows for a constant voltage across the output, regardless of the current being drawn by the load.

MULTIVIBRATOR CIRCUIT

Figure 1-124 is an op-amp with a resistive-capacitive (RC) coupling that uses positive feedback in a voltage comparator to form a free-running multivibrator or oscillator. In this example, the output voltage is divided between R2 and R3, and a fraction of that voltage is fed back into the non-inverting (positive) input as a reference voltage. The capacitor is charged through R1 until V1>V2 at which time the op amp switches to negative saturation. The time it takes for this to happen is determined by the resistance of R1 (in ohms) times the capacitor's capacitance (in farads), otherwise known as the RC time constant. The capacitor now charges in the opposite direction until V1<V2, at which point the op amp switches to positive saturation, and the cycle repeats itself producing a repeatable square wave at the output.

INTEGRATOR CIRCUIT

The free-running multivibrator circuit discussed in the previous section was characterized by a capacitor in the input circuit. However, if a capacitor, instead of a resistor, is inserted in the feedback loop, the circuit is classified as an integrator. An integrator amplifier circuit performs the mathematical operation of integration, such that its output voltage is proportional to that of its input voltage with respect to time. The advantage of the integrator circuit is that the feedback capacitor is charged by a constant current that can be controlled by a grounded voltage source. *(Figure 1-125)*

When an input voltage is first applied, the capacitor offers very little resistance, acting much like a voltage follower circuit. However, as the capacitor begins to charge, its reactance decreases. When the capacitor is fully charged, the ratio of reactance of C to the resistance of R1 is will be infinite, resulting in infinite gain which causes the amplifier to reach saturation. The value of the output voltage is determined by the length of time that a voltage is present at its input as the current flows through the feedback loop to charge and discharge the capacitor. The rate at which the output voltage increases is again determined by RC time constant.

An integrator can function as a ramp generator if a square wave is applied to the input causing the capacitor to charge and discharge in response to the changes in the input signal. This will result in a saw tooth waveform output signal based on the time constant of the RC network, as shown in *Figure 1-126*.

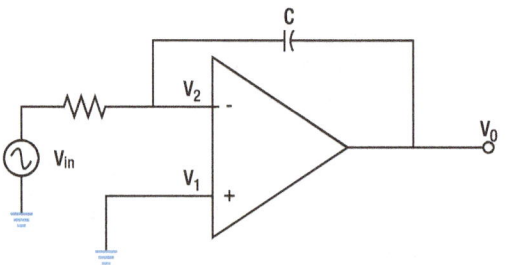

Figure 1-125. Integrator amplifier circuit.

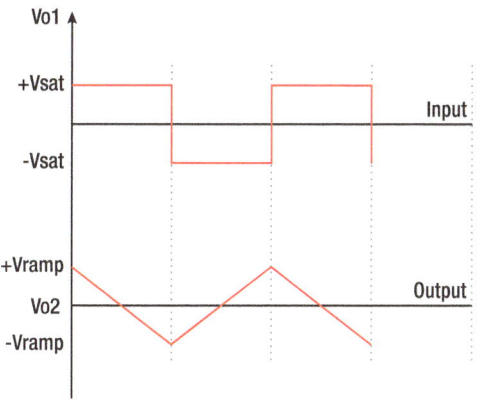

Figure 1-126. Ramp generator input and output waveforms.

DIFFERENTIATOR CIRCUIT

A differentiator performs the mathematic operation of differentiation, the opposite of integration, which is the process of finding a derivative. A derivative measures the instantaneous change of quantity (dependent variable) as determined by another quantity independent variable). For example, the derivative of the position of a moving aircraft with respect to time is velocity, or in the case of a differentiator amplifier, the value of the voltage output that is proportional to the rate of change of the input voltage.

A differentiator circuit is the exact opposite of the integrator circuit in that the position of the resistor and capacitor have been reversed such that the capacitor is at the input to the amplifier and the resistor provides the negative feedback. The capacitor only allows AC signals to pass whose frequency is dependent on rate of change of the input signal. At low frequencies, the reactance of the capacitor will be high resulting in low gain and low output voltage. At higher frequencies, the reactance of the capacitor is much lower resulting in higher gain and higher output voltage from the differential amplifier. *(Figure 1-127)*

A practical integrator and differentiator will have additional components added to their respective circuits to overcome instability (i.e., tendency to oscillate) and high-frequency noise issues that are inherent in op amps. These additional components will set the low frequency gain of the circuit to a small fixed value to prevent unwanted variations in the output voltage.

SCALE OF INTEGRATION

Integrated circuits are classified by their scale of integration, in other words, the number of transistors and other electronic components that they contain. Small-Scale Integration (SSI) circuits first appeared in the 1960's. They contained anywhere from 10 to 100 electronic components on a chip and were used to perform basic logic gate functions. *(Figure 1-128)*

Since the 1960's, there has been approximately a tenfold increase per decade on the number of transistors on a chip. For example, in the early-1970's, Medium-Scale Integration (MSI) circuits first appeared having anywhere from 100 to 3 000 electronic components per chip. MSI circuits are used for adders, counters, registers, comparators, encoders, decoders, multiplexers, de-multiplexers, etc. *(Figure 1-129)*

The first microprocessor, the 4-bit 4004 logic chip, appeared in 1971 in hand-held calculators. The 4004 chip contained 2 300 transistors running at a speed of 0.06 MIPS. *(Figure 1-130)* By the late 1970's, Large-Scale Integration (LSI) circuits with chips containing from 3 000 to 100 000 electronic components per chip

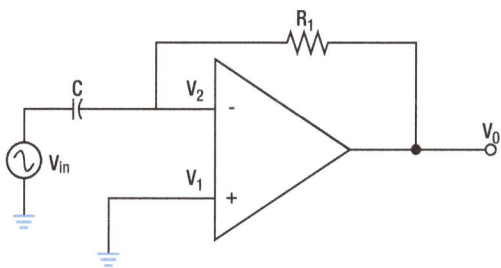

Figure 1-127. Differentiator amplifier circuit.

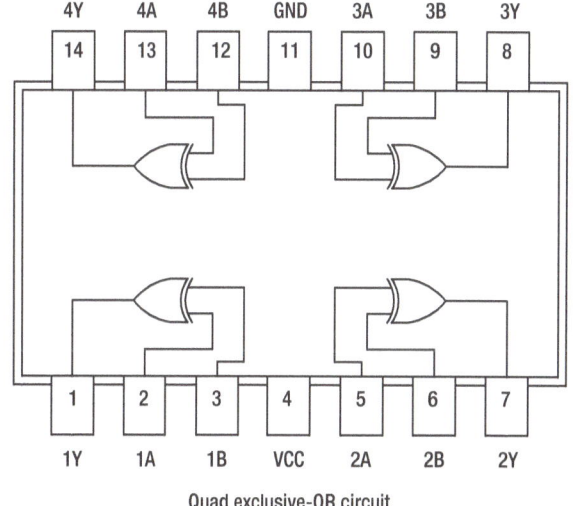

Figure 1-128. Small scale integration schematic form.

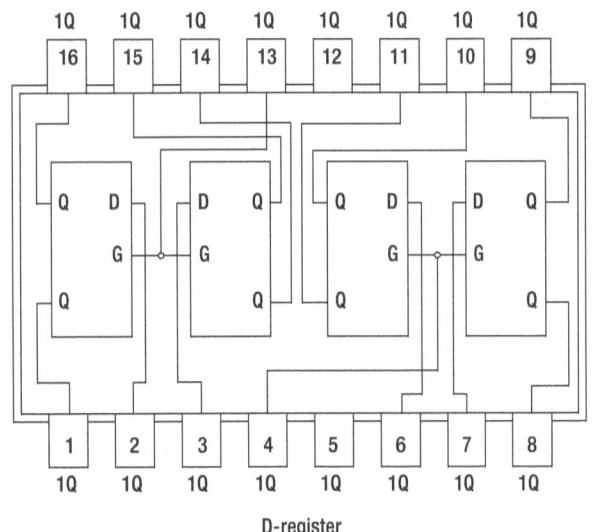

Figure 1-129. Medium scale integration schematic form.

were developed. These were used primarily for main memory modules and I/O controllers. In 1981, the first IBM Personal Computer appeared on the market with a 16-bit 8088 microprocessor chip, running at 0.75 MIPS and containing 29 000 transistors.

It's important to note that increasing the number of transistors on a chip increases the speed that the device can switch due to reduced gate delay times. However, the faster the chip operates, the more power it consumes, requiring heat-sinks to be installed over or under the IC package to reduce its operating temperature so that the component doesn't destroy itself.

In the 1980's, Very-Large-Scale Integration (VLSI) circuits with 100 000 to 1 000 000 electronic components per chip became available allowing much faster processors with greater memory capacity which gave rise to a burgeoning software industry producing operating systems, such as Windows, and a multitude of application programs that were previously unavailable. Finally, Ultra-Large-Scale Integration (ULSI) circuits with more than one million electronic components per chip were developed. By 1993, the 32-bit Intel Pentium microprocessor chip appeared on the market containing 3.1 million transistors and running at speeds up to 100 MIPS.

By 2012, System-On-Chip integration became a reality with entire electronic systems being produced on a single chip containing 9 million transistors with the width of the conductor between the components on the chips measured in tens of a nanometer (one nanometer = one billionth of a meter). Moore's Law says that every 18 months, processing speed will double. As can be seen from the previous examples, this prediction has held true. However, chip level integration is quickly coming to point where smaller component feature sizes are approaching the limits of physics.

Figure 1-130. Intel 4004 - The first microprocessor chip contained 2 300 transistors.

QUESTIONS

Question: 1-1
What are the advantages and disadvantages of solid-state devices over vacuum tubes?

Question: 1-5
What determines whether a doped silicon material becomes an N-type or a P-type semiconductor?

Question: 1-2
What is the difference between elemental and compound semiconductors?

Question: 1-6
What occurs at the depletion zone of the PN junction when a diode is forward-biased?

Question: 1-3
What characteristic does a material exhibit when its outer most shell has the maximum number of electrons?

Question: 1-7
What is leakage current?

Question: 1-4
What is a covalent bond and why is it important regarding the flow of electricity?

Question: 1-8
What is Peak Inverse Voltage?

ANSWERS

Answer: 1-1
Solid-state devices have replaced vacuum tubes in most applications due to their small size and weight, low operating voltages, lower power dissipation, higher reliability and extremely long life. In addition, there is no warm up-period. However, semiconductors typically do not perform as well as vacuum tubes for high-power, high-frequency operation, such as television broadcasting, and they are much more vulnerable to Electro-Static Discharge (ESD) during handling and operation.

Answer: 1-2
Elemental semiconductors, such as Silicon and Germanium, are made from a group of materials (group IV) having electrical conductivities that lie between metal conductors and non-metal insulators. Compound semiconductors do not appear in nature, but are synthesized using two or more elements from groups II through VI of the periodic table.

Answer: 1-3
The outer most orbital shell of any atom's electrons is called the valence shell. The number of electrons in the valence shell determines the chemical properties of the material. When the valence shell has the maximum number of electrons, it is complete and the electrons tend to be bound strongly to the nucleus. Substances with complete valence shells are known as good insulators because they resist the flow of electrons.

Answer: 1-4
A covalent bond is the method by which atoms complete their valence shells by sharing valence electrons with other atoms. Electrons in incomplete valence shells may move freely from valence shell to valence shell of different atoms or compounds. When electrons move freely from atom to atom or compound to compound, the substance is known as a conductor because it conducts the flow of electricity.

Answer: 1-5
When silicon is doped with an element or compound containing five electrons in its valence shell, the result is a negatively charged material due to the excess free electrons, and thus becomes an N-type semiconductor or donor material since it donates electrons. Doping silicon with an element that has only three valence electrons, causes an absence of the electrons, called holes, and thus becomes a P-type material or as an acceptor material since it accepts electrons in the holes.

Answer: 1-6
Applying a positive voltage to the P-type material and a negative voltage to the N-type material forces the holes and electrons toward the PN junction. The depletion zone becomes very narrow and electrons in the N-type material flow across into the P-type material. There, they combine with holes. The electron and holes continuously come together resulting in electric current flow.

Answer: 1-7
Leakage current, also known as the maximum reverse current, is the very small value of direct current that flows when a semiconductor diode is in reverse bias mode and is below the peak inverse voltage applied.

Answer: 1-8
Peak Inverse Voltage (PIV), is the maximum amount of voltage that the diode can withstand continually in the reverse-bias mode without causing a PN junction breakdown. It is the voltage at which a normal diode can no longer hold back the reverse current, and as a result, it fails. A zener diode is constructed to be able to handle the avalanche voltage and the resulting current, whereas avalanche voltage burns out an ordinary diode.

QUESTIONS

Question: 1-9
What do the numbers and letter represent in semiconductor identification codes?

Question: 1-10
What is the difference between silicon diodes and germanium diodes?

Question: 1-11
What happens when light photons strike a photocell?

Question: 1-12
What determines the color of light that Light Emitting Diodes (LED) emit?

Question: 1-13
What is the difference between a Schottky diode and a conventional silicon diode?

Question: 1-14
What purpose does a varistor serve?

Question: 1-15
How is the capacitance of the varactor inversely proportional to the applied reverse bias?

Question: 1-16
How can a series combinations of diodes be used to create a voltage regulator circuit?

ANSWERS

Answer: 1-9
The first number in the system indicates the number of junctions in the semiconductor device and is a number one less than the number of active elements. Thus 1 designates a diode; 2 designates a transistor (which may be considered as made up of two diodes); and 3 designates a tetrode (a four-element transistor). The letter "N" following the first number indicates a semiconductor. The 2- or 3-digit number following the letter "N" is a serialized identification number.

Answer: 1-10
Signal diodes can be made of either silicon or germanium diodes. Germanium signal diodes have a lower forward voltage drop (0.3v) across the PN junction than silicon signal diodes (0.7v), but have a higher forward resistance. Silicon diodes have higher forward current and higher reverse voltage peak values.

Answer: 1-11
When photons strikes a semiconductor atom, it raises the energy level above what is needed to hold its electrons in orbit. The extra energy frees an electron enabling it to flow as current. The vacated position of the electron becomes a hole. In photocells, this occurs in the depletion area of the reversed biased PN junction turning "on" the device and allowing current to flow.

Answer: 1-12
When an LED is reversed biased, no light is given off. When an LED is forward biased, the energy given off is visible in the color characteristic for the material being used. By using elements, such as gallium, arsenic, and phosphorous, an LED can be designed to radiate colors, such as red, green, yellow, blue and infrared light.

Answer: 1-13
A Schottky diode is not a pure semiconductor diode, but is a metal-semiconductor diode. It has no depletion zone, which means that the switching time is faster. Its reverse recovery time is much shorter, and it has a very low voltage drop (0.15 volts versus 0.7 volts for a silicon diode).

Answer: 1-14
A varistor has high resistance at low voltage, and low resistance at high voltage. Therefore, varistors are often used to protect circuits against excessive transient voltages. They are incorporated so that, when triggered, they shunt the current created by the high voltage away from sensitive components.

Answer: 1-15
The size of the insulation gap of the varactor, or depletion region, is similar to the distance between the plates of the capacitor. By varying the reverse-bias voltage applied to the varactor, the width of the "gap" may be varied. An increase in reverse bias increases the width of the gap which reduces the capacitance of the PN junction.

Answer: 1-16
The individual voltage drops across each diode are subtracted from the supply voltage to result in a pre-determined voltage potential across the load resistor. By adding more diodes in series, the voltage is reduced further.

QUESTIONS

Question: 1-17
How does a clamper circuit operate?

Question: 1-18
How does a diode behave as a rectifier?

Question: 1-19
Why is a bridge rectifier superior to both the half-wave and full-wave rectifier circuits?

Question: 1-20
Explain the operation of a voltage doubler circuit.

Question: 1-21
How are diodes typically tested?

Question: 1-22
Why is the binary numbering system used in digital electronics?

ANSWERS

Answer: 1-17
A clamper circuit is similar to the single-ended clipper, except that a capacitor is placed in series instead of a resistor. As a result, a clamping circuit places either the positive or negative peak of an AC sine wave at a desired DC level. It other words, it adds a DC component to the output without changing the shape or amplitude of the input AC signal.

Answer: 1-18
When AC current is applied to a diode, current flows during one cycle of the sine wave but not during the other cycle. The diode, therefore, becomes a rectifier and changes the AC current to a pulsating DC current.

Answer: 1-19
With a half-wave rectifier, only have of the AC sine wave is used to produce DC power. With a full-wave rectifier, the positive and negative cycles of the AC are used, but the magnitude of the AC voltage is half of what is supplied because of the center tap of the transformer. With a bridge rectifier, the entire applied AC voltage is used resulting in a non-interrupted DC pulse voltage at the output ready to be filtered to pure DC.

Answer: 1-20
A voltage doubler consists of a clamper circuit and a peak rectifier circuit. The peak rectifier circuit draws current from the voltage stored in the clamper's capacitor charging then peak rectifier's capacitor to twice the value of the clamper capacitor's value which causes the output voltage to be twice the peak-to-peak input voltage.

Answer: 1-21
The most convenient and quickest way of testing a diode is with an ohmmeter. To make the check, simply disconnect one of the diode leads from the circuit wiring, and make resistance measurements across the leads of the diode. The resistance measurements obtained depend upon the test-lead polarity of the ohmmeter; therefore, two measurements must be taken. The first measurement is taken with the test leads connected to either end of the diode and the second measurement is taken with the test leads reversed on the diode. The larger resistance value is assumed to be the reverse (back) resistance of the diode, and the smaller resistance (front) value is assumed to be the forward resistance. Measurement can be made for comparison purposes using another identical-type diode (known to be good) as a standard. Two high-value resistance measurements indicate that the diode is open or has a high forward resistance. Two low-value resistance measurements indicate that the diode is shorted or has a low reverse resistance. A normal set of measurements will show a high resistance in the reverse direction and a low resistance in the forward direction.

Answer: 1-22
The binary number system is used in digital electronics because the two basic conditions of electricity, ON and OFF, can represent the two digits of the binary number system. When a switch is ON, it represents the digit 1, and when it is OFF, it represents the digit 0.

QUESTIONS

Question: 1-23
Explain how to convert a decimal number to a binary number.

Question: 1-24
What is the difference between an inverter and a buffer?

Question: 1-25
Explain the logic function of the AND gate.

Question: 1-26
Explain the logic function of the OR gate.

Question: 1-27
Explain the logic function of the NOR gate.

Question: 1-28
What is the difference between the Negative OR and Negative AND gates and the NOR and NAND gates?

Question: 1-29
Explain the operation of a Half-Adder Logic Circuit.

ANSWERS

Answer: 1-23
To convert from decimal to binary, find the binary column that has the largest value but is equal to or smaller than the decimal number being converted. Place a 1 in that column and subtract the column value from the decimal number being converted. Look at the difference. Place a 1 in the column that has the largest value but is equal to or smaller than the decimal number difference of what was just subtracted. Now subtract this column value from the difference of the decimal number being converted and the previous column difference. If a column is not used, place a zero in it. Continue this operation until all of the binary place value columns with 1's, when added together, have the same value as the decimal number being converted. Write the number in binary form including a 1 or a 0 for each column.

Answer: 1-24
An inverter, also known as a NOT gate, inverts the input signal. In other words, if there was voltage at the input to the gate, there would be no output voltage. A buffer is a gate with the same output as the input used to isolate or amplify a signal.

Answer: 1-25
For an AND gate to have a Logic 1 output, all inputs have to be Logic 1. In an actual electronic circuit, this means that for a voltage to be present at the output, the AND gate circuit has to receive voltage at all of its inputs.

Answer: 1-26
In an OR gate, only one of the inputs needs to be Logic 1 for there to be an output of Logic 1. When both inputs are Logic 1, the OR gate has a Logic 1 output because it still meets the condition of one of the inputs being Logic 1.

Answer: 1-27
A NOR gate is an inverted OR gate. If there is to be a Logic 1 output, or output voltage, then neither input can be Logic 1 or have input voltage. This is the same as satisfying the OR gate conditions and then putting the output through a NOT gate.

Answer: 1-28
The output of a Negative AND gate is the same as a NOR gate, and the output of a Negative OR gate is the same as a NAND gate. However, the inputs are inverted in the Negative OR and Negative AND gates.

Answer: 1-29
A Half-Adder Logic Circuit consists of an Exclusive OR (XOR) gate and an AND gate with their inputs connected in parallel. Voltage applied to either input will cause the sum to be 1. Voltage applied to both inputs will cause sum to be 0 and the carry to be 1 forming the binary number 10, which is the decimal number 2. Note: Half-adders can only add two digits. A full-adder becomes necessary when a carry input must be added to the two binary digits to obtain a decimal sum of 3.

QUESTIONS

Question: 1-30
What is a comparator op amp circuit?

Question: 1-31
What is a voltage follower op-amp circuit?

Question: 1-32
What is the difference between an integrator and differentiator op amp circuit?

Question: 1-33
What are flip-flops and what purpose do they serve?

Question: 1-34
When using flip-flops, it is often desirable to establish the logic level outputs at a time other than when the signals are initially applied. How is this accomplished?

Question: 1-35
What is the advantage of a JK Flip-Flop over an RS Flip-Flop?

Question: 1-36
What is the purpose of a Comparator?

Question: 1-37
What is the difference between an Encoder and a Priority Encoder?

ANSWERS

Answer: 1-30
A comparator compares a signal voltage on one input with a reference voltage on the other input. If an AC sine wave is applied to one of the inputs, the op amp will act like a switch turning on when the AC voltage exceeds the DC reference voltage and turning off when falls below the DC reference voltage.

Answer: 1-31
Full negative feedback is achieved in a voltage follower circuit with direct coupling of the output to the input causing a voltage gain of 1. This is known as unity amplification, since the output voltage equals the input voltage in both magnitude and sign, providing a high impedance isolation between the source signal and the amplifier output.

Answer: 1-32
An integrator amplifier circuit performs the mathematical operation of integration. A differentiator performs the mathematic operation of differentiation, the opposite of integration, which is the process of finding a derivative. A differentiator circuit is the exact opposite of the integrator circuit in that the position of the resistor and capacitor have been reversed such that the capacitor is at the input to the amplifier and the resistor provides the negative feedback.

Answer: 1-33
Flip-flops are bi-stable multi-vibrator circuits that form basic storage units of sequential logic used in shift registers and counters. They have the ability to maintain their state without further application of a signal allowing them to store a bit of data or one place of a larger binary number. Their ability to set one condition and reset or change to an alternate condition results in a latch, also known as a flipflop.

Answer: 1-34
This is accomplished using a flip-flop circuit that is triggered by a clock input. The clock pulse acts as the control to allow the signals that appears at inputs of the S and R gates to pass to the cross-coupled flip-flop.

Answer: 1-35
The JK flip flop has the distinct advantage that they are no disallowed combinations as with the RS flip flops.

Answer: 1-36
Unlike a flip-flop that counts and stores binary numbers, the function of a comparator is to compare sets of binary numbers. Comparators are often used as parity checkers.

Answer: 1-37
The function of an encoder is to convert decimal numbers to binary numbers or binary-coded decimals. In systems where two or more inputs may simultaneously be HIGH, a priority encoder is used to establish which input will be used. A priority encoder produces an output signal in accordance with a priority scheme based on the magnitude of the decimal numbers appearing at the input of the encoder.

SUB-MODULE 02
PRINTED CIRCUIT BOARDS

PART-66 SYLLABUS LEVELS
CERTIFICATION CATEGORY → **B2**

Sub-Module 02
PRINTED CIRCUIT BOARDS
Knowledge Requirements

4.2 - Printed Circuit Boards
    Description and use of printed circuit boards.   2

PRINTED CIRCUIT BOARDS

An electric circuit is typically comprised of various components connected together by wire. In many cases, the circuit performs a function that doesn't require the circuit or the components to be large. The development of solid-state devices and the use of transistors have enabled many required electric functions on an aircraft to be carried out with small electronic circuits saving both space and weight. These circuits are often created on Printed Circuit Boards (PCB), which provides electrical connections as thin conductive metal tracks on a dielectric substrate, which also support the components. PCBs are used in nearly all electronic devices from a simple mouse *(Figure 2-1)* to the computer itself.

There are three types of printed circuit boards: single layered boards, double-layered boards, and multi-layered boards. Also, there are three technologies used to connect components to the circuits on the PCB: through hole, plated through hole, and surface mount. The following sections will discuss each of these board types and interconnection technology.

PCB MANUFACTURING PROCESS

All printed circuit boards are constructed from a thin sheet of non-conductive material often just 1/16 inch (1.5 mm) thick. The board can be sized as needed to contain the required circuit(s) and components or to fit the housing designed, such as the example of the mouse, to contain the PCB. Two common materials used to make PCBs are epoxy resin impregnated paper and epoxy resin impregnated fiber glass cloth, often called pre-preg. Typically, copper foil is bonded to the surface of the board in a heat press operation. The circuit traces are applied as a pattern using etch-resistive ink. Then, the unwanted copper is etched away using a photo sensitive chemical process (ammonium persulfate or ferric chloride) leaving only the conductive pathways of the circuits, called traces. *(Figure 2-2)*

SINGLE-LAYER BOARDS

Single layered boards have the electronic components mounted on the opposite side of the board where the copper traces are exposed. *(Figure 2-3)* Early PCB's had holes drilled at the connection points of the components. The conductive paths, or traces, were created with the copper foil on one side of the board and components located on the opposite side. Component leads were passed through the holes to be soldered to the copper foil traces on the other side of the board, as shown in *Figure 2-4*.

Through-hole technology later evolved into plated-through holes to provide better electrical properties and mechanical stability with the components mounted on the top on the PCB. The difference between non-plated through holes and plated through holes is the presence of copper inside the insulating board material. *(Figure 2-5)* Plated through holes have less resistivity at the joint and provide a degree of mechanical stiffness. PCBs with non-plated through holes are, of course, less expensive and take less time to manufacture.

DOUBLE-LAYERED BOARDS

Circuit boards can be single-sided, but more often are double-sided with copper circuit traces and components on both sides. Also, in the past, most components had lead wires that were inserted through corresponding holes on the PCB and then soldered. Through hole technology has since evolved to what is called Surface Mount Technology (SMT). Instead of placing the leads of the components through holes for soldering on to the copper traces, surface mount components are placed on the board as the same side as the copper traces and small leads that lie flat are soldered on to copper circuit pads, which provide not only an electrical connection, but mechanical rigidity as well. Surface mount technology allows more components and circuits to be placed on the same PCB since they are attached on both sides of the board. The only disadvantage is that it is more difficult to align and solder SMT components in place. *(Figure 2-6)*

Figure 2-1. Typical computer mouse printed circuit board.

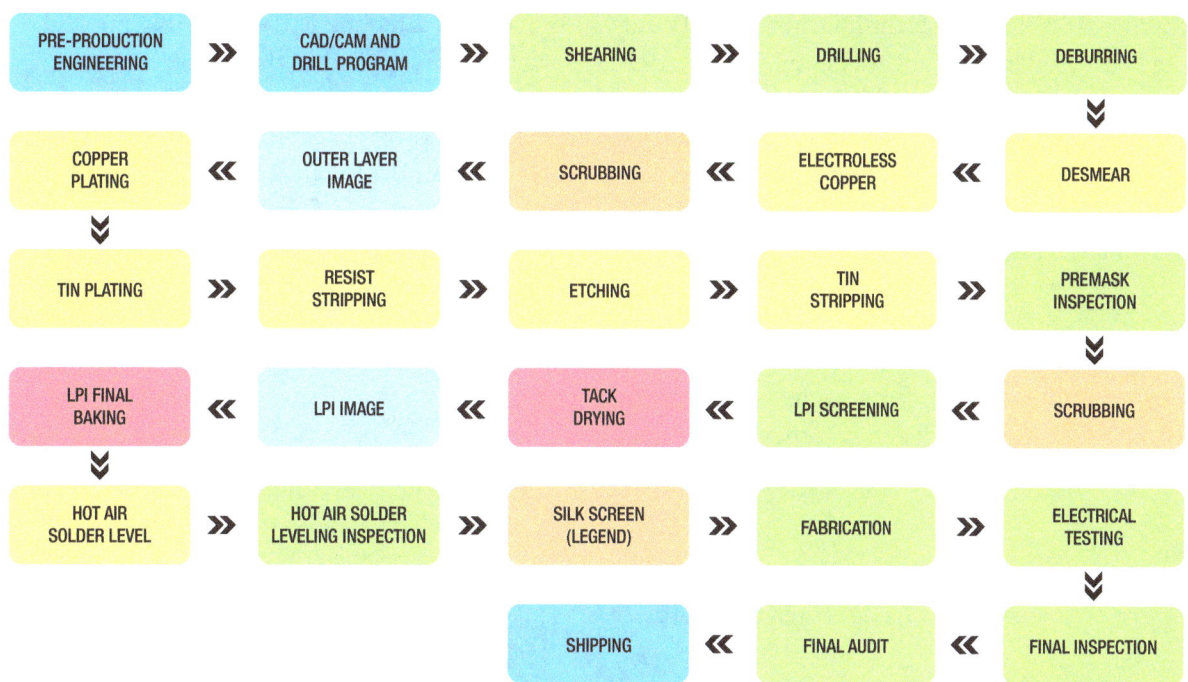

Figure 2-2. Printed circuit board manufacturing process.

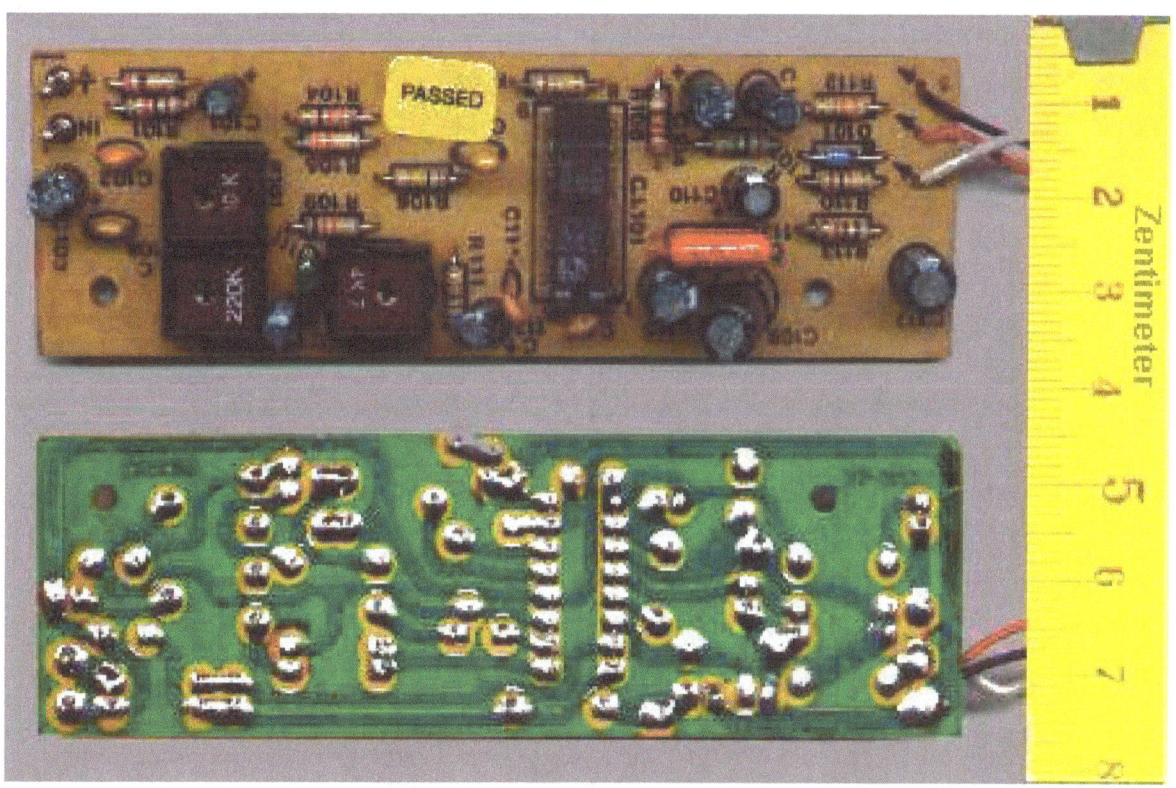

Figure 2-3. A single layer printed circuit board with traces and solder connections on one side and the soldered components on the other side.

A variation of surface mount technology that takes up even less space on the board is Ball Grid Arrays (BGA) components. *(Figure 2-7)* In this type of package, the leads are replaced with small solder balls located on the bottom of the component. BGA packages have the advantage of higher pin density compared to other methods, but it requires special equipment, instead of a simple soldering iron, to install or remove BGA components.

The changes in mounting technology have brought with them changes in soldering techniques as well. Hand soldering with soldering irons was common practice long ago, especially with single-layered circuit boards. That has since evolved into two automated soldering principles used today, flow soldering and the reflow method. In high volume manufacturing, a robot will pick and place the various electronic components from assorted bins and place them on PCBs at pre-programmed locations on the board. The circuit board is then moved to a conveyor belt where the board is dipped in molten tin-lead solder and the solder is sucked up through the plated-through holes to form the joints, as shown in the top illustration in *Figure 2-8*.

With the introduction of surface mounted technology components came the reflow soldering method, whereby solder paste is applied to the copper mounting pads and the components are picked and placed on to the board and held in place with an adhesive. The board is then subject to controlled heat using a reflow oven to melt the solder paste and form a electrical connection and mechanical bond with the copper pads on the PCB. *(Figure 2-8 bottom)*

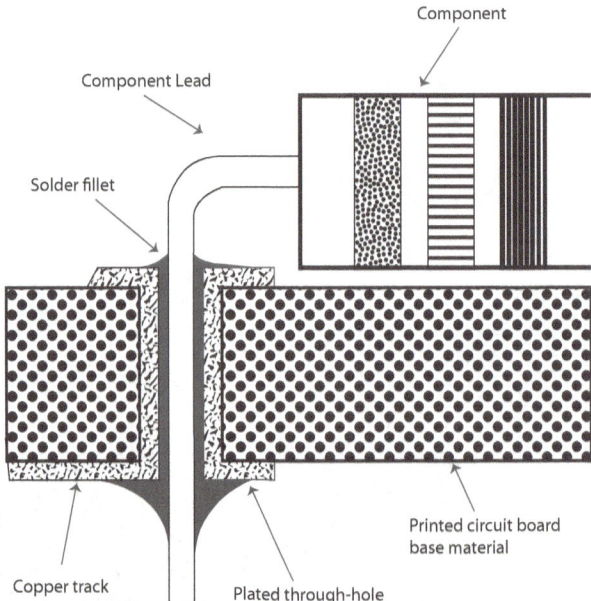

Figure 2-5. Plated through holes offer better electrical conductivity and mechanical stability.

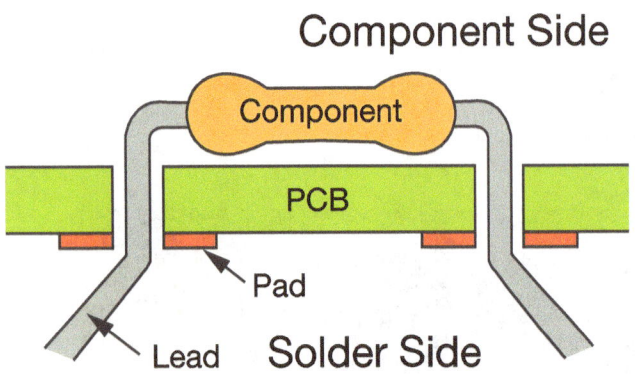

Figure 2-4. Components mounted on one side and soldered on the opposite side.

Figure 2-6. Surface-mounted technology solders components on to traces on the same side.

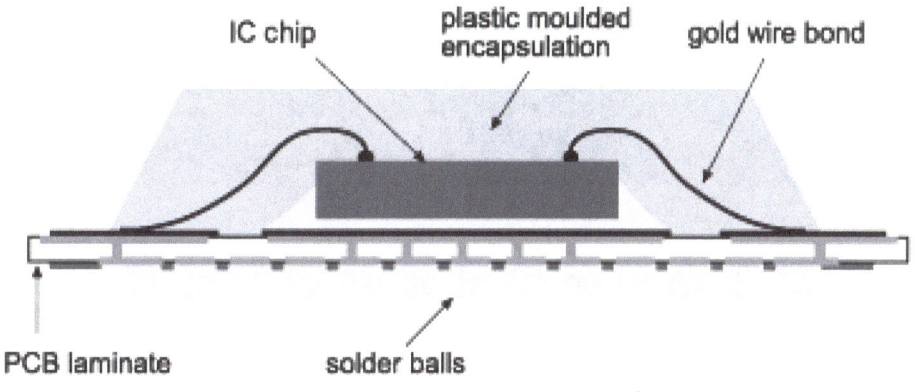

Figure 2-7. A Ball Grid Array SMT component.

☐ **Soldering using through hole technology and flow method**

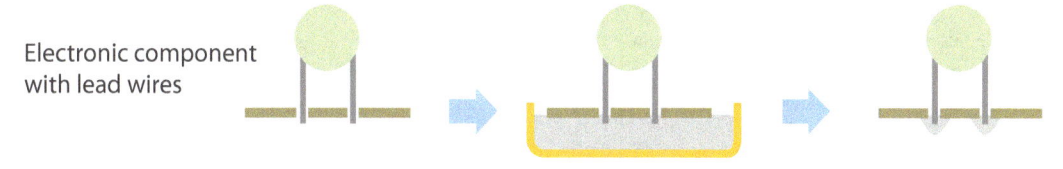

☐ **Soldering using surface mount technology and reflow method**

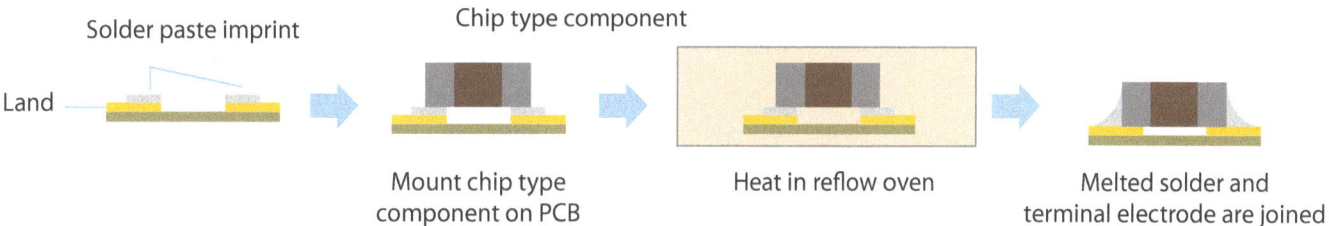

Figure 2-8. PCB soldering techniques.

MULTI-LAYERED BOARDS

As previously discussed, miniaturization has been a key driving force in the electronic industry since the diode and transistor first replaced the vacuum tube in the 1960's. As electronic components have reduced is size, so have the methods used to connect them, principally through the evolution of the printed circuit board to multi-layer technology. Multi-layered PCBs are used where several layers of boards are stacked to provide an even greater density of components. *(Figure 2-9)*

Multi-layered boards are joined electrically by what looks like a hollow rivet, called a via. Vias resemble the early holes used to attach components, but are actually conductive paths between layers of the circuit boards. Corresponding positions on different layers of the board that are electrically connected through a hole in the board is where vias are found. The hole is made conductive through electroplating or by inserting a hollow rivet. *(Figure 2-10)*

A through-hole via (1) consists of a conductive tube and two pads at each end of the barrel connected to the circuit trace. High density boards may have blind vias (2) that are exposed to only one side of the board, or buried vias (3) that connect internal layers without being exposed to either surface. Thermal vias are used to carry heat away from power devices and are typically arranged in an array. Multi-layer PCBs are designed by computer software programs due to their complexity and requirements for extremely precise registration of circuit traces between the various layers. Very complex circuits are possible with the attachment of all types of electronic devices, including resistors, transistors, and integrated circuits in dual-in line and BGA packages, and microprocessors in BGA packages. *(Figure 2-11)*

It is important to note that as circuit designs have become more complex and constraints on space have increased, problems have occurred in multi-layer board designs, particularly for high frequency applications,

Figure 2-9. Multi-layered boards typically have one layer for Vcc and another for ground.

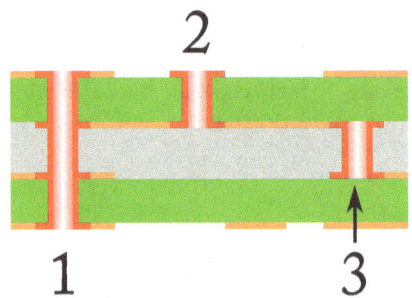

Figure 2-10. The gray and green layers are non-conductive pre-preg material while the thin orange layers (copper foil traces) and the vias are conductive.

due to various unintended capacitive and inductive coupling mechanisms that appear between the various layers. As such, modern PCB design uses computer modeling to mitigate such issues. For example, at a frequency of 100MHz, any circuit trace smaller than 30 square centimeters can cause radio frequency coupling interference.

PCB REPAIR

The soldering process required for attaching components to printed circuit boards requires special equipment with precise heat control and is not performed in the field. Removable PCBs, or Line Replaceable Modules (LRMs), allow replacement of defective units or repair in an equipped shop by knowledgeable technicians. *(Figure 2-12)* Often, the boards with components attached are coated with a protective laminate substance that must be removed before repairs can be made. The following sections will discuss the risks and possible damage to electronic components and how they must be handled when conducting a PCB repair.

RISKS AND POSSIBLE DAMAGE

Static electricity is a simple fact of nature. It is around us all the time and is caused by friction. Most work environments have non-conductive floors and no means of controlling the humidity. As the humidity drops below 20%, a static charge builds up on a person's body. The faster the person walks, the higher the charge. Simply walking across a carpet can generate 1 500 volts of static electricity at 65% relative humidity and up to 35 000 volts of static electricity at 20% relative humidity. Plastics used in most products will produce charges from 5 000 to 10 000 volts. Once the person sits down at the work station, the electrostatic field surrounding their body is enough to cause damage to sensitive electronic components without even touching them. However, when the person touches the component, an electrostatic discharge or spark occurs, and zap, the component is most certainly destroyed. *(Figure 2-13)*

Electro-Static Discharge (ESD) is defined in U.S. military handbook DOD-HKBK-263 as "transfer of electrostatic charges between bodies at different potentials caused by direct contact or induced by an electrostatic field". In other words, an electrostatic charge on one body can be imparted to another body through induction from an electromagnetic field, or through conduction via physical contact. If an electronic component that is charged is then suddenly grounded, the charge will dissipate to ground, but in the process, the component will be damaged due to excessive heat from breakdown of the dielectric material within the component.

Figure 2-11. A multilayer printed circuit board with LED's, microprocessors and various other components and traces mounted on both sides of the board.

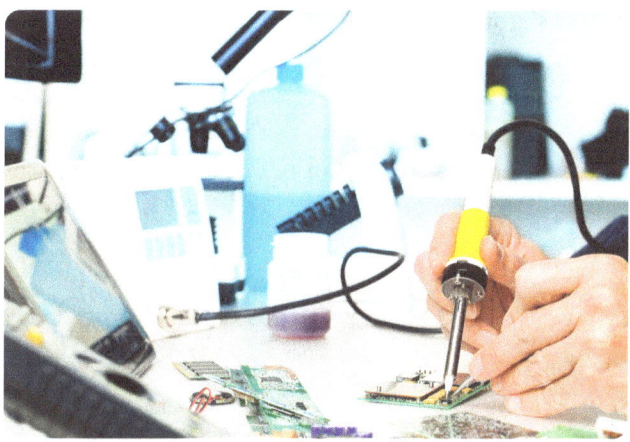

Figure 2-12. Repair of a printed circuit board.

Electrostatic induction occurs when a charged object induces the redistribution of charges in another object. A classic example of this is picking up pieces of paper using a comb that was rubbed against fur. In **Figure 2-14**, the comb is charged negative, meaning that there exists an excess of electrons built up on the comb. The side of the paper closest to the comb will end up being slightly positive due to the attraction of opposite charges, while the opposite side of the paper will be slightly negative due to the repulsion of similar charges.

Figure 2-13. Electrostatic discharge.

MIL-STD-1686C is the U.S. military standard for "ESD control programs for the protection of electrical and electronic parts, assemblies, and equipment". It recognizes two classes of ESD-sensitive items: Class I for 100 to 1 000 volts and Class II for 1 001 to 4 000 volts sensitivity. Most electronic components are in Class I. For example, bi-polar transistors are susceptible to ESD between 380 to 7 000 volts; CMOS devices are susceptible between 250 volts and 3 000 volts; and EPROMs, used in computer memories, are susceptible to as low as 100 volts.

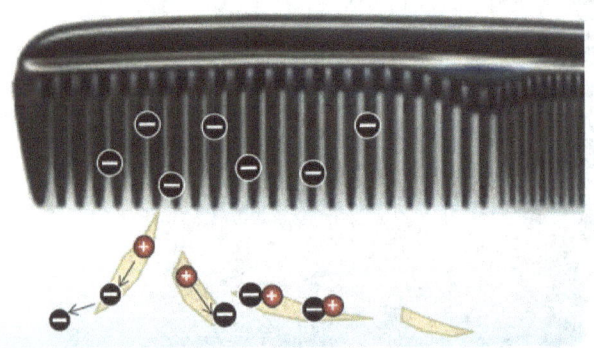

Figure 2-14. Electrostatic induction.

Figure 2-15. Warning sign for an ESD controlled area.

The ESD issue is not going away. In fact, the problem is getting much worse. As component technology continues to advance to achieve higher speeds and greater functionality, their physical geometries are shrinking, which is causing components to become even more susceptible to lower discharge voltages. The following section will discuss special handling of ESD-sensitive components and anti-static protection devices which must be used to protect these sensitive electronic components from the dangers of electrostatic discharge.

ANTI-STATIC PROTECTION

Controlled Environment

Static electricity can't be eliminated. It can only be controlled. Therefore, it is essential to only handle ESD sensitive devices in static-safe controlled environment. Signage must be placed outside any ESD controlled areas to warn people that special precautions must be taken before entering the controlled environment. *(Figure 2-15)* Any insulating materials, such as nylon, mylar, vinyl, rubber, mica, ceramics, fiberglass, wood, styrofoam, and plastic, will store static electricity, and therefore, should be kept out of the work area. Technicians should only enter the work area wearing anti-static (steel mesh) smocks and conductive (leather-soled) footwear. If wearing an anti-static heel strap in place of conductive shoes, the grounding cord must run into the sock in order to make contact with the skin.

Static-Safe Workstation

Conductive materials, including personnel, must be grounded. The floor surface should be covered with conductive paints or coatings, anti-static floor finishes, or anti-static vinyl flooring. As shown in *Figure 2-16*, the work station should have a static dissipative floor mat and table-top mat that have a surface resistivity of 105 to 1 012 ohms per square inch. The conductive mat not only provides a surface that is free of static charge on which to work, but must also remove the static charge from conductive items placed on it. Both the floor and table-top mats should be connected through a 1 mega-ohm resistor connected to a common ground point. The resistor is required to protect personnel in the event the ground becomes electrically live.

Anti-Static Wrist Straps

The same safety requirement holds true for the anti-static wrist strap *(Figure 2-17)* in that the coil cord must be plugged or clipped into a receptacle with a 1 mega-ohm resistor connected to a common ground point. The wrist strap must be secure around the wrist at all times while seated at the work station so that it makes good electrical connection with the skin to dissipate any electrical charge to ground before touching sensitive electronic components.

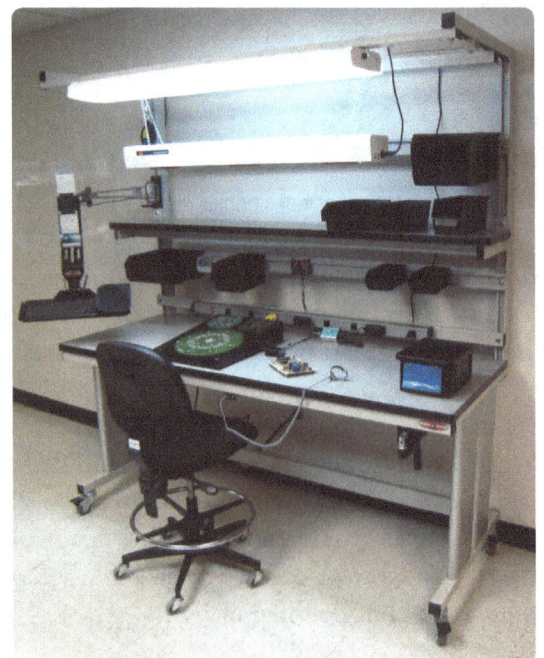

Figure 2-16. Static-safe workstation.

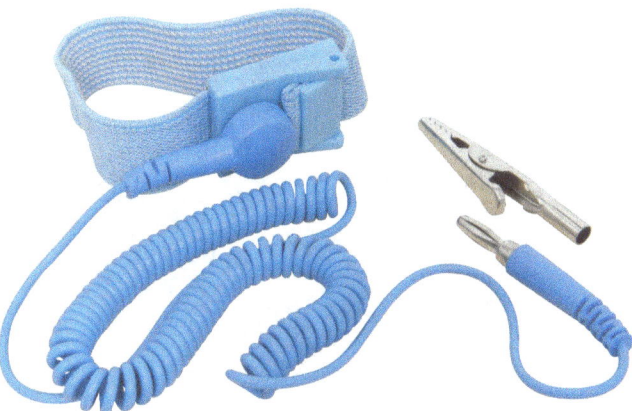

Figure 2-17. Anti-static electricity grounding wristband.

Grounding Test Stations

All anti-static devices should be tested before entering the static-safe controlled environment. *Figure 2-18* is a picture of a typical grounding test station used to determine whether the anti-static devices are working properly. A green indicator light means that the wrist strap is worn properly and is working as intended. The test station can also be used to test footwear, heal straps, and coil cords as well.

Ionizers

Since it is not practical to raise the relative humidity to high levels due to operator discomfort and the fact that it would cause metals to rust, the controlled environment should be equipped with ionizers to neutralize any charged insulators commonly found in the work environment. Because positively or negatively charged surfaces will attract ions of the opposite charge, an air stream containing both positive and negative

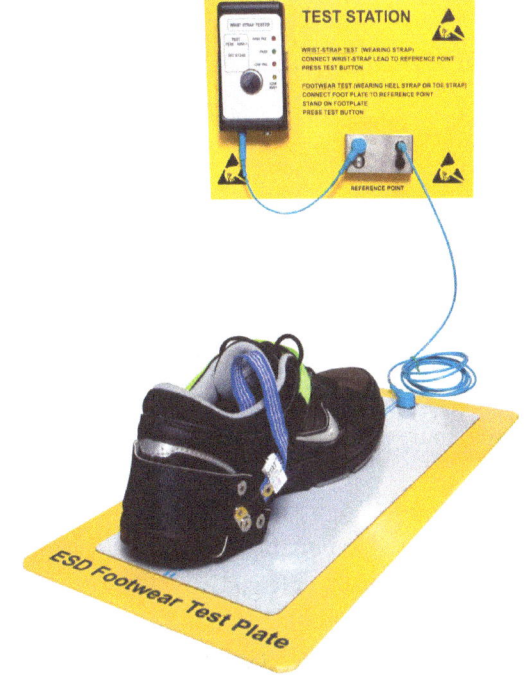

Figure 2-18. Typical grounding test station.

ions is used to neutralize the charged surface. Once the surface is neutralized, it remains so as long as the ion stream is present.

Ionizers are available in high-pressure, low-volume air guns for periodic localized cleaning, and low-pressure, high-volume wall-mounted units designed to be suspended over the work station with the ionized air blowing down over the area to be protected against an ESD event. *(Figure 2-19)*

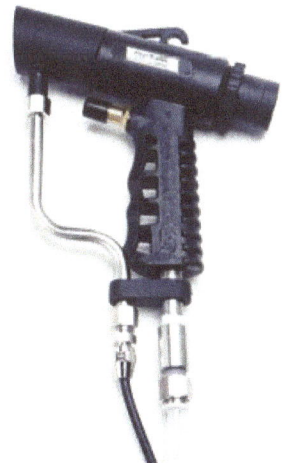
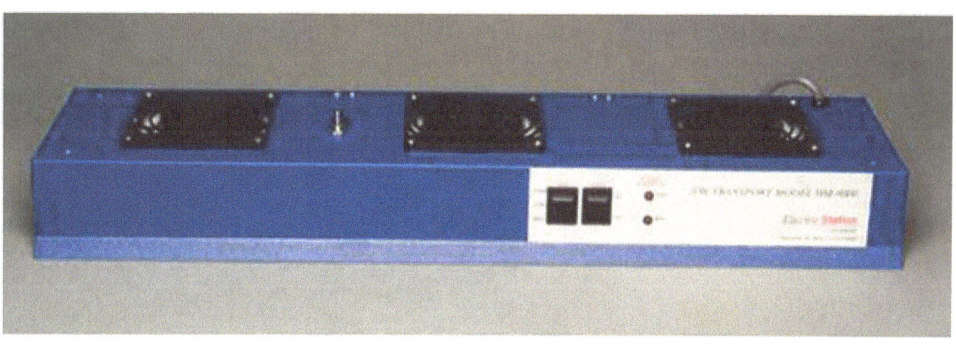

Figure 2-19. Hand-held and wall-mounted ionizers.

Module 04 B2 - Electronic Fundamentals

Designed to cover a work station area, the ionizer will neutralize even the highest electrostatic charge. Normally the system is mounted 30"-36" above the area to be controlled, producing a balanced ionization pattern of approximately 36" wide x 48" long. It is highly recommended to use an electrostatic field meter to detect static charges in the work area to be assured that the ionizer is functioning properly before handling sensitive components. If the ionizer is not working properly, topical anti-stats should be sprayed in the work area to control the generation and accumulation of electrostatic charges.

Special Handling

All ESD sensitive components should transported in a closed conductive container (e.g., LRU or a tote box). The container must be stored on a grounded rack, and when moved to the work station, it must make contact with the grounded table mat. Any accumulated charge on the human body should first be discharged, by wearing the grounded anti-static wrist strap, before opening the protective container containing the ESD sensitive component. Also, always use a grounded soldering iron to install ESD sensitive components.

All ESD sensitive components should be packaged is an electrostatic shielded conductive bag. These laminated bags are made from an outer layer of transparent metalized sheet or an aluminum foil material, a middle insulation layer, and an inner anti-static layer. Finally, the bag is sealed with a label warning that there is an ESD sensitive component inside. *(Figure 2-20)*

Figure 2-20. Laminated metalized bag for storing ESD sensitive components.

QUESTIONS

Question: 2-1
Describe how printed circuit board traces are made.

Question: 2-2
What is the difference between single-layer boards and double-layer boards?

Question: 2-3
What are the advantages of plated-through holes?

Question: 2-4
Describe surface mount technology components.

Question: 2-5
How the soldering techniques different for through hole technology components versus surface mount technology components?

Question: 2-6
Describe the three different types of vias used in multi-layer boards.

Question: 2-7
What causes static electricity and electrostatic induction?

Question: 2-8
What is Electro-Static Discharge (ESD) and what are the ways that it can damage electronic components?

ANSWERS

Answer: 2-1
Copper foil is bonded to the surface of the pre-preg board in a heat press operation. The circuit traces are applied as a pattern and using etch-resistive ink. Then, the unwanted copper is etched away using a photo sensitive chemical process (ammonium persulfate or ferric chloride) leaving only the conductive pathways of the circuits, called traces.

Answer: 2-2
Single-layer boards have the traces with the copper foil on one side of the board and components mounted on the opposite side. Double-layer boards have circuit traces on both sides of the board, and can also have components mounted on both sides as well.

Answer: 2-3
The difference between non-plated through holes and plated through holes is the presence of copper inside the insulating board material. Plated through holes have less resistivity at the joint and provide a degree of mechanical stiffness.

Answer: 2-4
Instead of placing the leads of the components through holes for soldering on to the copper traces, surface mount components are placed on the board as the same side as the copper traces and small leads that lie flat are soldered on to copper circuit pads, which provide not only an electrical connection, but mechanical rigidity as well. Surface mount technology allows more components and circuits to be placed on the same PCB since they are attached on both sides of the board. A variation of surface mount technology that takes up even less space on the board is Ball Grid Arrays (BGA) components. In this type of package, the leads are replaced with small solder balls located on the bottom of the component.

Answer: 2-5
For through-hole technology components, the circuit board is then moved to a conveyer belt where the board is dipped in molten tin-lead solder and the solder is sucked up through the plated-through holes to form the joints. With surface mounted technology a solder paste is applied to the copper mounting pads. The board is then subject to controlled heat using a reflow oven to melt the solder paste to form solder joints.

Answer: 2-6
A through-hole via consists of a conductive tube and two pads at each end of the barrel connected to the circuit trace. High density boards may have blind vias that are exposed to only one side of the board, or buried vias that connect internal layers without being exposed to either surface.

Answer: 2-7
Static electricity is caused by friction. Simply walking across a carpet can generate 1 500 volts of static electricity at 65% relative humidity and up to 35 000 volts of static electricity at 20% relative humidity. Electrostatic induction occurs when a charged object induces the redistribution of charges in another object.

Answer: 2-8
ESD is the transfer of electrostatic charges between bodies at different potentials caused by direct contact or induced by an electrostatic field. If an electronic component that is charged is then suddenly grounded, the charge will dissipate to ground, but in the process, the component will be damaged due to excessive heat and/or from breakdown of the dielectric material within the component.

QUESTIONS

Question: 2-9
How susceptible are electronic components to damage from ESD?

Question: 2-10
What precautions must be taken when working in an ESD controlled environment?

Question: 2-11
How does one maintain a static-free workstation?

Question: 2-12
What is the reason for using ionizers?

Question: 2-13
What precautions should be used when handling ESD sensitive components?

ANSWERS

Answer: 2-9
Bi-polar transistors are susceptible to ESD between 380 to 7 000 volts; CMOS devices are susceptible between 250 volts and 3 000 volts; and EPROMs, used in computer memories, are susceptible to as low as 100 volts.

Answer: 2-10
Any insulating materials, such as nylon, mylar, vinyl, rubber, mica, ceramics, fiberglass, wood, styrofoam, and plastic, will store static electricity, and therefore, should be kept out of the work area. Technicians should only enter the work area wearing anti-static (steel mesh) smocks and conductive (leather-soled) footwear.

Answer: 2-11
The work station should have a static dissipative floor mat and table-top mat that are connected through a 1 mega-ohm resistor to a common ground point. The wrist strap must be secure around the wrist at all times while seated at the work station so that it makes good electrical connection with the skin to dissipate any electrical charge to ground before touching sensitive electronic components. The wrist strap cord must be plugged into a receptacle with a 1 mega-ohm resistor connected to the same common ground point.

Answer: 2-12
A controlled environment should be equipped with ionizers to neutralize any charged insulators commonly found in the work environment. Because positively or negatively charged surfaces will attract ions of the opposite charge, an air stream containing both positive and negative ions is used to neutralize the charged surface. Once the surface is neutralized, it remains so as long as the ion stream is present.

Answer: 2-13
All ESD sensitive components should transported in a closed conductive container (e.g., LRU or a tote box). The container must be stored on a grounded rack, and when moved to the work station, it must make contact with the grounded table mat. Any accumulated charge on the human body should first be discharged, by wearing the grounded anti-static wrist strap, before opening the protective container containing the ESD sensitive component. All ESD sensitive components should be packaged is an electrostatic shielded conductive bag.

Sub-Module 03
SERVOMECHANISMS
Knowledge Requirements

4.3 - Servomechanisms
(a) Understanding of the following terms:
 Open and closed loop systems, feedback, follow up, analogue transducers;
 Principles of operation and use of the following synchro system components/features:
 resolvers, differential, control and torque, transformers, inductance and capacitance transmitters.

(b) Understanding of the following terms: Open and closed loop, follow up, servomechanism, analogue, transducer, null, damping, feedback, deadband;
 Construction operation and use of the following synchro system components: resolvers, differential, control and torque, E and I transformers, inductance transmitters, capacitance transmitters, synchronous transmitters;
 Servomechanism defects, reversal of synchro leads, hunting.

2

SERVOMECHANISMS

A servomechanism is an electric control system for an automatic powered mechanism that produces motion or force using a low energy input signal. The amplified system typically drives an electric or hydraulic motor; however, the motion can be rotary or linear depending on the mechanical transmission of the force. Servomechanisms are integral in Automatic Flight Control Systems (AFCS), also commonly known as autopilots. *(Figure 3-1)* They are also used in flight instrumentation, autothrottle systems, radar antenna systems, etc. The discussion that follow focuses on autopilot systems, but the principles are the same for any servomechanism. It will begin with a discussion of the basic principles of servomechanisms; followed by the operation of various servomechanism components, such as transducers, synchros, and transmitters.

FEEDBACK: OPEN-LOOP AND CLOSED-LOOP SYSTEMS

In the previous submodule, it was discussed how feedback is used to control amplifier gain. Feedback occurs when output of a system is "fed back" as an input as part of a cause-and-effect chain that forms a circuit or loop. An open-loop system is one that does not have any feedback mechanism. An example of an open-loop system is a conventional voltmeter. Here, voltage applied across the input terminals creates a current through a moving coil, which in turn, generates a magnetic field. The field, acting with a permanent magnet, creates a torque which displaces the moving coil with its attached pointer until a counter-torque from the coiled spring balances the system. Ideally, the voltmeter indication is an accurate indication of the source voltage. Unfortunately, its accuracy depends on the accuracy of each of the components and will vary based on spring tension, magnet strength, coil impedance, bearing friction, and unbalance. As such, a voltmeter must be calibrated and constantly monitored to changes in the environment that could limit its performance as a precision measuring instrument.

A closed-loop system is different from an open-loop system in that there is a feedback mechanism present. In other words, the output is continually compared to the input and any difference is applied to control the output in such a way to reduce the difference to zero, which is called the "null". A common example of a closed loop system is illustrated in *Figure 3-2*. In this example, a

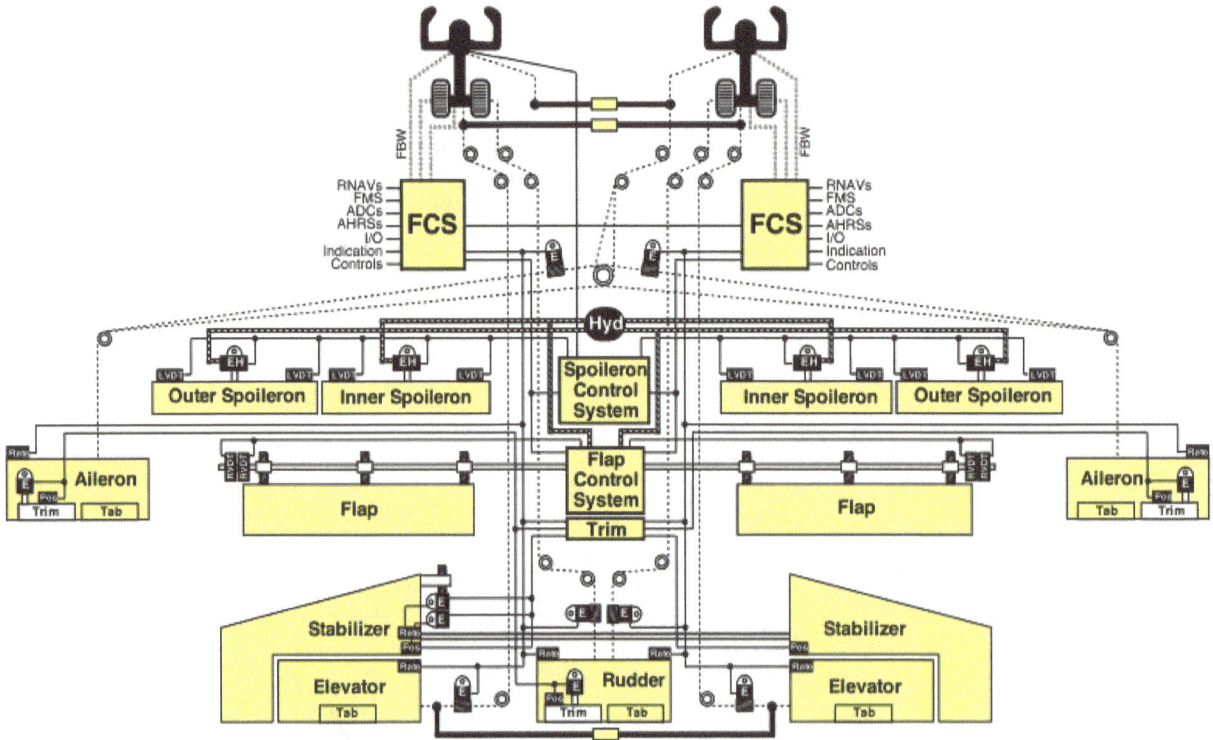

Figure 3-1. AFCS controllers send commands to actuator servomotors which physically move the aircraft control surfaces to the desired position.

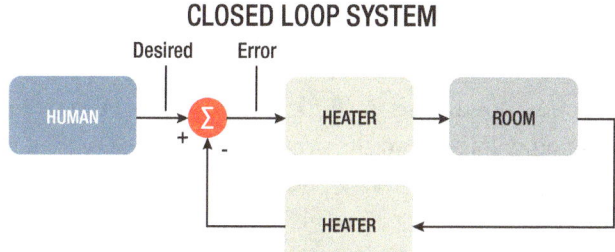

Figure 3-2. A closed-loop system uses feedback to provide an error signal to the controller.

person adjusts the thermostat control to the desired temperature. The controller sends a signal to the heater to command it produce heat. All closed-loop systems have an error detector, known as a "follow-up", which calculates the difference between the desired input and the actual measured state. At some point, the output signal from follow-up sensor (thermometer) is equal and opposite to the input control signal, producing zero voltage which shuts the heater down until such time that an imbalance once again occurs between the desired temperature and actual temperature which starts the cycle over again.

Let's apply the previous example of open-loop and closed-loop systems to aircraft flight controls. First let's begin with an open-loop system. When the cockpit controls are set to a selected setting, the signal produced in the AFCS controller is amplified to operate a two-phase AC servomotor which moves the flight control surfaces to the desired setting. If there is something that prevents the controlled unit from actually reaching the desired setting, the control system does not know this since there is no feedback loop. Bearing friction, wind resistance, and other factors may cause the setting of the flight control surfaces on the controller to not actually be achieved. For that reason, open loop systems are not used on automatic flight control systems since flight safety is of paramount importance.

However, in a closed-loop control system, the actual position of the unit is fed back as a signal input to the controller so that adjustments can be made to achieve or maintain the original selected settings. In the simplified example shown in *Figure 3-3*, the input potentiometer is set to provide a desired control signal, which is then amplified to drive the servomotor, which positions the load, in this case, a flight control surface such as an aileron, elevator, or rudder.

The feedback potentiometer is mechanically coupled to the servomotor to measure its angular position, which provides a signal to the error detector (follow-up) circuit. Note that the voltage feeding the two potentiometers is reversed. Therefore, when the feedback signal is equal and opposite to the control signal, the voltage at the summing point of the error detector (TP3) is zero, and the servomotor stops in place. The summing circuit is a resistor network used to add up the follow-up and control voltages to provide a difference signal to the amplifier.

The purpose of the amplifier is to increase the low-level signal from the follow-up to a level that can be used to drive the servomotor. One phase of the servomotor is

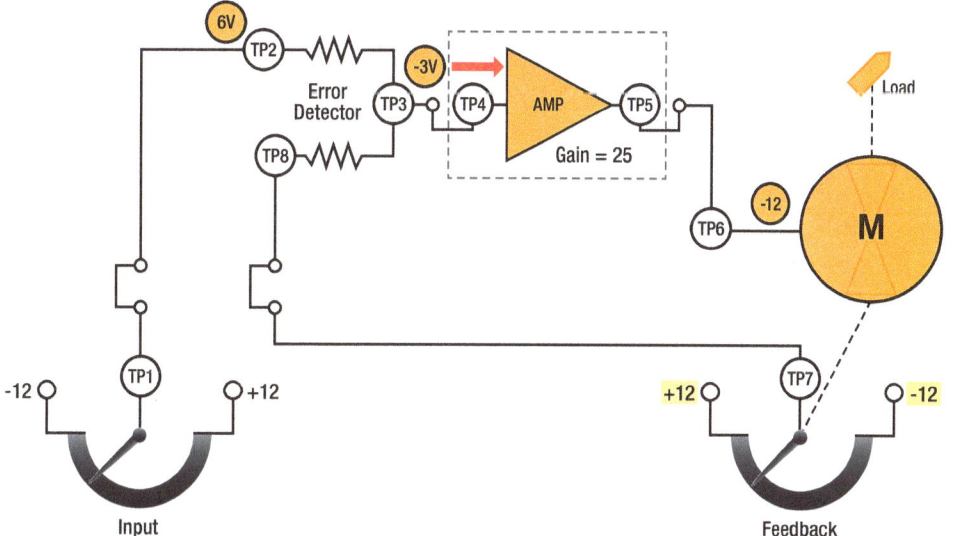

Figure 3-3. A closed-loop control system provides feedback so that adjustments are made automatically to the output to match the desired input setting.

energized by a fixed reference voltage and the other is coupled to the amplifier output to produce torque to drive the output towards zero error. Often, a gear train is used to couple the servomotor to the output or load to amplify the torque output sufficiently to move the flight control surface.

If during flight, turbulence moves the flight control surface to an un-commanded position, the servomotor, with its coupled feedback potentiometer, will also rotate sending a feedback signal to the error detector, which will cause the amplifier to drive the servomotor until such time that the voltage at the summing point (input to the amplifier) again returns to zero, thereby once again stopping the servomotor in place.

ANALOG TRANSDUCERS

The information regarding the position of a controlled device is often accomplished with an analog transducer in place of a potentiometer. A transducer is a device which converts the differing position of the physical flight control surface in to a variable electric output signal that can be processed by the controller. It is basically a transformer with two secondary induction coils and a moving core that is attached to the controlled unit. As the unit moves, the core moves, which changes the value of the voltage induced in the two secondary coils. The differential of the output voltages of the coils is the feedback signal sent to the controller.

Figure 3-4 depicts a cutaway view of a Linear Variable Differential Transducer (LVDT) and a schematic diagram showing its operation as the armature moves inducing voltage from the primary coils to the secondary coils to provide the voltage output.

A Rotary Variable Differential Transducer (RVDT) measures angular motion, instead of linear motion. RVDTs are devices that function by the motion of a rotor within the electro-magnetic field of the stator. This produces an AC output signal which has a known relationship with the mechanical motion. The amplitude of the signal is proportional to the rotor angular position. An RVTD is basically a transformer with one primary input winding and two stationary output windings. When the armature is placed equally between the two stator secondary coils, the induced voltage in each secondary coil cancels out, since they are equal and opposite, resulting in zero output. *(Figure 3-5)*

Since there is only an inductive connection between the primary and secondary coils, variable coupling transducers are very stable devices that operate accurately and reliably for long periods of time. The core of the transducer, which is mechanically linked to the flight controls, or other unit whose movement is being controlled, is the only moving part.

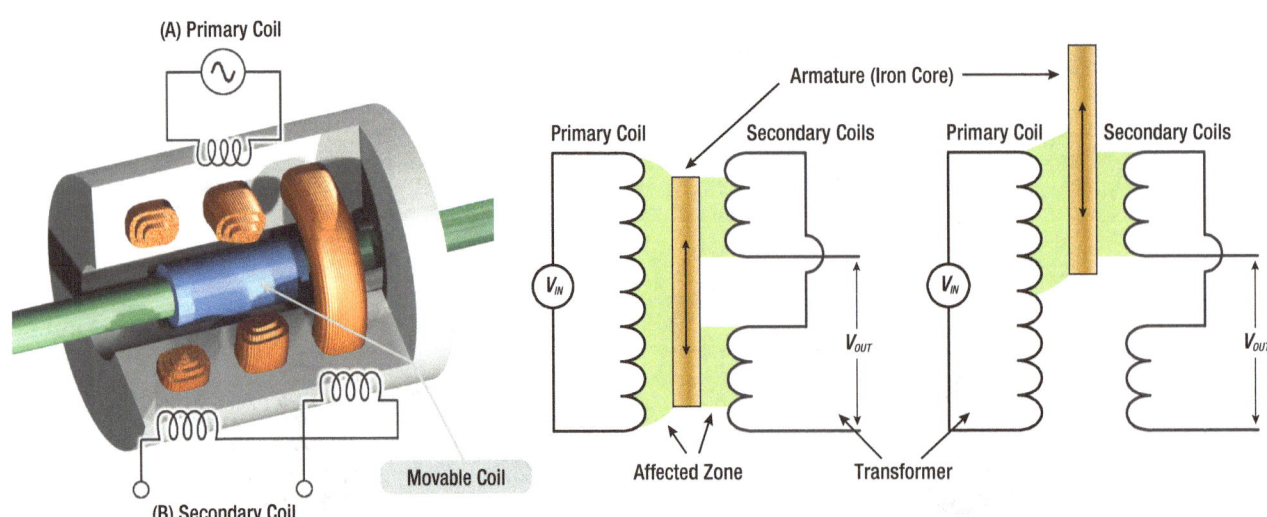

Figure 3-4. Current is driven through the primary coil at A of the LVDT, causing an induction current to be generated through the secondary coils at B.

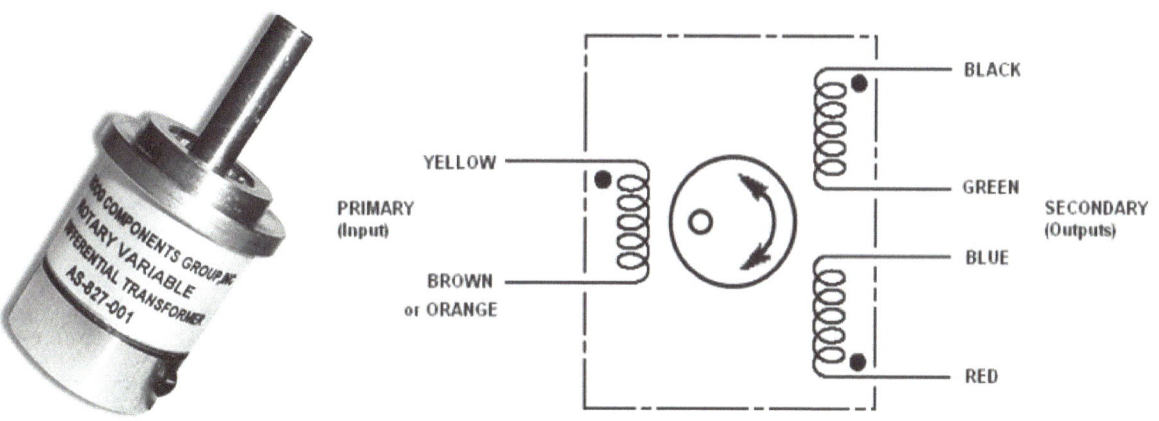

Figure 3-5. Schematic diagram and illustration of a RVDT.

SYNCHRO SYSTEMS

Another type of position monitoring system that incorporates feedback is known as a synchro system. A synchro system is a servomechanism used for transmitting information from one point to another. The word "synchro" is a shortened form of the word "synchronous", and refers to any one of a number of similarly operating two-unit electrical systems capable of measuring, transmitting, and indicating a certain parameter and then sending the signal, via a synchronous transmitter, to a synchronous receiver that could be used to display the information on an indicator dial. *(Figure 3-6)*

The most common types of synchro systems in use today are the DC Selsyn, AC Autosyn and AC Magnesyn systems. These three syncho systems are similar in construction, and all operate by exploiting the consistent relationship between electricity and magnetism. Their basis of operation relies on the fact that electricity can be used to create magnetic fields that have definite direction, and that these magnetic fields can interact with magnets and other electromagnetic fields.

The following description of a DC synchro system provides the basic concept of how a synchro system works on light aircraft. AC systems are more refined, and therefore, are more commonly found on transport category aircraft. Most remote analog position-indicating instruments are designed around a synchro system, such as a flap position indicator or flap position indictor. Fluid pressure indicators may also use synchro systems.

DC SELSYN SYSTEMS

Aircraft with only a Direct Current (DC) electrical power system have no other choice but to use a DC selsyn system. Selsyn is an abbreviation for "self-synchronous". The DC selsyn system consists of a transmitter, an indicator, and connecting wires. The transmitter consists of a circular resistance winding and a rotatable contact arm. The rotatable contact arm turns on a shaft in the center of the resistance winding. The two ends of the arm are brushes and always touch the winding on opposite sides. *(Figure 3-7)* With position indicating systems, the shaft to which the contact arm is fastened protrudes through the end of transmitter housing and is attached to the unit whose position is to be transmitted (e.g., flaps or landing gear).

The transmitter is often connected to the moving unit through a mechanical linkage. As the unit moves, it causes the transmitter shaft to turn. The arm is turned so that voltage is applied through the brushes to any two points around the circumference of the resistance winding. However, if the DC selsyn system is measuring data other than angular position from an outside unit, the rotor shaft may not protrude outside of the housing. In this case, the sensing device, which imparts rotary motion to the shaft, could be located inside the transmitter housing.

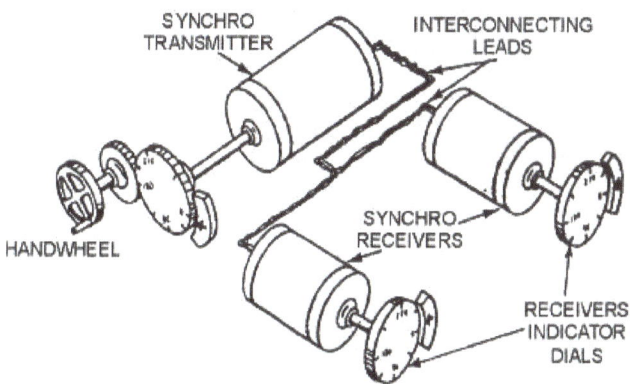

Figure 3-6. Synchronous Transmitter output signal moves receiver indicator dials in unison.

Referring to *Figure 3-7*, note that the resistance winding of the transmitter is tapped off in three fixed places, 120 degrees apart. These taps distribute current through the toroidal windings of the indicator motor. When current flows through these windings, a magnetic field is created. Like all magnetic fields, a definite north and south direction to the field exists. As the transmitter rotor shaft is turned, the voltage-supplying contact arm moves. Because it contacts the transmitter resistance winding in different positions, the resistance between the supply arm and the various tapoffs changes. This causes the voltage flowing through the tapoffs to change as the resistance of sections of the winding become larger or shorter. The result is that varied current is sent via the tapoffs to the three windings in the receiver indicator motor.

The resultant magnetic field created by current flowing through the indicator coils changes as each receives varied current from the transmitter tapoffs. The direction of the magnetic field also changes. Thus, the direction of the magnetic field across the receiver indicating element corresponds in position to the moving arm in the transmitter. A permanent magnet is attached to the centered rotor shaft in the indicator, as is the indicator pointer. The magnet aligns itself with the direction of the magnetic field and the pointer does as well. Whenever the magnetic field changes direction, the permanent magnet and pointer realign with the new position of the field. Thus, the position of the aircraft control surface, such as the flaps, is indicated.

The receiver incorporates a damping device to prevent hunting, which is the overshoot and undershoot that can occur when the receiver tries to match the transmitter signal. Without the damping device, the receiver would go slightly past the desired point, return past the desired point slightly in the opposite direction, and would continue to oscillate back and forth until finally coming to rest. The damper prevents hunting by feeding back some of the signal, thus slowing down the approach to the desired indication point.

Landing gears contain mechanical devices that lock the gear up or down, called an up-lock or down-lock. When the DC selsyn system is used to indicate the position of the landing gear, the indicator can also show that the up-lock or down-lock is engaged. This is done by again varying the current flowing through the indicator's coils. Switches located on the actual locking devices close

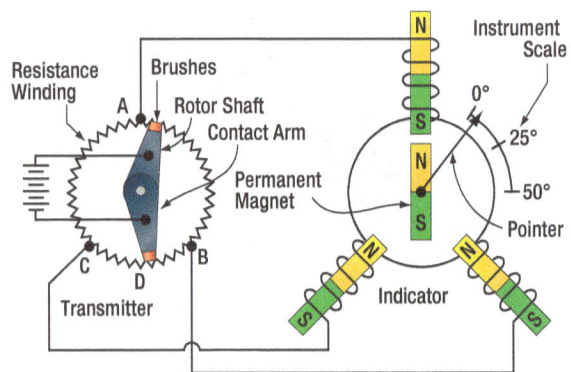

Figure 3-7. A schematic diagram of a DC selsyn synchro remote indicating system.

when the locks engage. Current from the selsyn system, described above, flows through the switch and a small additional circuit. The circuit adds an additional resistor to one of the transmitter winding sections created by the rotor arm and a tapoff. This changes the total resistance of that section. The result is a change in the current flowing through one of the indicator's motor coils. This, in turn, changes the magnetic field around that coil. Therefore, the combined magnetic field created by all three motor coils is also affected, causing a shift in the direction of the indicator's magnetic field. The permanent magnet and pointer align with the new direction and shift to the locked position on the indicator dial. *Figure 3-8* shows a simplified diagram of a lock switch in a three-wire selsyn system and an indicator dial.

AC SYNCHRO SYSTEMS

Aircraft with Alternating Current (AC) electrical power systems make use of autosyn or magnasysn synchro remote indicating systems. Both operate in a similar way to the DC selsyn system, except that AC power is used. Thus, they make use of electric induction, rather than resistance current flows defined by the rotor brushes. Magnasyn systems use permanent magnet rotors, such as those found in the DC selsyn system. Usually, the transmitter magnet is larger than the indicator magnet, but the electromagnetic response of the indicator rotor magnet and pointer remains the same. It aligns with the magnetic field set up by the coils, adopting the same angle of deflection as the transmitter rotor. *(Figure 3-9)* Again, the flight control surface, or other unit whose position is being monitored, is attached to the transmitter rotor.

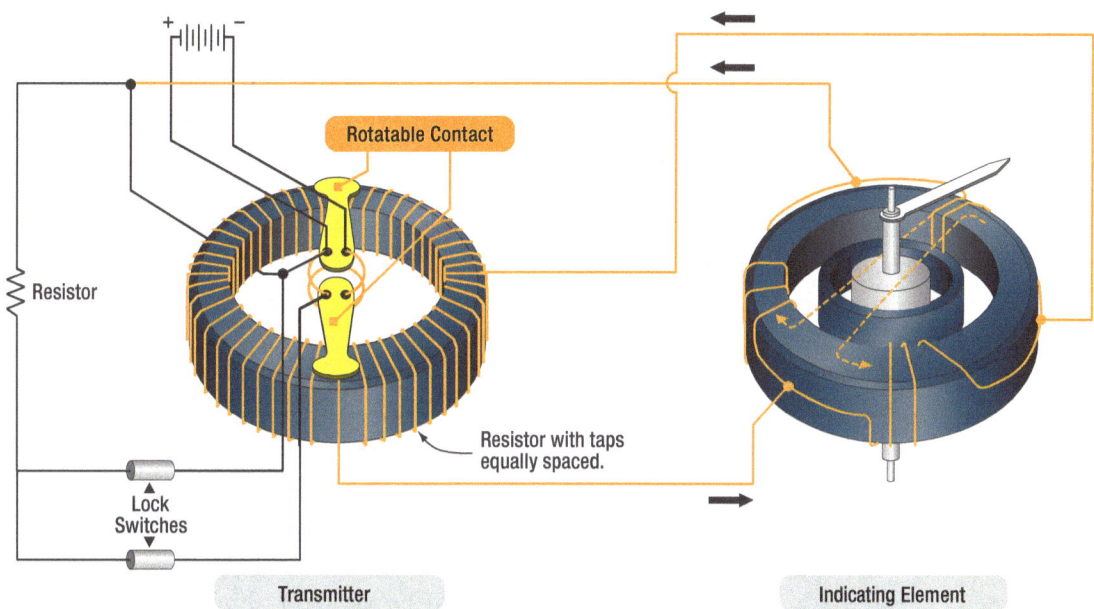

Figure 3-8. A lock switch circuit can be added to the basic DC selsyn synchro system when used to indicate landing gear position and up- and down-locked conditions on the same indicator.

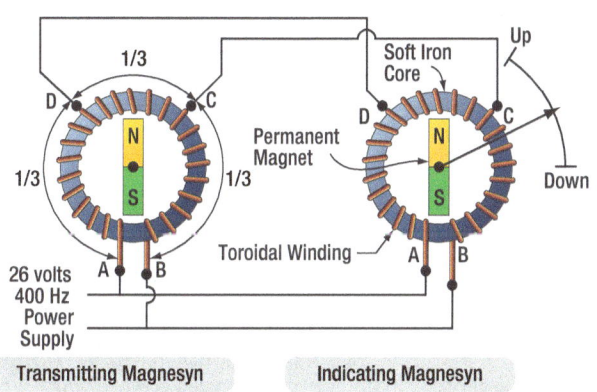

Figure 3-9. A magnasysn synchro remote-indicating system uses AC. It has permanent magnet rotors in the transmitter and indictor.

AC synchros function as rotary transformers, that is, if the transmitter and receiver are at the same shaft angle, the phases of the induced stator voltages will be identical, and no current will flow. However, if the transmitter rotor shaft moves out of place, the stator voltages will differ between the two synchros, which will generate a current in the receiver stator and produce a torque to align its angle to match that of the angle of the transmitter. Either the transmitter or the receiver may be turned to rotate the other unit. *(Figure 3-10)*

Autosyn systems are further distinguished by the fact that the transmitter and indicator rotors used are electro-magnets, rather than permanent magnets. Nonetheless, like a permanent magnet, an electro-magnet aligns with the direction of the magnetic field created by current flowing through the stator coils in the indicator. Thus, the indicator pointer position mirrors the transmitter rotor position. Autosyn transmitters and receivers are identical in that they both contain single-phase AC energized rotors and three-phase stators, which are not externally energized. The stators are wound with three-phase windings brought out to external terminals. The single stator winding leads are brought out by brushed slip rings.

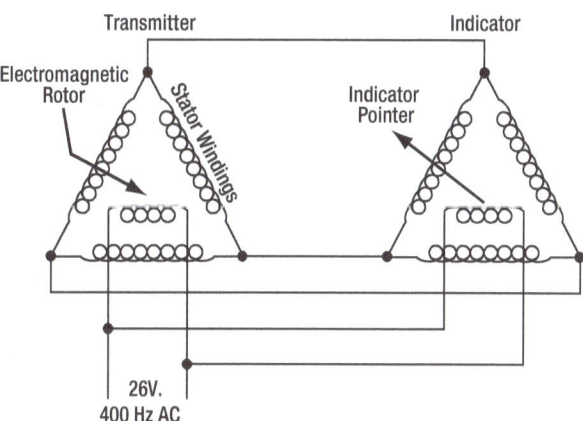

Figure 3-10. An autosyn remote-indicating system utilizes the interaction between magnetic fields set up by electric current flow to position the indicator pointer.

In summary, AC synchro systems are wired differently than DC systems. The varying current flows through the transmitter and indicator stator coils are induced as the AC cycles through zero and the rotor magnetic field flux is allowed to flow. The important characteristic of all synchro systems is maintained by both the autosyn and magnasyn systems. That is, the position of the transmitter rotor is mirrored by the rotor in the indicator. These AC synchro systems are used in many of the same applications as the DC synchro systems. Since they are usually part of instrumentation for high performance aircraft, adaptations of the autosyn and magnasyn synchro systems are frequently used in directional indicators and in autopilot systems.

TORQUE SYNCHRO SYSTEMS

AC synchro systems include variants of the AC synchros just described. A torque synchro system was alluded to above. The transmitter synchro sets up the electromagnetic field in the receiver synchro and the electromagnetic rotor of the receiver, responding to the field, has enough torque to move the indicator pointer or some other small-torque device. The torque synchro is designed to provide a light torque output without additional servo components. Torque is generated as a result of the interaction of the stator field and rotor field in the receiver which drives the rotor of the receiver into alignment with that of the transmitter. The misalignment curve over 360 degrees is at maximum value of opposite polarity at 90 and 270 degrees.

CONTROL SYNCHRO SYSTEMS AND SYNCHRONOUS TRANSMITTERS

A control synchro system is designed to minimize errors in the output signal due to current loading, magnetic non-linearity, or temperature variations. It consists of a pair of synchros, namely a synchronous transmitter driving a receiver, known as a control transformer. The control transformer has three equally spaced stator windings; however, its rotor is wound with more turns than a typical synchro transmitters and receivers to make it more sensitive at detecting a null as it is rotated by a mechanical connection to a servo motor moving a load.

As shown in *Figure 3-11*, a mechanical command input is connected to the shaft of the Control Transmitter (TX) and the mechanical response output is connected to the shaft of the Control Transformer (CT). By exciting the control transmitter with a fixed AC reference voltage, an error voltage is obtained from the control transformer which is proportional to the angular difference between the TX and CT. As such, the control transformer measures the difference between the input and the output, and produces a voltage that is proportional to that difference to achieve a null.

If an null is not present, the CT detects sends an error signal to a servo amplifier that amplifies the signal from the CT which then turns a servo motor to position an indicator, or more typically, a larger device or heavier load. The signal produced in the CT is an error voltage which represents the amount and direction that the load

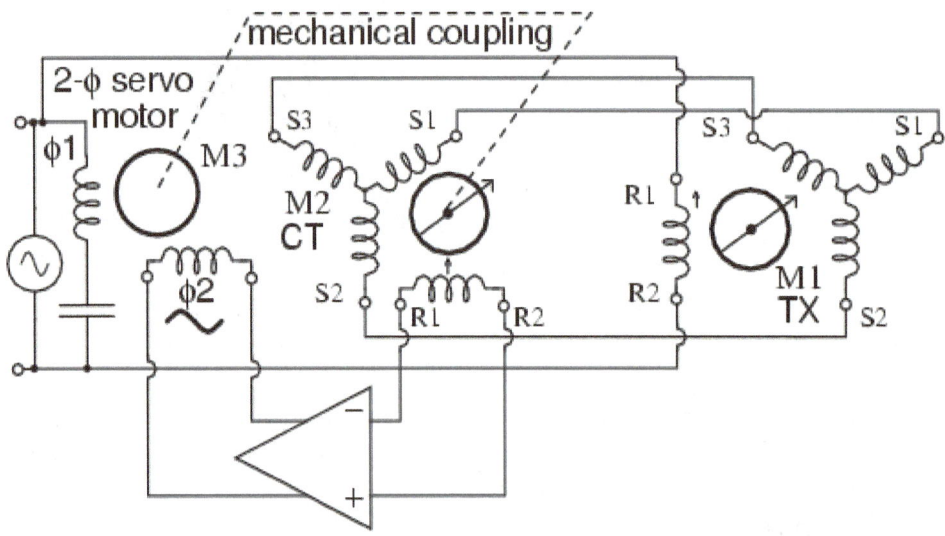

Figure 3-11. A control transformer compares commanded to actual position and signals the servo amplifier to drive the motor until the commanded angle is achieved.

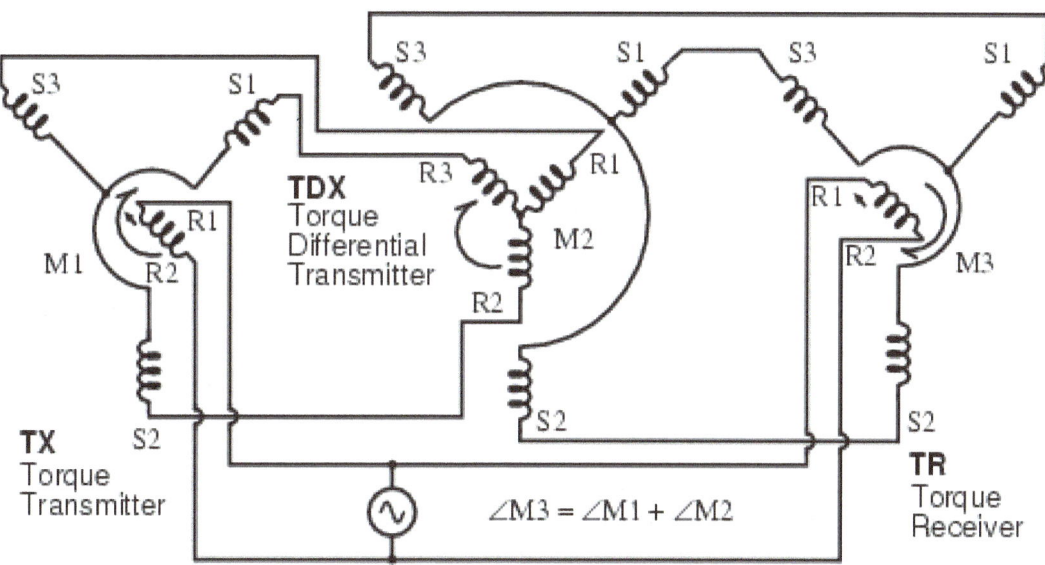

Figure 3-12. A differential synchro system consists of three synchros.

is out of alignment with the control input. It is this error signal that is used to ultimately move the load with the servo motor once the signal has been amplified. The rotor output is zero (null) when the CT detects it is oriented at 90 degrees to the axis of the stator magnetic field.

DIFFERENTIAL SYNCHRO SYSTEMS

A synchro system is not always as simple as positioning an indicating device in response to information received from a single transmitter. For example, an AFCS receives positioning inputs, not only from movements of the crew station control stick or column, but also from the Attitude and Heading Reference System (AHRS) as well. The signals from the AHRS correspond to the aircraft's actual track, due to wind speed and direction, and the cockpit control inputs correspond to aircraft's desired track. As such, the system must compare the two signals and position the flight control surface actuators based on the difference between these two signals.

A differential synchro system *(Figure 3-12)* includes not only a Torque Transmitter (TX) and Torque Receiver (TR), but also a Torque Differential Transmitter (TDX) between the two. The basic concept is that the TDX has a three-phase winding on the rotor that accepts two position inputs simultaneously, such that it adds the shaft angle input to an electrical angle input on the rotor inputs, outputting the sum on the stator outputs. The TDX stator electrical angle is displayed by sending it to an TX. For example, a TDX can accept one mechanical input (e.g., control stick), and one electrical input (e.g., AHRS) from the TR, and the sum of the inputs turns the TX rotor. Reversing the stator leads (S1-S3) between the TX and the TDX and between TDX and TR sends the angular difference voltage, instead of the sum of the two position inputs to the receiver. In other words, it subtracts the two angular positions.

Figure 3-13(A) depicts a Torque Differential Transmitter. Here the magnetic field created by the currents in the stator will position the rotor shaft of the TDX to correspond to the magnetic field of the transmitter providing the input signal. However, if the rotor position changes in response to a mechanical input, the voltage induced in the windings will also change. Therefore, the output voltage varies as a result of either a change in the input stator voltage, or a change in the mechanical input to the rotor.

Figure 3-13 (B) depicts a Torque Differential Receiver (TDR). A TDR is similar to a TDX, except that a TDR accepts two electrical inputs, one on the stator and one on the rotor, and produces one mechanical angular output, which produces torque on the TDR shaft. Both the TDR and TDX are electrically identical. The only difference in their construction is that the receiver has a damper that prevents the rotor from oscillating. The application; however, is different in that the differential receiver provides one mechanical output as the sum or difference of electrical signals from two transmitters. Again, whether the angular output of the receiver is the sum or difference of the two input signals depends on how the stator wires are connected.

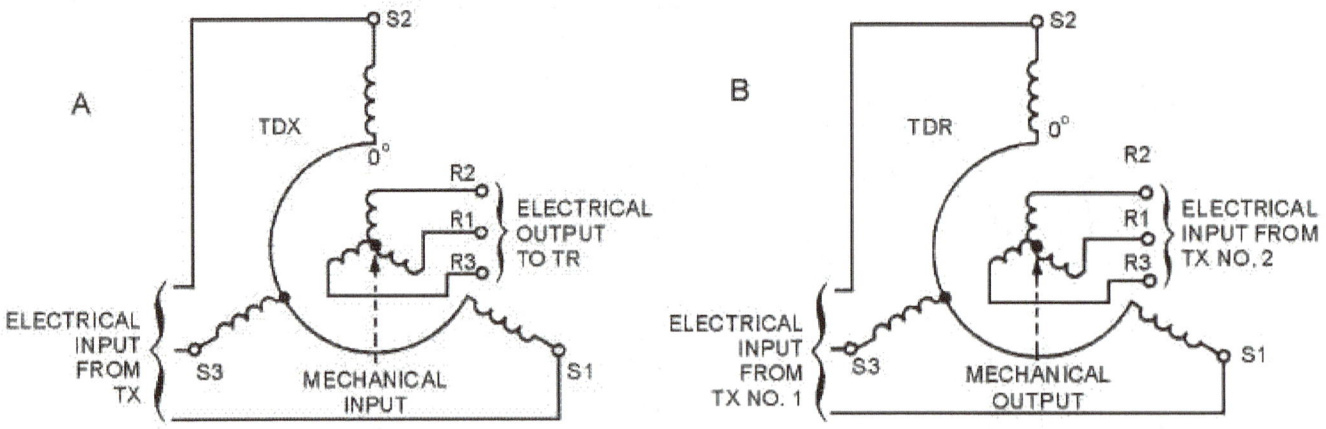

Figure 3-13. The Torque Differential Transmitter (A) receives a mechanical input and an electrical input to provide an electrical output. The torque differential receiver (B) two electrical inputs to provide a mechanical output.

RESOLVER SYNCHRO SYSTEMS

A resolver is another type of synchro system. Resolvers are used to transmit angular position data from one location to another where a high degree of accuracy is required. Resolvers are essentially variable transformers in which the coupling between windings varies with rotor position. A resolver has two stator windings placed at 90 degrees to each other, and a single rotor winding that is energized. *(Figure 3-14)* An angular input to the rotor shaft produces rectangular coordinates on the stator windings as their outputs are related by sine and cosine functions to the angular positions being measured.

Unlike those synchro systems previously described, the stator windings on a resolver are at 90 degree angles to each other, instead of 120 degrees. The 90 degree spacing provides sine and cosine stator outputs that represent the angular displacement of the rotor attached to the device being sensed. If, for example, a radar detects the distance to a target as a proportion sine wave voltage fed to the rotor, and the bearing to the target as the resolver shaft angle, the Cartesian coordinates (X, Y) of the target will be available on the resolver stator outputs.

Resolvers are generally considered to be most robust of all angular measurement devices and provide the highest reliability. Signals from resolvers are typically input into Analog to Digital Converters (ADC). Digital signals from the ADC are sent to AFCS computers to be processed into control outputs to drive actuator servo motors.

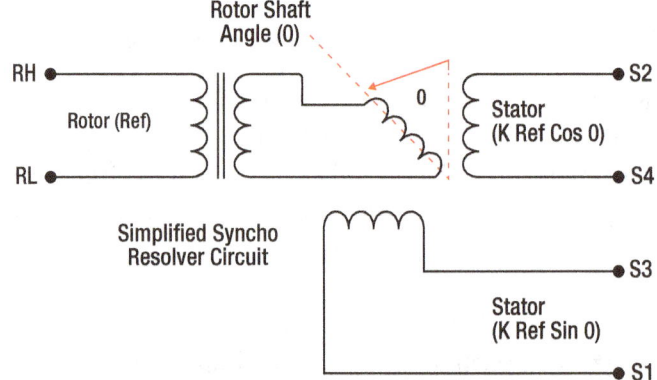

Figure 3-14. A simplified synchro resolver circuit.

E-I INDUCTIVE TRANSMITTERS

There are other methods of transmitting condition information other than using synchronous transmitters just described. Inductance transmitters are used in older instruments, acceleration sensors, and air data computers. It uses inductance windings, similar to a synchro, but the shape and spatial location of the laminated core is that of a capital letter "E" and capital letter "I". The magnetic field is concentrated by the core, and nearly all of the magnetic flux will pass from the primary through the windings of the secondary where a voltage will be induced. The core in this case is typical of the construction of an "E" and "I" transformer. *(Figure 3-15)*

The center limb of the E shape is fed primary voltage and the upper and lower limbs contain the secondary windings. An I-shaped bar of conductive material pivots in sync with the position of the element being sensed and is located at the open end of the E. The space between the upper and lower limbs of the E changes as the bar pivots. The voltage induced in the secondary coils on these limbs also changes due to the bar's influence on the

Figure 3-15. E-I transformer core.

electromagnetic field. The varied output of the secondary windings is interpreted as the sensor position. *Figure 3-16* shows the inductance transmitter set up with the pivoting sensor/bar in three different positions.

CAPACITANCE TRANSMITTERS

A capacitance transmitter is another type of device used on aircraft to transmit condition. It is found most often in transport category aircraft fuel quantity systems. Since a capacitor is a device that stores electricity, the amount it can store depends on three factors: the area of its plates, the distance between the plates, and the dielectric constant of the material separating the plates.

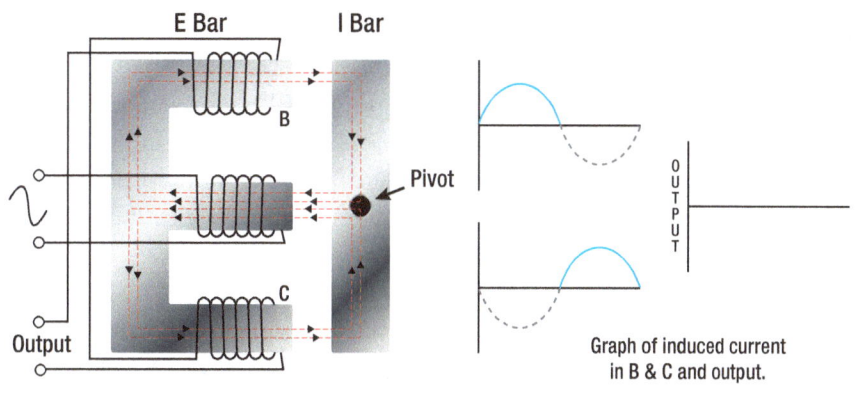

(A) I Bar - Neutral Position.

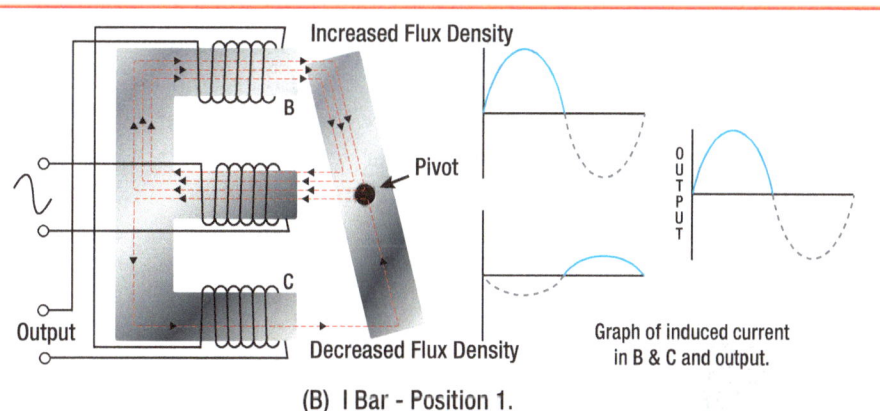

(B) I Bar - Position 1.

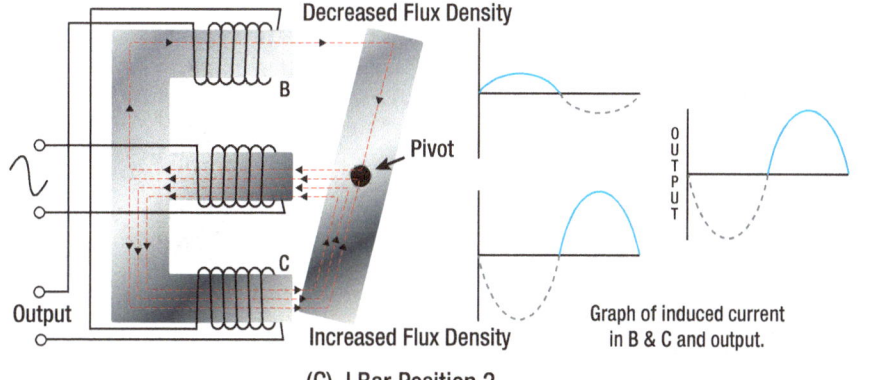

(C) I Bar Position 2.

Figure 3-16. Configuration of an inductance transmitter.

Module 04 B2 - Electronic Fundamentals

A fuel tank unit contains two concentric plates that are a fixed distance apart. Therefore, the capacitance of a unit can change if the dielectric constant of the material separating the plates varies. The units are open at the top and bottom so they can assume the same level of fuel as is in the tanks. Therefore, the material between the plates is either fuel (if the tank is full), air (if the tank is empty), or some ratio of fuel and air depending on how much fuel remains in the tank. The voltage stored in a reference capacitor completely submerged in fuel is compared to the transmitter capacitor or group of capacitors wired in parallel. The difference is a signal which is transmitted for display on the fuel quantity indicator in the cockpit. The transmitter and its bridge circuit are illustrated in *Figure 3-17* and *Figure 3-18*.

STABILITY: NULL HUNTING, DEADBAND, AND DAMPING

Stability is a problem facing any closed-loop system. The output voltage from the amplifier causes the servomotor to accelerate. At some point in time, the control voltage applied to the servomotor is zero due to the feedback voltage applied to the follow-up. However, the momentum of the motor causes the output to coast beyond the desired displacement. At this point, the error voltage reverses phase and the output is decelerated until it stops and reverses direction. It now accelerates towards the null point, but again, due to its inertia it overshoots the null and the process is repeated. Successive oscillations typically reduce in amplitude and eventually dampen out so that the system becomes stable. *(Figure 3-19)*

However, conditions can exist where such successive oscillations increase in amplitude such that the system becomes unstable, especially in the case where there is inadvertent lead reversal of the feedback signal to the follow-up such that a stable state can never be achieved.

The interval in the signal domain of a transducer where there is a null, or no output present, is called the "deadband". For example, the deadband for a variable coupling transducer would be measured by the amount of linear or angular motion allowed on either side of the null before a signal begins to appear in the secondary transformer outputs. This interval determines the precision or accuracy of the control system. A small interval is said to have a "tight" deadband, and results in high degree of precision. However, if the deadband is too tight, it will cause oscillations to occur due to the inertia of the output. As a result, the transducer will successively "hunt" back and forth to converge on its null point and achieve control system stability.

Damping is required to prevent a control system from becoming unstable; in other words, to keep it from hunting back and forth and overshooting its null point. All though there is some inherent damping in the servomotor and its load, that is not sufficient. Therefore, a generator is typically designed into the servomotor as one integral assembly that causes the motor to begin decelerating its output before it is in agreement with the input control signal, thereby reducing the overshooting problem. As the output is accelerated, the generator feeds back a voltage proportional to the velocity attained. This voltage subtracts from the error voltage resulting in a

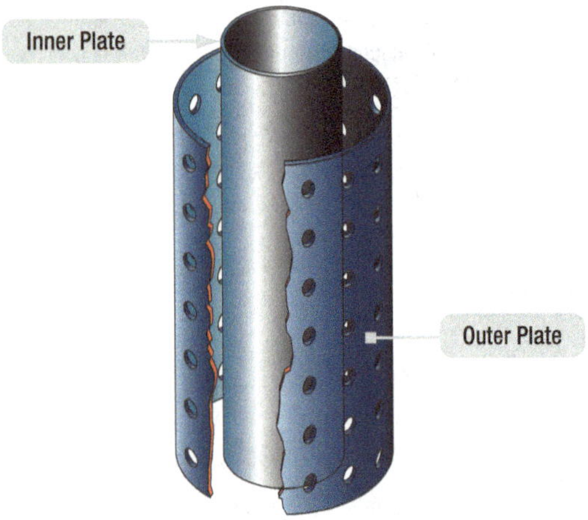

Figure 3-17. The capacitance of tank probes varies in a capacitancetype fuel tank indicator system as the space between the inner and outer plates is filled with varying quantities of fuel and air depending on the amount of fuel in the tank.

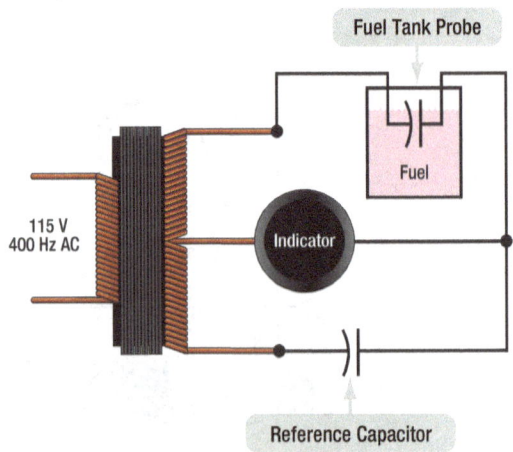

Figure 3-18. A simplified capacitance bridge circuit for a fuel quantity system.

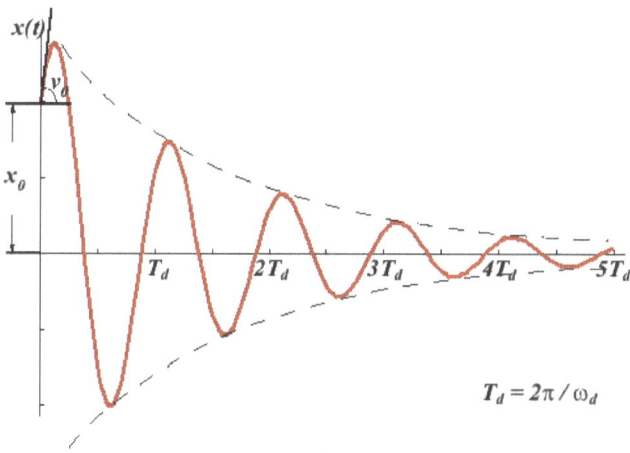

Figure 3-19. Successive oscillations typically reduce in amplitude and eventually dampen out.

$$T_d = 2\pi / \omega_d$$

reduced acceleration; consequently, the output response gradually reduces as the servomotor approaches its null point. The degree of damping is controlled by the amount of generator feedback voltage that is input into the summing circuit. The summing circuit is an electrical network used to add the follow-up and the generator voltages. The follow-up voltage is proportional to the system error, and the generator voltage is proportional to the output velocity. The sum of these voltages is applied to the amplifier input to drive the servomotor.

A viscous damper, or inertial damper, is sometimes used in place of a damping generator to lower the servomotors speed. The viscous damper, like the generator, is connected to the servomotor in one integral assembly. It consists of either a low inertia drag cup made from conducting material connected to the motor shaft and a rotating permanent-magnetic flywheel. As the motor builds us speed, viscous torque is developed that is proportional to the relative velocity between the drag cup and the flywheel. This torque acts as a drag on the motor to provide the desired damping. The viscous damper does not adversely affect the motor starting voltage or stall torque, but does increase its inertia and reduces its slew speed. An alternate design uses an inertia ring that attempts to compress fluid within the damper housing causing the fluid to dissipate the energy stored in the oscillation. *(Figure 3-20)*

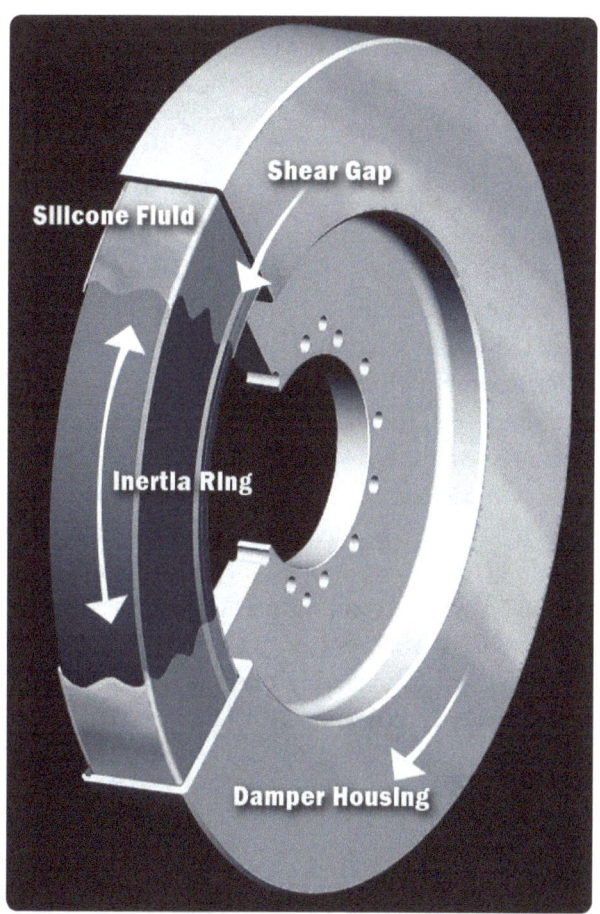

Figure 3-20. A vicious damper dissipates the energy stored in oscillation.

SERVOMECHANISM DEFECTS

Servomechanism systems are by their very nature nonlinear systems whose behavior can be unpredictable based on many variables. Previously discussed were issues with hunting whereby a servomotor can overshoot its null due to inertia, and how damping is employed to mitigate against this defect. However, gear train stiffness and load friction can also have an effect on stability, as well as motor starting voltage, amplifier gain saturation, and transient response.

Synchros are subject to two types of defect errors: inherent electrical errors based on design limitations, such as winding distribution, and random manufacturing defects that vary from unit to unit. An unsymmetrical winding distribution causes the magnetic flux wave in the air gap to deviate from an ideal sinusoidal wave resulting in a series of superimposed flux waves having multiple poles. While the amplitude of the flux wave distribution will be alternating with the input current, in the absence of saturation, the space distribution of the wave will remain unchanged, thereby tending to flatten out the sine wave at the 90 degree and 270 degree intervals. Errors in the flux waveform due to the nonsinusoidal character of the flux distribution yield undesirable characteristics that affect the synchro system accuracy.

One of the most common manufacturing defects in synchros is air gap inaccuracies. Even minor air gap irregularities causes major distortion in the flux distribution pattern. One of the most common geometric irregularities that affects air gap is ellipticity of the stator. Another common manufacturing defect is unbalancing the stator winding impedance by winding too many turns on one of the stator legs. The net effect of any imbalance is a nonuniformity in flux amplitude. Most defects will, of course, manifest themselves in maintenance logs as components age, and therefore, it is imperative that synchronous systems be monitored and maintained within operating tolerances as stated in the manufacturer's specifications.

QUESTIONS

Question: 3-1
What is a servomechanism?

Question: 3-5
What is the difference between a selsyn, a magnasysn, and an autosyn synchro?

Question: 3-2
What is the difference between an open-loop system and a closed-loop system?

Question: 3-6
Describe the operation of an AC synchro system.

Question: 3-3
What is the purpose of a follow-up?

Question: 3-7
Why purpose does the damping device serve in a synchro receiver?

Question: 3-4
Describe the operation of an analog transducer.

Question: 3-8
What is the purpose of a control synchro system and what function does it perform?

ANSWERS

Answer: 3-1
A servomechanism is an electric control system for an automatic powered mechanism that produces motion or force using a low energy input signal. The amplified system typically drives an electric or hydraulic motor; however, the motion can be rotary or linear depending on the mechanical transmission of the force.

Answer: 3-2
A closed-loop system is different from an open-loop system in that there is a feedback mechanism present. In other words, the output is continually compared to the input and any difference is applied to control the output in such a way to reduce the difference to zero, which is called the "null".

Answer: 3-3
All closed-loop systems have an error detector, known as a "follow-up", which calculates the difference between the desired input and the actual measured state. When the feedback signal is equal and opposite to the control signal, the voltage at the summing point of the error detector is zero, and the servomotor stops. The summing circuit is a resistor network used to add up the follow-up and control voltages to provide a difference signal to the amplifier that drives the servomotor.

Answer: 3-4
An analog transducer is a device which converts the differing position of the physical flight control surface in to a variable electric output signal that can be processed by the controller. It is basically a transformer with two secondary induction coils and a moving core that is attached to the controlled unit. As the unit moves, the core moves, which changes the value of the voltage induced in the two secondary coils. The differential of the output voltages of the coils is the feedback signal sent to the controller.

Answer: 3-5
The selsyn uses DC power and the magnasysn and autosyn used AC power. Thus, the AC synchros make use of electric induction, rather than resistance current flows defined by the rotor brushes. Magnasyn systems use permanent magnet rotors, such as those found in the DC selsyn system. Aurosyn systems use electromagnetic rotors.

Answer: 3-6
A synchro system is a servomechanism used for transmitting information from one point to another. AC synchros function as rotary transformers, that is, if the transmitter and receiver are at the same shaft angle, the phases of the induced stator voltages will be identical, and no current will flow. However, if the transmitter rotor shaft moves out of place, the stator voltages will differ between the two synchros, which will generate a current in the receiver stator and produce a torque to align its angle to match that of the angle of the transmitter. Either the transmitter or the receiver may be turned to rotate the other unit.

Answer: 3-7
The receiver incorporates a damping device to prevent hunting, which is the overshoot and undershoot that can occur when the receiver tries to match the transmitter signal. Without the damping device, the receiver would go slightly past the desired point, return past the desired point slightly in the opposite direction, and would continue to oscillate back and forth until finally coming to rest. The damper prevents hunting by feeding back some of the signal, thus slowing down the approach to the desired indication point.

Answer: 3-8
A control synchro system is designed to minimize errors in the output signal due to current loading, magnetic nonlinearity, or temperature variations. It consists of a pair of synchros, namely a synchronous transmitter driving a receiver, known as a control transformer. The control transformer has three equally spaced stator windings; however, its rotor is wound with more turns than a typical synchro transmitters and receivers to make it more sensitive at detecting a null as it is rotated by a mechanical connection to a servo motor moving a load.

QUESTIONS

Question: 3-9
What is a differential synchro system and how does it operate?

Question: 3-10
What is a resolver and what purpose does it serve?

Question: 3-11
Explain the operation of an Inductive Transmitter.

Question: 3-12
How does a Capacitance Transmitter measure fuel quantity?

Question: 3-13
Explain the principle of deadband.

Question: 3-14
Explain the operation of a viscous damper.

Question: 3-15
Name some of the most common type of Synchro defects.

ANSWERS

Answer: 3-9
A differential synchro system has not only a Torque Transmitter and Torque Receiver, but also a Torque Differential Transmitter (TDX) between the two. The basic concept is that the TDX has a three-phase winding on the rotor that accepts two position inputs simultaneously, such that it adds the shaft angle input to an electrical angle input on the rotor inputs, outputting the sum or difference on the stator outputs. The TDX stator electrical angle is displayed by sending it to the Torque Receiver.

Answer: 3-10
A resolver is another type of synchro system. Resolvers are used to transmit angular position data from one location to another where a high degree of accuracy is required. Resolvers are essentially variable transformers in which the coupling between windings varies with rotor position. A resolver has two stator windings placed at 90 degrees to each other, and a single rotor winding that is energized. An angular input to the rotor shaft produces rectangular coordinates on the stator windings as their outputs are related by sine and cosine functions to the angular positions being measured.

Answer: 3-11
The center limb of the E shape is fed primary voltage and the upper and lower limbs contain the secondary windings. An I-shaped bar of conductive material pivots in sync with the position of the element being sensed and is located at the open end of the E. The space between the upper and lower limbs of the E changes as the bar pivots. The voltage induced in the secondary coils on these limbs also changes due to the bar's influence on the electromagnetic field. The varied output of the secondary windings is interpreted as the sensor position.

Answer: 3-12
The amount of voltage that a capacitor can store it can store depends on three factors: the area of its plates, the distance between the plates, and the dielectric constant of the material separating the plates. A fuel tank unit contains two concentric plates that are a fixed distance apart. Therefore, the capacitance of the unit will change if the dielectric constant of the material (i.e., the amount of fuel) separating the plates varies.

Answer: 3-13
The interval in the signal domain of a transducer where there is a null, or no output present, is called the "deadband". For example, the deadband for a variable coupling transducer would be measured by the amount of linear or angular motion allowed on either side of the null before a signal begins to appear in the secondary transformer outputs. This interval determines the precision or accuracy of the control system. A small interval is said to have a "tight" deadband, and results in high degree of precision. However, if the deadband is too tight, it will cause oscillations to occur due to the inertia of the output. As a result, the transducer will successively "hunt" back and forth to converge on its null point and achieve control system stability.

Answer: 3-14
A viscous damper, or inertial damper, is sometimes used in place of a damping generator to lower the servomotors speed. The viscous damper, like the generator, is connected to the servomotor in one integral assembly. It consists of either a low inertia drag cup made from conducting material connected to the motor shaft and a rotating permanentmagnetic flywheel. As the motor builds us speed, viscous torque is developed that is proportional to the relative velocity between the drag cup and the flywheel. This torque acts as a drag on the motor to provide the desired damping.

Answer: 3-15
Synchros are subject to two types of defect errors: inherent electrical errors based on design limitations, such as winding distribution, and random manufacturing defects that vary from unit to unit. One of the most common manufacturing defects in synchros is air gap inaccuracies. One of the most common geometric irregularities that affects air gap is ellipticity of the stator. Another common manufacturing defect is unbalancing the stator winding impedance by winding too many turns on one of the stator legs. The net effect of any imbalance is a nonuniformity in flux amplitude.

ACRONYM INDEX (ACRONYMS USED IN THIS MANUAL)

AC	/	Alternating Current
ADC	/	Analog-to-Digital Converter
AFCS	/	Automatic Flight Control System
AHRS	/	Attitude and Heading Reference System
As	/	Arsenic
B	/	Base (transistor)
BGA	/	Ball Grid Arrays
BJT	/	Bipolar Junction Transistor
BCD	/	Binary Coded Decimal
C	/	Carbon
C	/	Collector (transistor)
CB	/	Common base
CC	/	Common collector
CdSe	/	Cadmium-Selenium
CdHgTe	/	Cadmium-Mercury-Tellurium
CdTe	/	Cadmium-Tellurium
CE	/	Common emitter
CMOS	/	Complementary Metal-Oxide Semiconductor
CT	/	Control Transformer
D	/	Drain (FET)
DC	/	Direct Current
DIP	/	Dual In-line Package (integrated circuit)
E	/	Emitter (transistor)
ESD	/	Electro-Static Discharge
FET	/	Field Effect Transistor
$f_R = 1 / 2\Pi \sqrt{L \times C}$	/	Resonant Frequency Formula (L = inductance, C = capacitance)
GaAlAs	/	Gallium-Aluminum- Arsenide
GaAs	/	Gallium-Arsenide
GaN	/	Gallium-Nitride
GaP	/	Gallium-Phosphide
Ge	/	Germanium
G	/	Gate (FET)
HEMT	/	High Electron Mobility Transistors
IFAV	/	Maximum (Average) Forward Current
IFSM	/	Maximum (Peak or Surge) Forward Current
IC	/	Integrated Circuit (chip)
InP	/	Indium-Phosphorus
InSb	/	Indium-Antimony
IR	/	Maximum Reverse Current
JFET	/	Junction Field Effect Transistor
LC	/	Inductor Capacitor (tank circuit)
LCD	/	Liquid Crystal Display
LED	/	Light-Emitting Diode
LRM	/	Line Replaceable Module
LRU	/	Line Replaceable Unit
LSB	/	Least Significant Bit

ACRONYM INDEX *(ACRONYMS USED IN THIS MANUAL)*

LSI	/	Large-Scale Integration (chip)
LVDT	/	Linear Variable Differential Transducer
MOSFET	/	Metal-Oxide Field Effect Transistor
MESFET	/	Metal Semiconductor FET
MSB	/	Most Significant Bit
MSI	/	Medium-Scale Integration (chip)
NPN	/	Negative-Positive-Negative (transistor junction)
Op Amp	/	Operational Amplifier
P	/	Phosphorus
$P = I^2R$	/	Ohm's Law (P = power, I = current, R = resistance)
PCB	/	Printed Circuit Board
PN	/	Positive-Negative (diode junction)
PNP	/	Positive-Negative-Positive (transistor junction)
RFC	/	Radio Frequency Choke
RL	/	Load Resistor
RVDT	/	Rotary Variable Differential Transducer
RS	/	Reset-Set (flip-flop logic circuits)
RX	/	Receiver
S	/	Source (FET)
SCR	/	Silicon Controlled rectifier
Si	/	Silicon
SiC	/	Silicon Carbide
SMT	/	Surface Mount Technology
SSI	/	Small-Scale Integration (chip)
T = RC	/	Time Constant (R= resistance, C= capacitance)
TDR	/	Torque Differential Receiver
TDX	/	Torque Differential Transmitter
Trr	/	Reverse Recovery Time
TR	/	Torque Receiver
TTL	/	Transistor-Transistor Logic
TX	/	Control or Torque Transmitter
UJT	/	Unipolar Junction Transistor
ULSI	/	Ultra Large-Scale Integration (chip)
Vcc	/	Supply Voltage
VF@IF	/	Maximum Forward Voltage Drop at Indicated Forward Current
VR	/	Maximum Reverse Voltage
VREF	/	Reference Voltage
Vs	/	Source Voltage
VLSI	/	Very Large-Scale Integration (chip)
XOR	/	EXCLUSIVE OR (gate)
ZnS	/	Zinc Sulfer

INDEX

A

AC Synchro Systems	3.6
Adder Logic Circuits	1.53
Aircraft Logic Gate Applications	1.51
Analog Transducers	3.4
AND Gate	1.49
Anti-Static Protection	2.8
Anti-Static Wrist Straps	2.8

B

Basic Amplifier Circuits	1.37
Biasing	1.34
Binary-Coded Decimals	1.47
Binary Numbering System	1.44
Binary Number System Conversion	1.46
Bipolar Junction Transistors	1.28
Bridge Rectifier Circuit	1.23
Buffer Gate	1.48

C

Capacitance Transmitters	3.11
Cascade Amplifiers	1.39
Characteristics And Properties	1.2
Clamper Circuit	1.22
Class A Amplifiers	1.37
Class AB Amplifiers	1.38
Class B Amplifier	1.38
Class C Amplifier	1.38
Clipper Circuit	1.21
Common-Base Configuration	1.36
Common-Collector Configuration	1.36
Common-Emitter Configuration	1.36
Comparator Logic Circuits	1.55
Configurations	1.36
Construction And Operation Of Transistors	1.28
Controlled Environment	2.8
Control Synchro Systems And Synchronous Transmitters	3.8

D

DC Selsyn Systems	3.5
Decoder Logic Circuits	1.57
Description, Characteristics, Properties and Symbols	1.25
DIACS And TRIACS	1.34
Differential Synchro Systems	3.9
Differentiator Circuit	1.63
Diode Identification	1.11
Diode Maintenance And Testing	1.19
Diode parameters	1.9
Diodes In Series And Parallel	1.21
Diode Symbols	1.10
Direct Coupling	1.39
Double-Layered Boards	2.2

E

Effects of Impurities on P and N Type Materials	1.5
E-I Inductive Transmitters	3.10
Electron Behavior In Valence Shells	1.4
Encoder Logic Circuits	1.56
Exclusive NOR Gate	1.51
Exclusive OR Gate	1.51

F

Feedback And Stabilization	1.39
Feedback: Open-Loop And Closed-Loop Systems	3.2
Field Effect Transistors	1.30
Flip-flop Circuits	1.43
Flip-Flop Logic Circuits	1.53
Forward-Bias PN Junction	1.8
Full-Wave Rectifier Circuit	1.23

G

Grounding Test Stations	2.9

H

Half-Wave Rectifier Circuit	1.22

I

Impedance Coupling	1.40
Integrated Circuits	1.43
Integrator Circuit	1.62
Ionizers	2.9

INDEX

L

Light Emitting Diodes	1.13
Linear Circuits And Operational Amplifiers	1.57
Logic Circuits	1.53
Logic Gates	1.48

M

Majority And Minority Carriers	1.6
Metal Oxide Field Effect Transistors	1.31
Multi-Layer Ed Boards	2.5
Multi-Layer Semiconductor Devices	1.32
Multivibrator Circuit	1.62
Mutivibrators	1.43

N

NAND Gate	1.50
Negative Logic Gates	1.51
NOR Gate	1.51
NOT Gate	1.48

O

OR Gate	1.49
Oscillators	1.41

P

PCB Manufacturing Process	2.2
PCB Repair	2.6
Photodiodes	1.13
Place Values	1.46
PN Junctions And The Basic Diode	1.7
Positive and Negative Feedback	1.61
Power Rectifier Diodes	1.15
Printed Circuit Boards	2.2
Push-Pull Amplifiers	1.41

R

Resistive-Capacitive Coupling	1.40
Resolver Synchro Systems	3.10
Reverse-Biased PN Junction	1.9
Risks And Possible Damage	2.6

S

Scale Of Integration	1.63
Schottky Diodes	1.16
Semiconductor Diodes	1.9
Semiconductor Materials	1.3
Semiconductors	1.2
Servomechanism Defects	3.13
Servomechanisms	3.2
Shockley Diodes	1.32
Signal Diodes	1.12
Silicon Controlled Rectifiers	1.32
Simple Circuits	1.34
Single-Layer Boards	2.2
Special Handling	2.10
Stability: Null Hunting, Deadband, And Damping	3.12
Static-Safe Workstation	2.8
Synchro Systems	3.5

T

Testing of Transistors	1.26
Torque Synchro Systems	3.8
Transformer Coupling	1.40
Transistors	1.25
Types Of Diodes	1.11

U

Unbiased PN Junction	1.7
Unipolar Junction Transistors	1.28

V

Varactor Diodes	1.17
Varistor	1.16
Voltage Doublers And Triplers	1.24
Voltage Follower Circuit	1.61